THE SOUTHERN ALPS

THE SOUTHERN ALPS

Photographs by Craig Potton

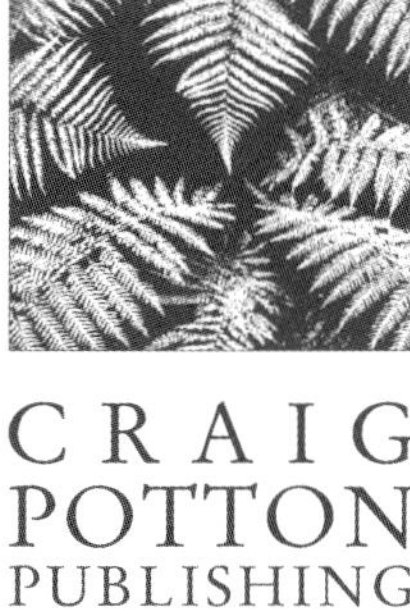

CRAIG
POTTON
PUBLISHING

Acknowledgements

This collection of aerial photographs would never have got off the ground without the skill of the helicopter pilots I have flown with, and in particular I'd like to acknowledge Alfie Speight of Heliworks, Richard Hayes of Southern Lakes Helicopters, and Trevor McGowan of Nelson. The original idea for this book came from Tony Moores of Paper Plus, for which I'm very grateful. James Brown, Dave Chowdhury and Andy Dennis have all contributed enormously to the text and I thank them for that. Finally I would like to acknowledge Paul Huston from Industrial Light and Magic, Paul Lasaine and Alan Lee, who were contracted to Weta Workshop when I was working with them, for their companionship and inspiration when many of these photographs were taken.

First published in 2005 by Craig Potton Publishing
98 Vickerman Street, PO Box 555, Nelson, New Zealand
www.craigpotton.co.nz

© Craig Potton

ISBN 1-877333-30-1

Editing by James Brown
Captions by Dave Chowdhury and Andy Dennis
Scanning by Image Centre, Auckland, New Zealand
Printed in China by Midas Printing Co. Ltd

Contents

Gazing at the Southern Alps

Craig Potton

I drive south in winter to look at the mountains, to seek out the great stretching wave upon wave of rock, ice and snow that we call the Southern Alps. In the cold of the shortest days when they stand mantled in a blanket of pure white, they are a line of extraordinary clarity above the varied hue and complexity we live in below. I come again and again to look and each time return home with resounding afterimages of their beauty.

I'm not alone in this compulsive desire to peer in from the edge. Many come. Few wish to penetrate the mountains' inner sanctums and even fewer will climb to their summits. As a sometime mountaineer, at times I gaze and wish myself on their faces and ridges. Even from the distance of the lowlands, they are seductive sirens whose unbidden disclosures compel me to pull over in my car, stopping dead in my tracks near Hokitika when, as a mirage, Aoraki/ Mt Cook and Mt Tasman float like white spectral pyramids above the shimmering ocean. I've been similarly stopped at Okarito, Mapourika and Matheson by the dazzling white sheets of snow that levitate above the dark forests and cast immaculate reflections in lagoon and lake. From eastern approaches I've pulled over in the Mackenzie basin just beyond Lake Tekapo caught by Aoraki/Mt Cook floating above the tussocks, and later by Mt Sefton when it fills the car's front window at the entrance to the national park.

These winter days of mountain gazing are to me a reverse of hibernation: I wake to life revitalised by the shutting-down cold. Whenever the road wanders near the Alps my heart quickens. At Arthur's Pass and on the Milford road I linger shivering by the car door, staring at the mountain walls that loom over me. Again and again I'm drawn down all those gravel, back-country roads, which suck you up great river valleys farther and farther into those 'thousand mountains shining'[1]. Little wonder I feel enticed up these remote valleys; they lead, after all, into the central spine, the core of our land—inhospitable yet extraordinarily alluring.

For me to succumb again and again to their magnetic beauty I can only assume that they must meet some inner need. It is as if they offer some compelling truth which is always just out of reach. In an attempt to fathom this I have looked backwards into my past, and at the writings of those who have also heard the mountains' voices:

> From time immemorial the mountains have been the dwelling place of the great sages; wise men and sages have all made the mountains their own chambers, their own body and mind. And through these wise men and sages the mountains have been actualised. However many great sages and wise men we suppose have assembled in the mountains, ever since they entered the mountains no one has met a single one of them. There is only the actualisation of the life of the mountains; not a single trace of their having entered remains.[2]

I became enchanted gazing at the mountains well before I had any inclination to climb among them. What caused that original impulse? Something deep-rooted; something hard-wired into my soul? I suspect my affair with the mountains began well before I was consciously aware of it, when I first stared wide-eyed at the sky and began to sense how fathomless and far beyond me it was. And in that amazing panorama I saw also a long range of mountains settling solidly on the lowest edge of the open sky. It was the Arthur Range, to the west of my childhood home in Nelson. Out there was a land quite unlike the perennially sunlit green and vibrant world close at hand. It was always blue with a sky often gathering clouds, and held all the fear and promise of somewhere else.

Gazing at the mountains filled me with a very different feeling than that of gazing at the sky and sea—the other great verities of my horizon. The sky was just too abstract, conjuring up the incomprehensible fright of infinity. I sensed it went on forever and even at night, when the stars reflected back an inkling of reassurance that there *was* something solid out there, they were still too far away, too cold, too lonely and surrounded by too much blackness. The sea was a less scary proposition and I quickly saw myself playing on its fringe. But it too spread rapidly beyond my depth: that inviting border and sparkling surface was a ruse disguising a hidden abyss. So it was always easier to daydream about the mountains, for, although far away, they were clearly made of the same solid earth that I was standing on.

It was comforting to see something you could imagine walking across—an ethereal form that certain lights revealed as a solid, complex terrain. They were neither so different nor so remote that I couldn't see myself exploring their strangeness. At dusk and on moonlit nights I went to those mountains many times in my mind, long before I actually visited them.

Was it also their particular shades of blueness that drew me in? Up close blue is not overtly seductive; in fact it casts a pallor that suggests sickness and unease. There is none of the warmth or sensuality of red and yellow. Yet all that changes with distance. Since astronauts first sent back those epiphanous images of our blue planet glimmering quietly in the black of space, blue, as the colour of atmosphere, has become the most life-affirming hue. On the horizon where great masses of sky, mountains and sea meet, blue becomes the warmest of colours. Leonardo da Vinci, Joachim Patinier and Piero della Francesca were among the first painters to recognise that with distance the other colours of the spectrum are filtered away. Now the smoky blue haze over Leonardo's mountains and the wintry, clear blues in Patinier and della Francesca are recognised as realistic depictions. It is their use of blue that banished the surreal gold leaf surrounds that had previously enthroned Madonnas, saints and other saviours, and grounded the spiritual firmly in the world. So although skies may briefly flame red and yellow at sunrise and sunset or sulk into grey on wet days, it is the far blue of clear days, horizons and mountains that we are most consistently comforted by. As the Chinese poet Tu Fu said of deep meditative rest: 'I sit in the blue of the hills.'

Whatever personal responses we may have to the mountains, our 'blue remembered hills'[3] also form part of the backbone of our culture. The Southern Alps, like all great mountain chains, have a kind of mythic stature as the embodiment of the elemental and timeless nature of our particular land. To both Maori and Pakeha they are imbued with character. We talk about them with admiration, respect and fear. Their size, solidity and beauty admonishes our pettiness by putting our daily existence into perspective. We respect them for their longevity, having come into existence long before our human habitation, and they will continue unchanged throughout our frantic comings and goings.

The Southern Alps are an ever-present feature of our culture and history. To Maori they are demi-gods, rohe markers and backdrops to greenstone trails. To Pakeha they are the terrain of early exploration stories, impediments to easy gold and pasturage, and brute faces and ridges to be scaled. And yet they out-distance our myths as much as they do our eyes. They overspread the horizon calling into question our sense of scale, our sense of place, our sense of ourselves.

All cultures have stories involving mountains as revered sources of spiritual energy from which sacred rivers often run. Such stories are central to the culture's mythology and carry deep chthonic symbolism.

The earliest writing on Sumerian and Akkadian seals, and many stories from ancient oral traditions extol the power of a central, mythical mountain. The mountain is always referred to as 'our mountain', the one behind 'our village'. Or it may not physically exist. In the speculative cultures of Hinduism and Buddhism, for example, Mount Meru, the ideal mountain and source of the mother river, was originally nowhere, and thereby everywhere, but has gradually come to be sited as Mount Kailas in Tibet.

Mythical mountains are generally beyond ascent; that is, they remain off-limits to all but a chosen few. For those individuals, such as Moses and Milarepa, occasionally permitted to climb (and even then sometimes only partially), the journey was usually undertaken with great trepidation because the toll on the mind and body could be extreme. Nevertheless, the self-shattering illuminations to be gained were considered necessary for the culture as a whole and therefore justified the risk to the sage. Thus the eyes of the general population were constantly drawn upwards into the realms reserved for souls or sages, conjuring what Michael Tobias calls 'Mankind's oldest dizziness'[4].

Throughout history and across cultures, gods have chosen mountains as points of contact between themselves and the earth, so it is hardly surprising that places of worship—temples, steeples, pyramids—echo their ascending form. The association of spiritual voices with mountains is universal[5]. This spiritual purity stems partly from an absence of people. Mythical peaks are literally above and beyond human endeavour; like gods, they are primarily to be gazed on from afar.

These distant or inaccessible mountains seem to touch each culture with a generative power. In many ways they succour us. The Jewish Golem tales, to take a European example, tell how only through the soil from an untouched mountain and the fresh water of a virgin spring could the invocation of God's name create new life. From this the medieval rabbis of Eastern Europe created folktales about mythical beings made of clay, whose intercessional powers would give hope to generations of Jews during times of persecution.

Although it was not possible for the average person to attempt an outward ascent of the sacred peak, there were other ways to gain enlightenment. By turning one's mountain gaze inward on the mind's eye, the peak could be encouraged to 'grow within'. No one has surpassed the thirteenth century Japanese Zen priest Dogen (see endnote 2) for his sheer audacity in this aesthetic/physical inversion. Many other intellectual and religious thinkers have steered our focus away from the exterior wilderness to one within us, but the extremity of Dogen's insight could only have evolved from a particular strand in Chinese art and philosophy.

Long before Chinese artists flicked their brushes across rice paper, Chinese poets exalted their mountains and rivers as exemplars of unadulterated life forces. Their cosmology was founded on the notion of a primordial breath of life which divided the original chaos into two vital forces, yin and yang, whose continual interplay governed the workings of the ten thousand beings of the created world. The yang was the active force, the yin the receptive; thus the sky was yang, the earth yin, and it was the mountain's yang that reacted with the water's yin. There is even evidence that the words yin and yang themselves may originate in the complementary opposites of the shaded and sunny slopes of mountain ranges.

To the Chinese, in the universal order of the natural world these antinomies continually engage in erotic interplay, each seeking the other's qualities. Mountain and water contend when a rock face interacts with mist and rain. In some prescient awareness of tectonic geology, early Chinese thinkers described the arrested wave of energy in a mountain range and the solid flow of energy present within the collective water particles of a river.

In at least 500 BC, an unknown poet sang in the *Book of Songs*:

Heaven sustain your course in quietness
to abound and rise as mountain hill and range
constant as rivers flow that all augment
a steady increase in ever cyclic change.

In the traditions of Taoism and Buddhism, schools of poetry and painting (shan-shui) arose that explored these insights through meditation on rivers and mountains. Early in the eighth century, great poets like Wang Pei, Li Po and Tu Fu looked for the mountains behind their houses and found them in their hearts. They walked country paths, sat under trees, drunk and sober, taking in the sublime rocky heights before them. In their banishment or self-imposed exile from court and culture they saw in the power of nature an alternative order to the ideal Confucian society. This long lineage of philosophic poetry served Dogen well. Looking directly at a mountain, or its image, he saw that what was constant and abiding was also in a continual state of change, which he called 'the blue mountains constantly walking'. Reflecting on the river's continual state of change, he recognised its unending nature and saw constancy, stating 'water penetrates everywhere', and in so doing prefigured the modern paradox that change is the only constant.

As for mountains, there are mountains hidden in jewels; there are mountains hidden in marshes, mountains hidden in the sky; there are mountains hidden in mountains. There is a study of mountains hidden in hiddenness. An ancient Buddha has said, 'Mountains are mountains and rivers are rivers.' The meaning of these words is not that mountains are mountains, but that mountains are mountains. Therefore, we should thoroughly study these mountains. When we thoroughly study the mountains, this is the mountain training. Such mountains and rivers themselves spontaneously become old men and sages.[6]

We look to the mountains because they hold mysteries that the urban and rural vistas which dominate our social and self-obsessed lives don't always radiate. Gazing at mountainscapes we are able to see ourselves in a new perspective. How temporary and insignificant our individual lives can suddenly appear, while at the same time how destructive and long-lasting the sum of human endeavour. Yet staring into spaces so beautiful and unsullied can also be enormously uplifting and restorative, upending our tired ideas and restoring our minds with hope. Mountains are a source, an enigma for the imagination to work with, and the responses they elicit can be both moral and aesthetic.

We may debate the moral and metaphysical importance of mountains, skies and oceans until we too are blue, but it seems unarguable that they are great reservoirs of unattainable beauty. No one inhabits their far reaches, visits are brief and tentative, and yet no effort of ours could make arenas so pleasurable to gaze upon. It is this thought that so exasperated the poet Byron: 'Mountains, why are you so beautiful? I cannot love you…'[7]. Being a man of words and deeds who loved to grasp the object of his desire, the note of desperation in his cry is clear. Yet some of us too are compelled to gaze upon mountains with the same perplexity, our eyes searching them out, finding their faces mesmerising, their forms sometimes sensual, sometimes classical, their dark and dangerous masks sublime. They may be temptations before which we are frequently struck dumb and have no answer but to stare. All we can resolve is whether our gaze will be out of frustrated desire or composed reverie.

Our lives seem brief and full of fragility when measured against the endurance of a mountain. Soon I will be too old to climb among them and will have to return permanently to my childhood vision where the mountains are once more a distant, untouchable verity. But like Dogen, or perhaps more like the poet Shelley writing to his friend Thomas Medwin, I hope to accept the pleasure of the distant gaze with good grace:

> I see the mountains, the sky, and the trees from my windows, and recollect as an old man does the Mistress of his youth, the raptures of a more familiar intercourse, but without regrets for their forms are living in my mind.[8]

ENDNOTES

1 The phrase 'the thousand mountains, shining' comes from the poem 'Hawk over Bowen Peak' by Charles
   Brasch.
2 Japanese Zen master Dogen (1200-1253), *Treasury of the True Dharma Eye: Book XXIX, The Mountains and
   Rivers Sutra*, translated by Carl Bielefeldt: MA thesis, University of California, Berkeley, 1972. This book
   is included in Dogen's collection of writings called *Shobogenzo*, and represents one of the earliest Japanese
   texts of the Zen movement, which had long been prominent in China.
3 From A.E. Housman's poem 'Into my heart an air that kills'.
4 Michael Tobias, *The Mountain Spirit*, London: Victor Gollancz, 1980.
5 Edwin Bernbaum, *Sacred Mountains of the World*, Sierra Club, 1996.
6 Dogen, *The Mountains and Rivers Sutra*.
7 From Lord Byron's poem 'Manfred'.
8 Percy Bysshe Shelley in a letter to Thomas Medwin from Pisa, 1820.

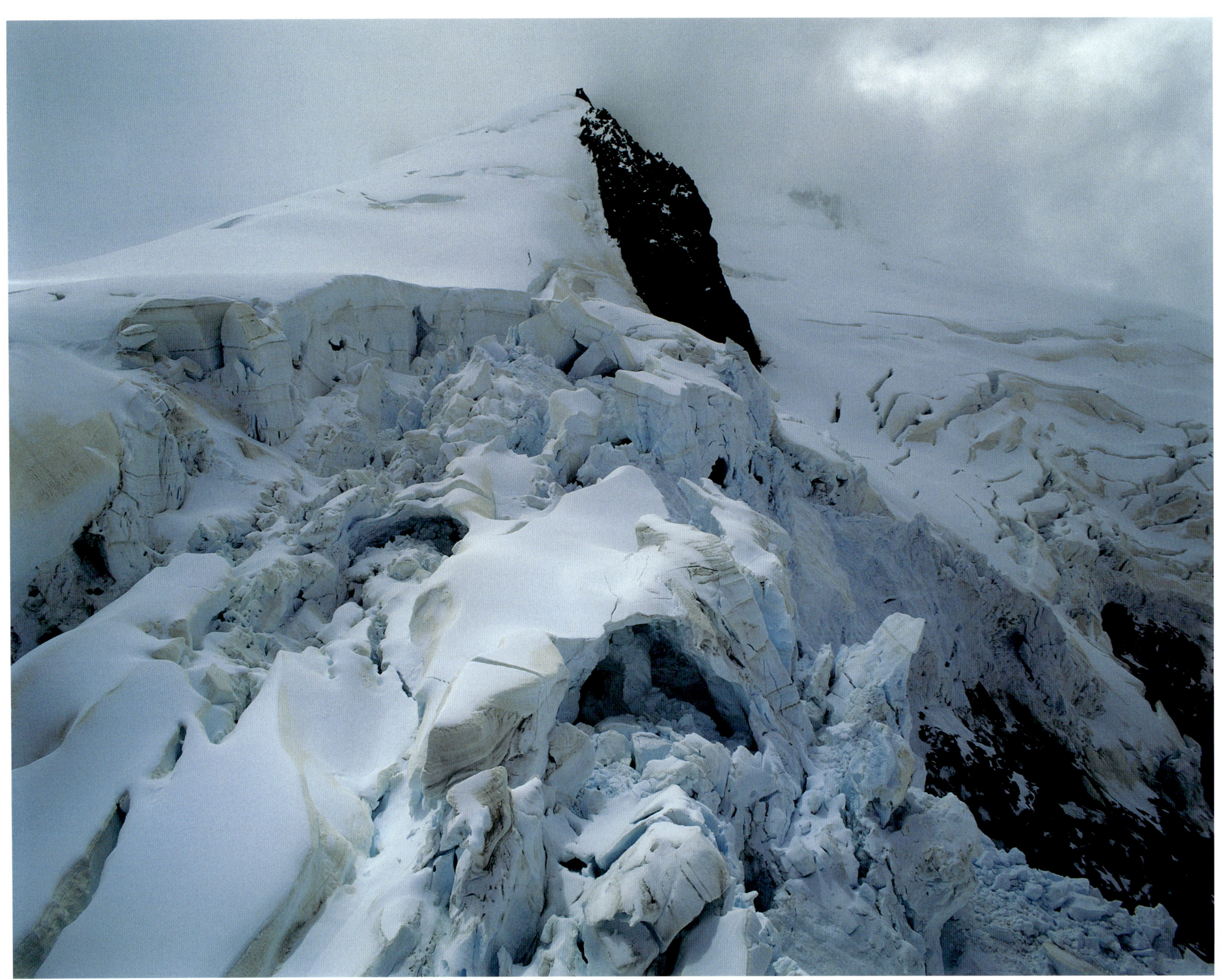

Icefall, Mt Tutoko, Darran Mountains

Fiordland to Mount Aspiring

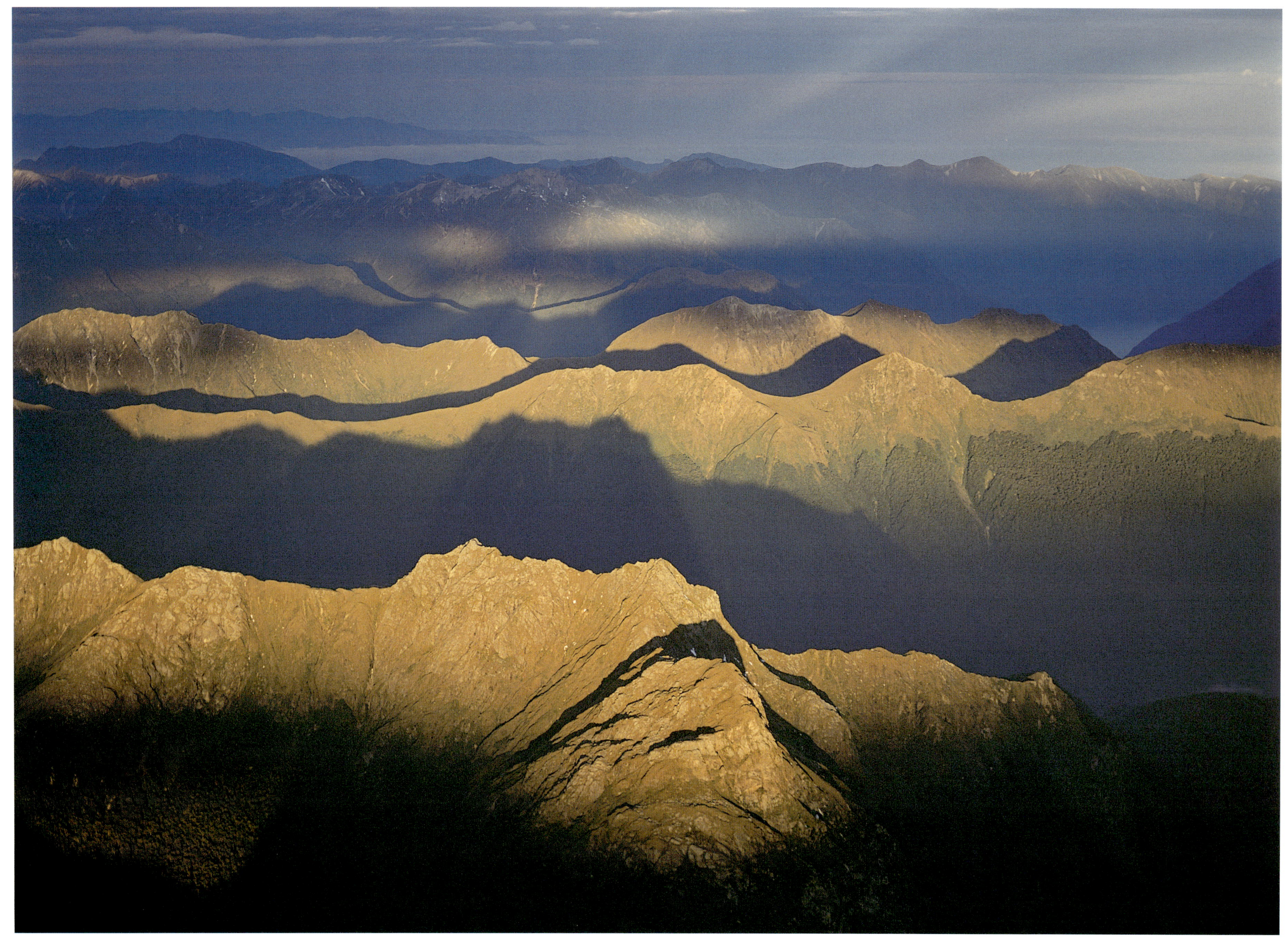

Heath Mountains, Fiordland National Park

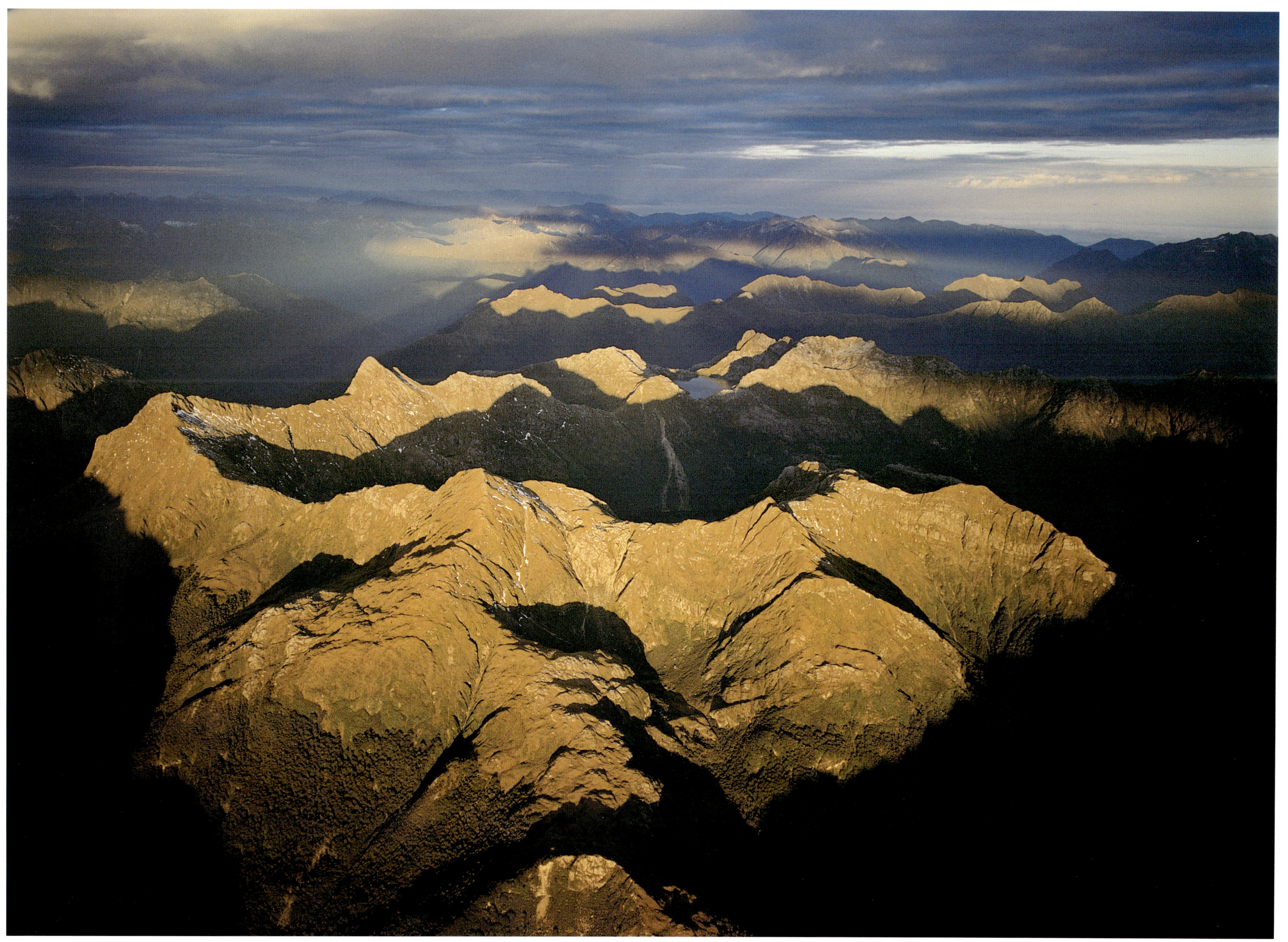

Heath Mountains, Fiordland National Park

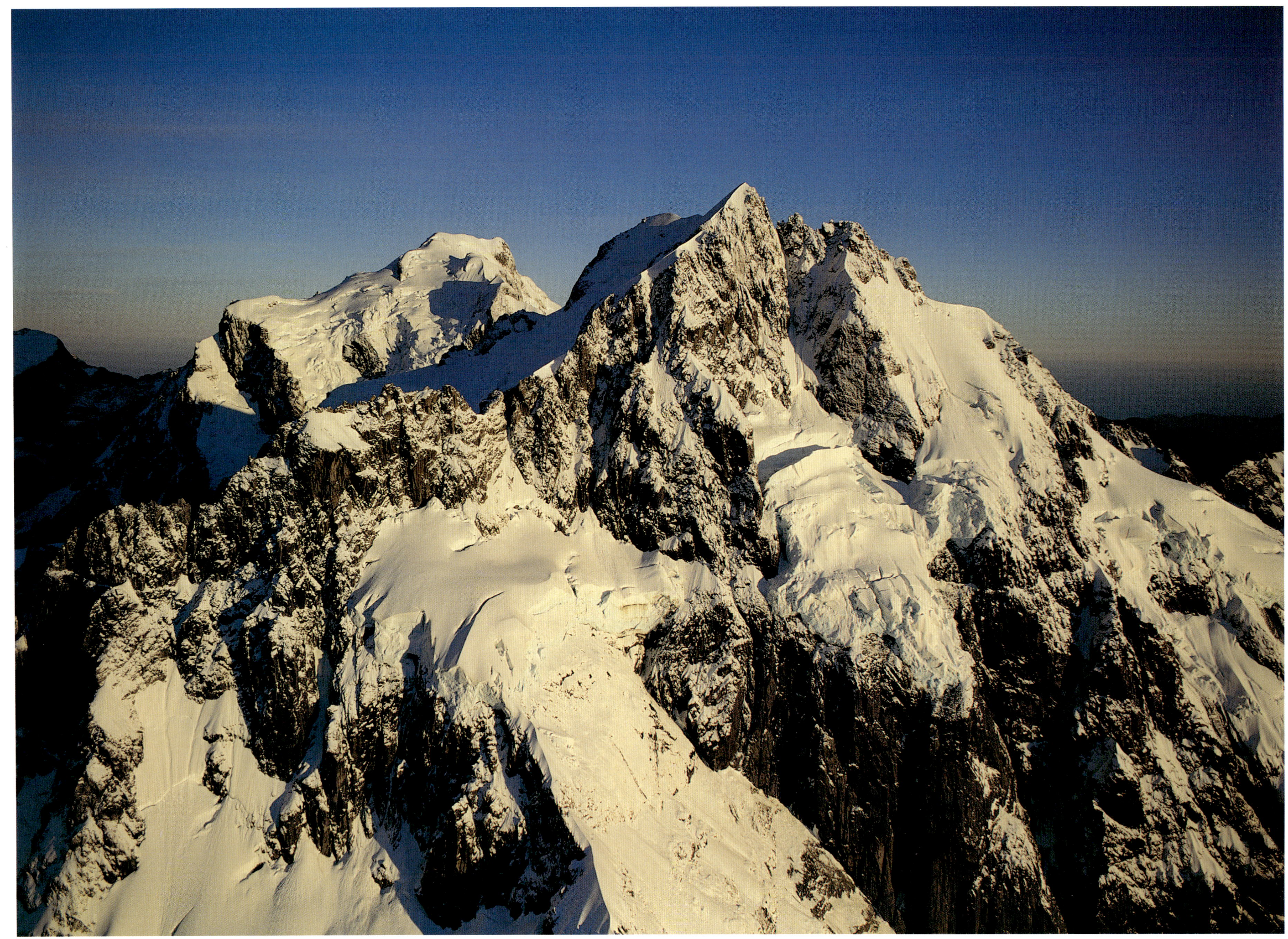

Mts Tutoko and Madeline, Darran Mountains

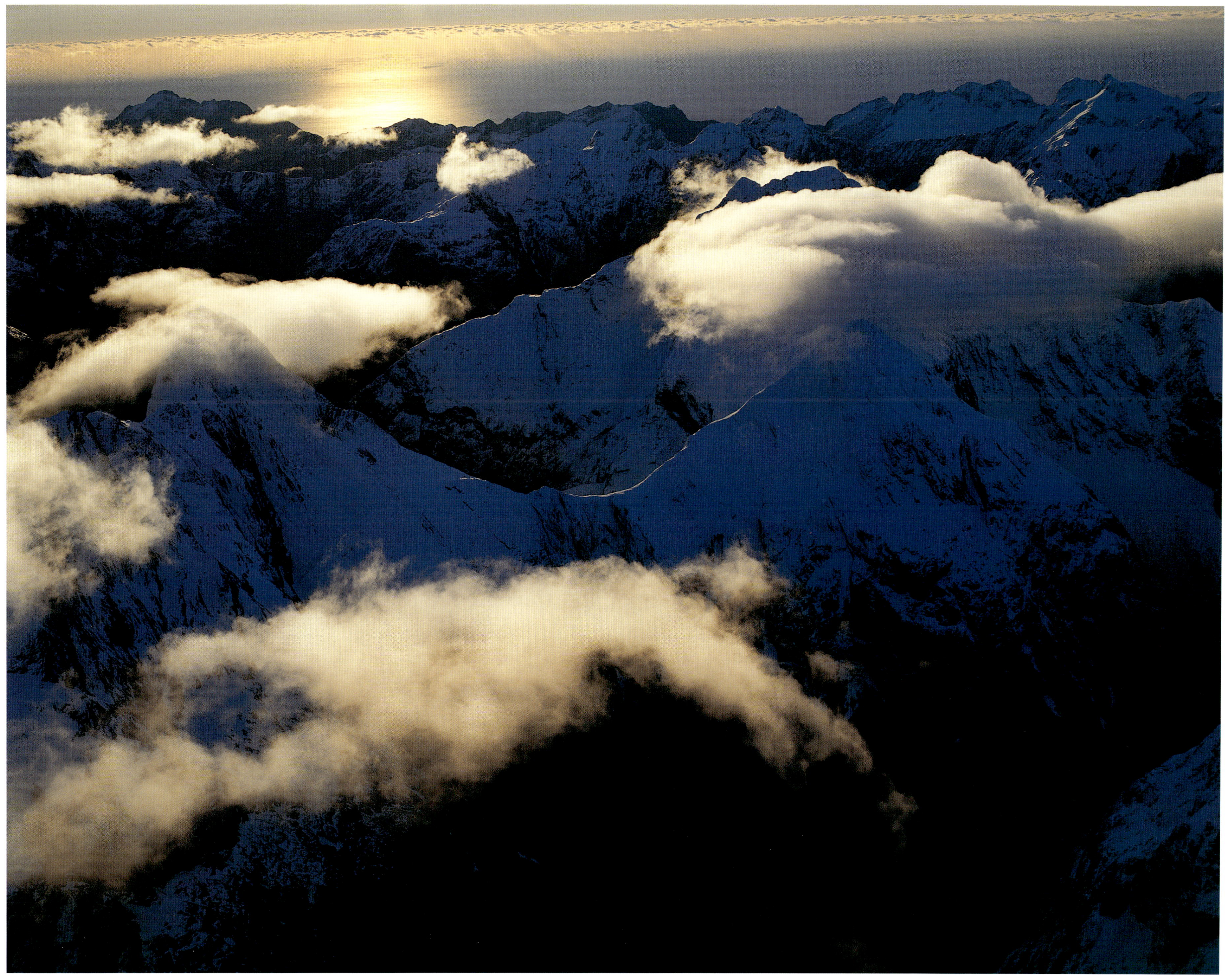

Mountain ranges south of Milford Sound

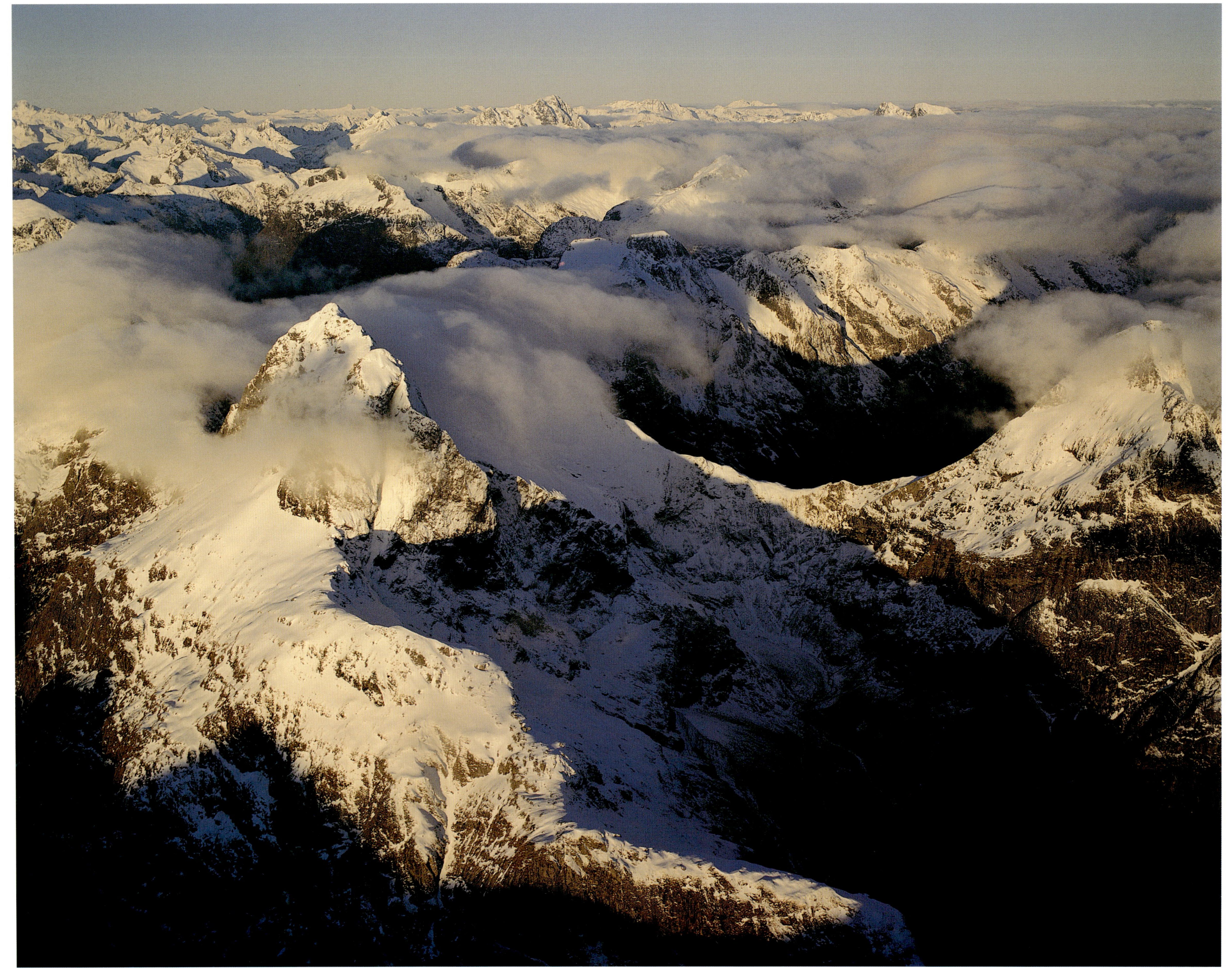

Darran Mountains

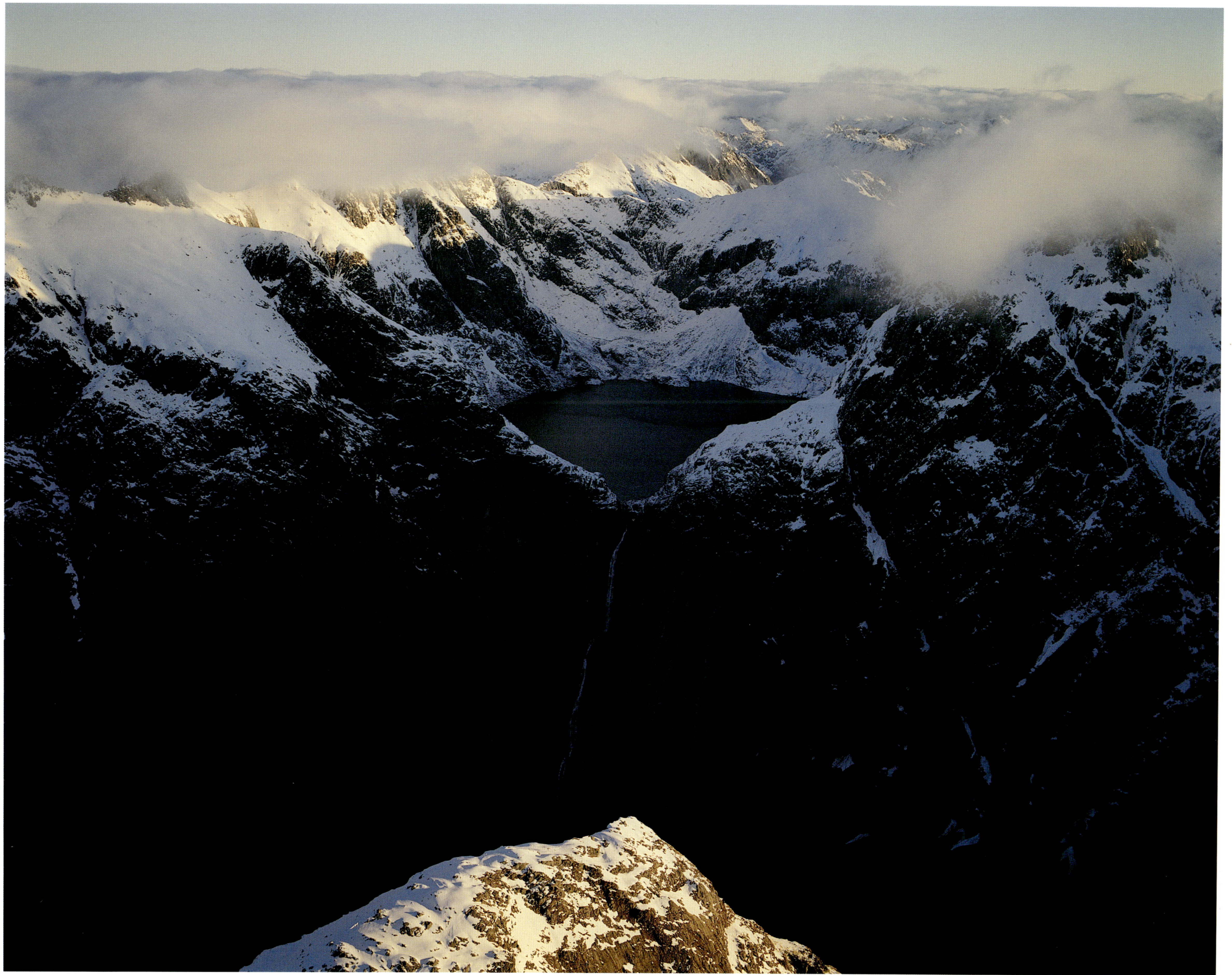

Lake Quill and Sutherland Falls

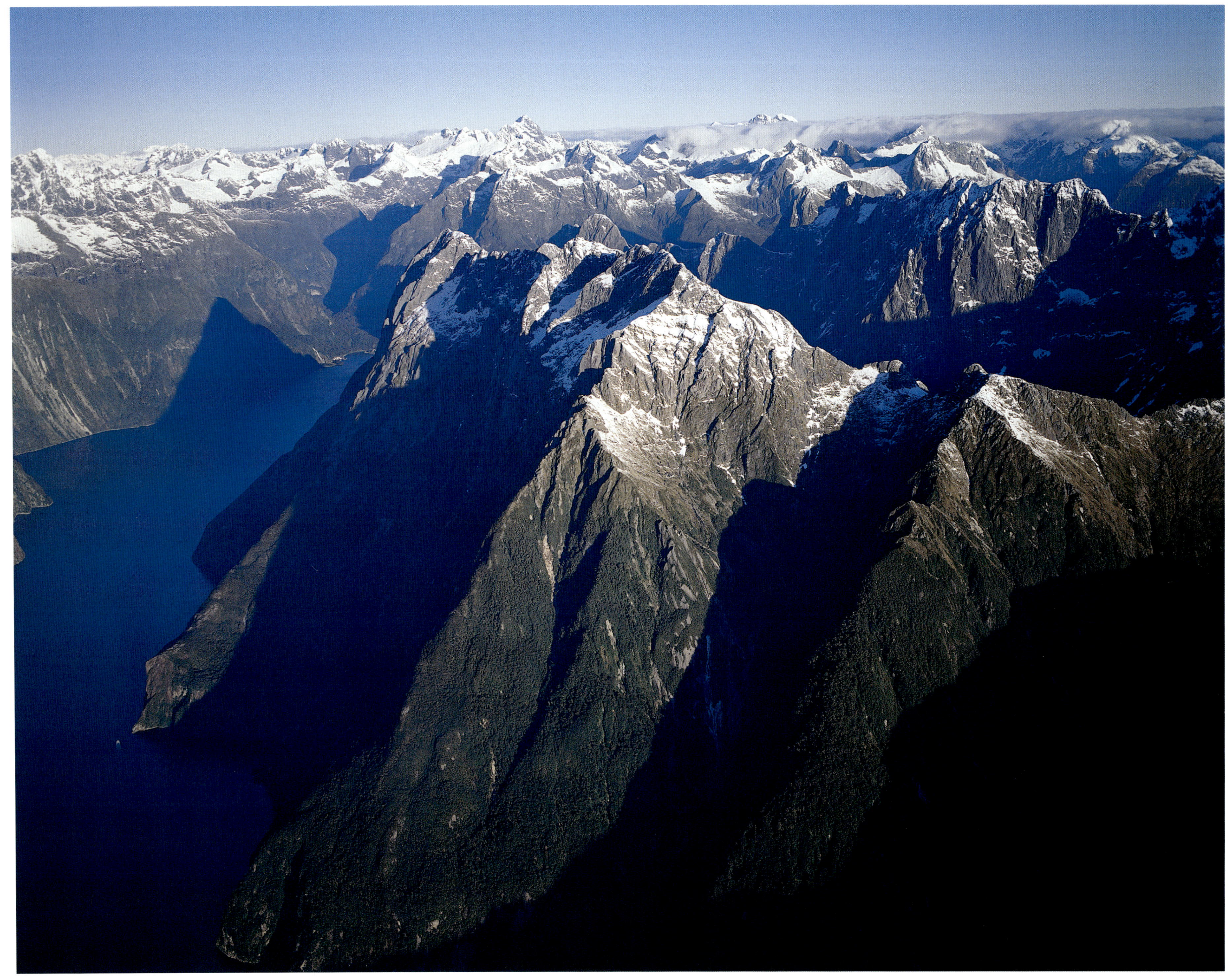

Mitre Peak, Milford Sound

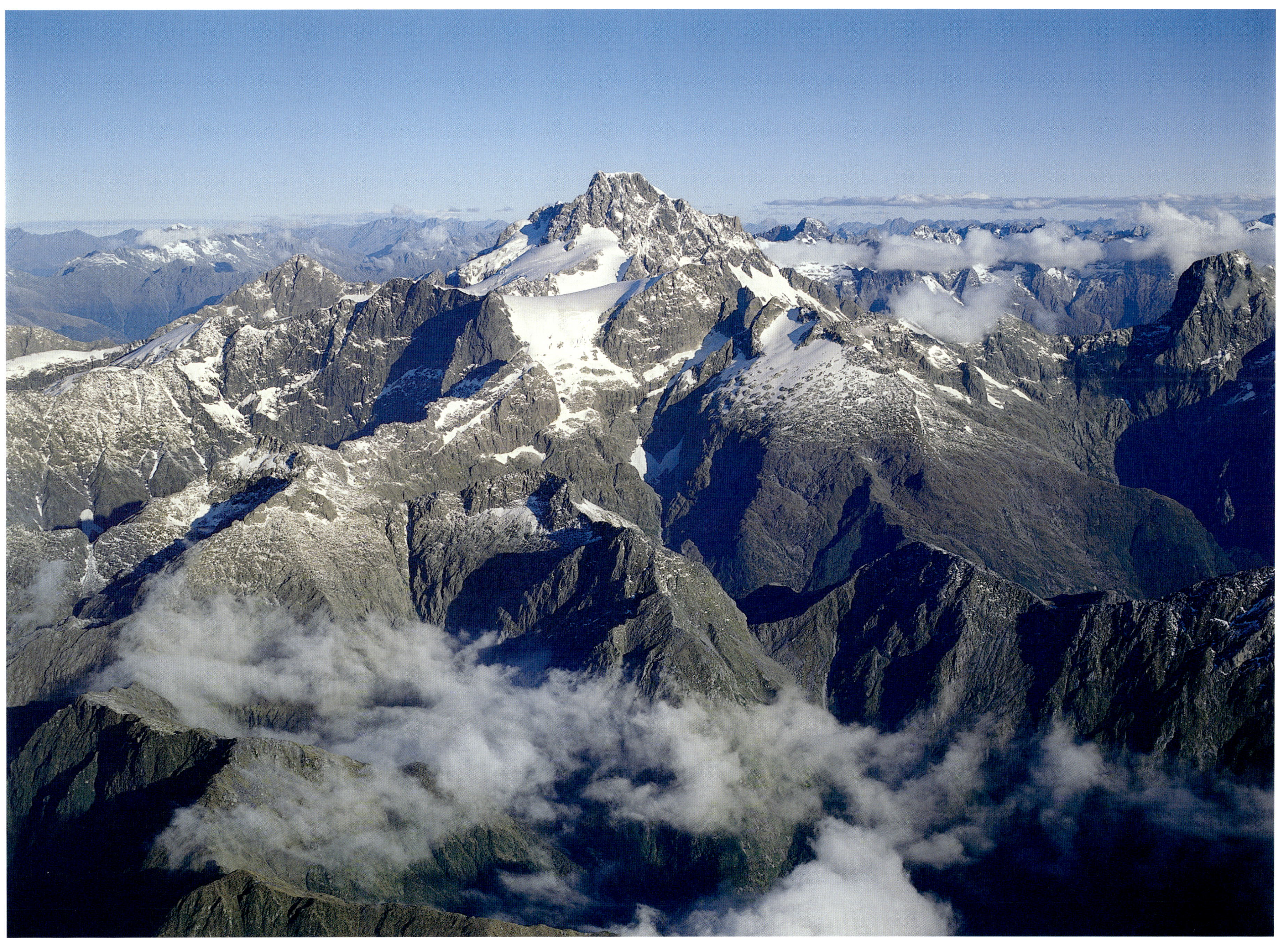

Mt Tutoko from the west

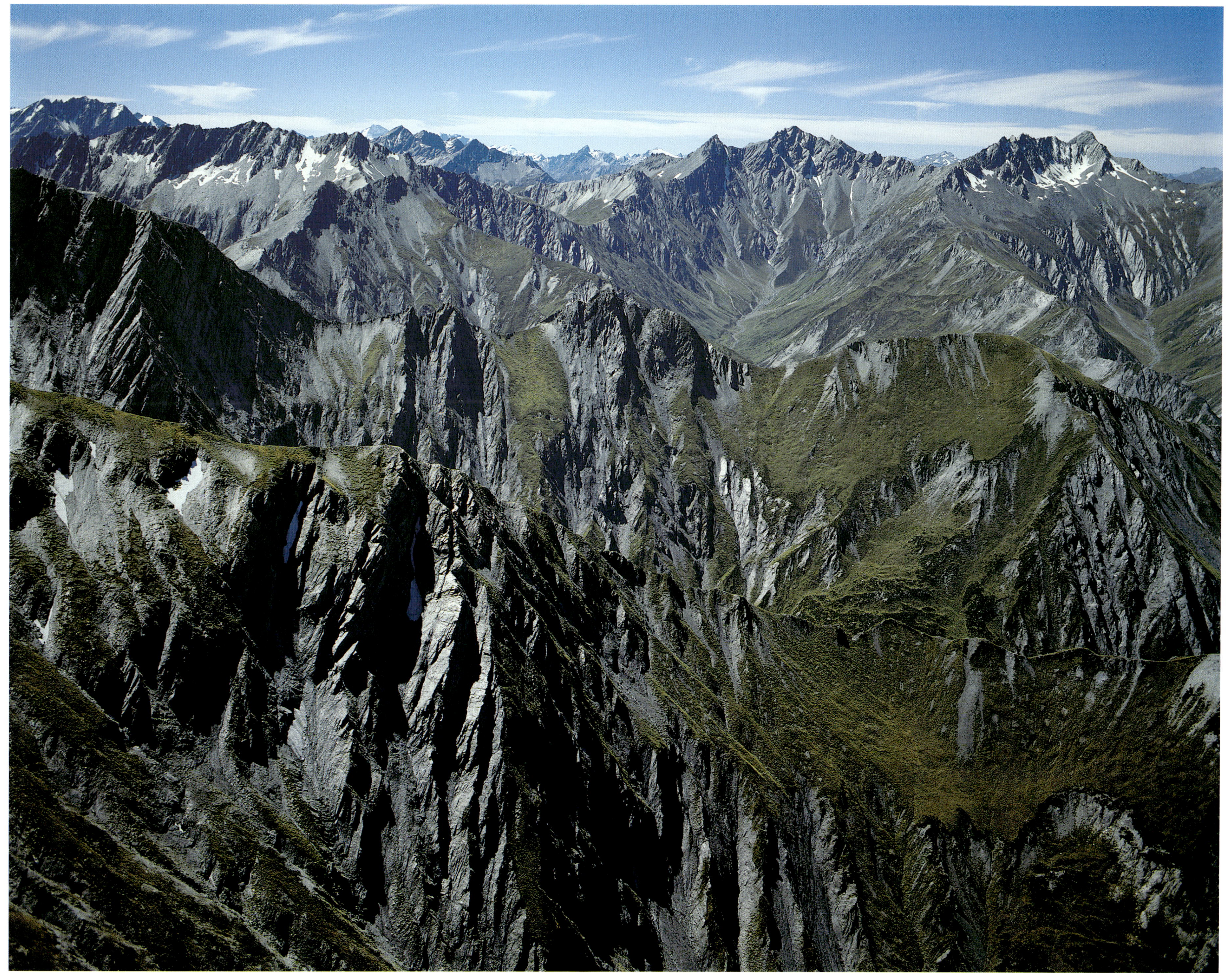

Harris Mountains

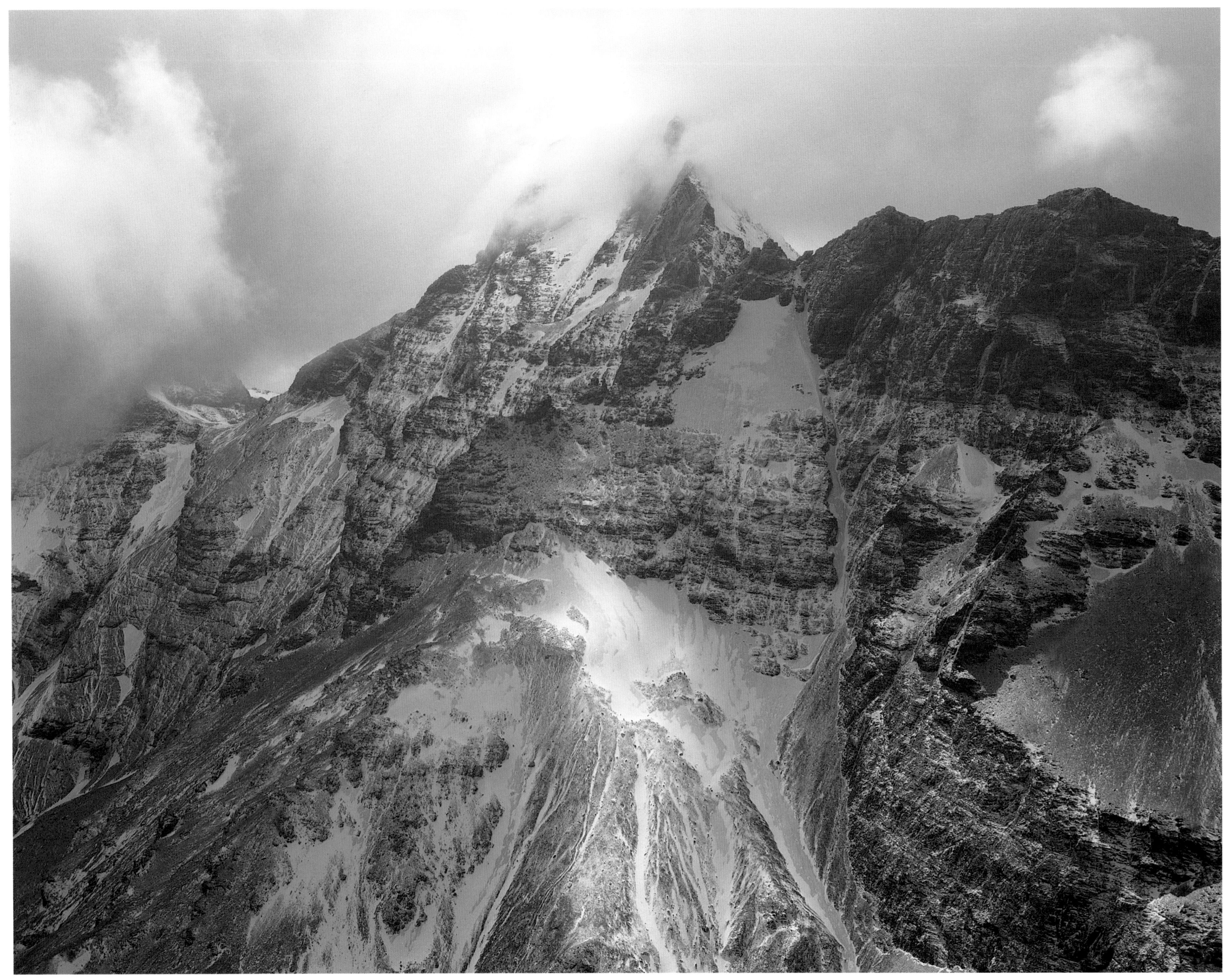

West Peak, Pikirakatahi/Mt Earnslaw

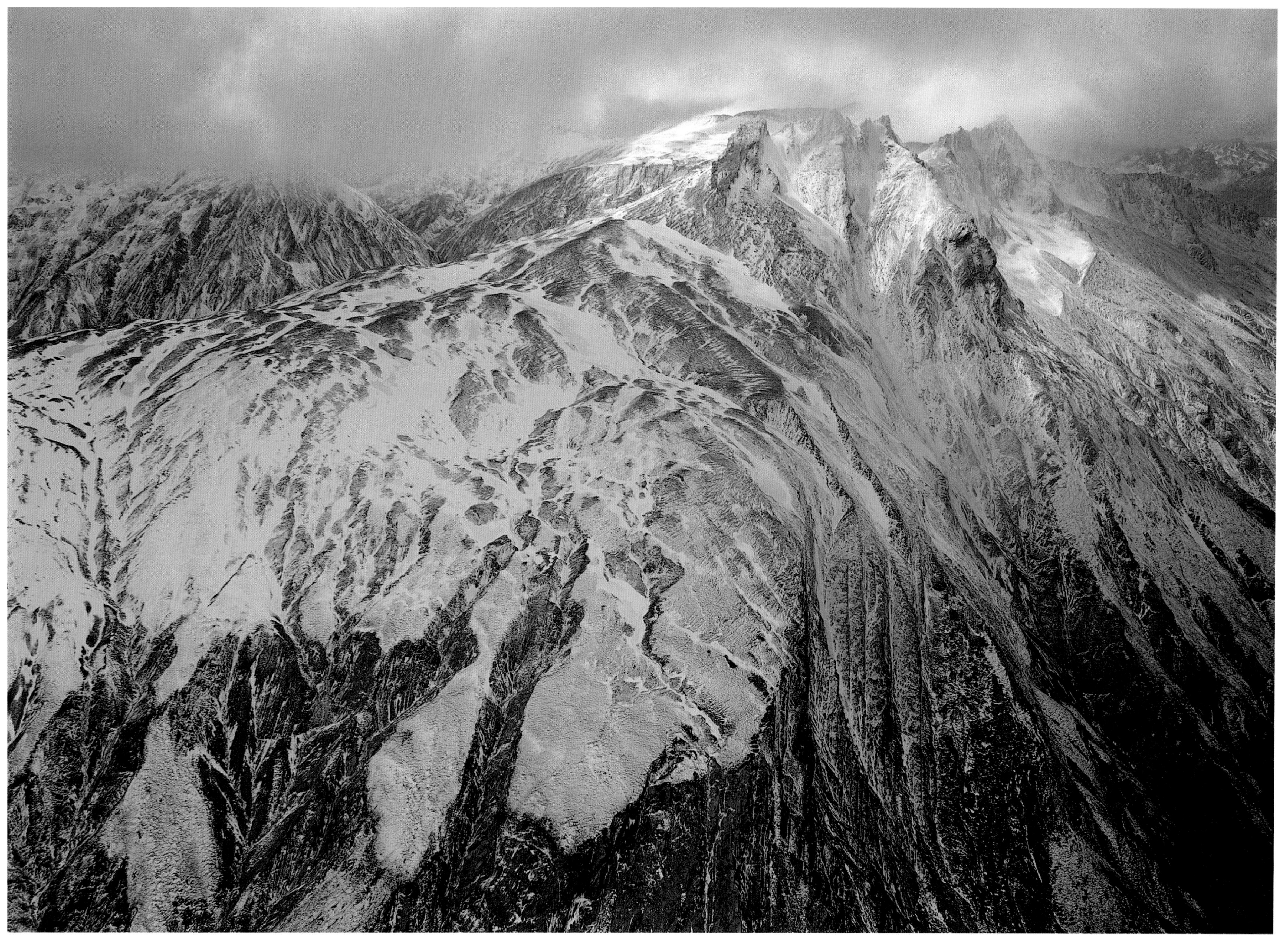

Richardson Mountains—ridge above Lochnagar

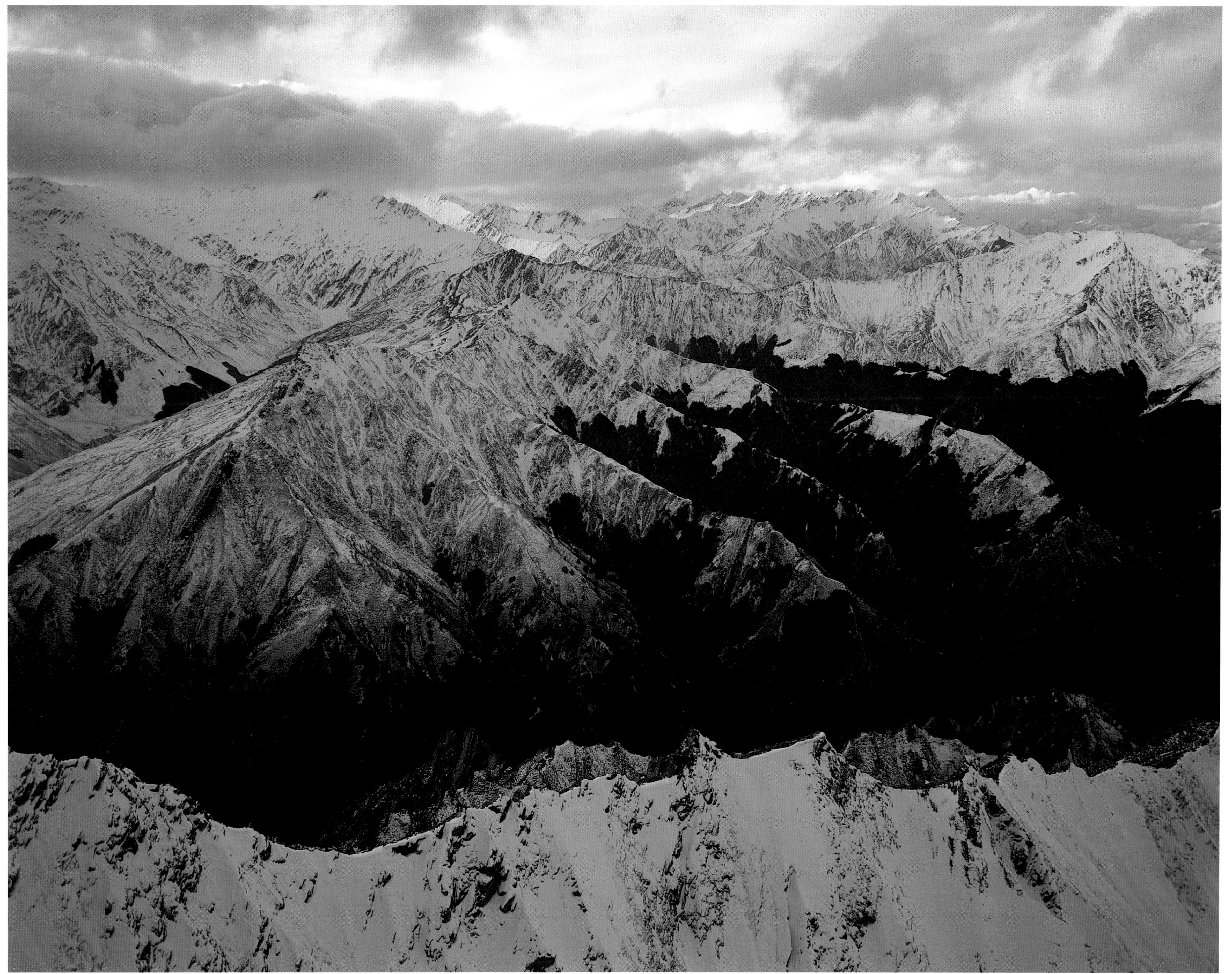

Richardson Mountains

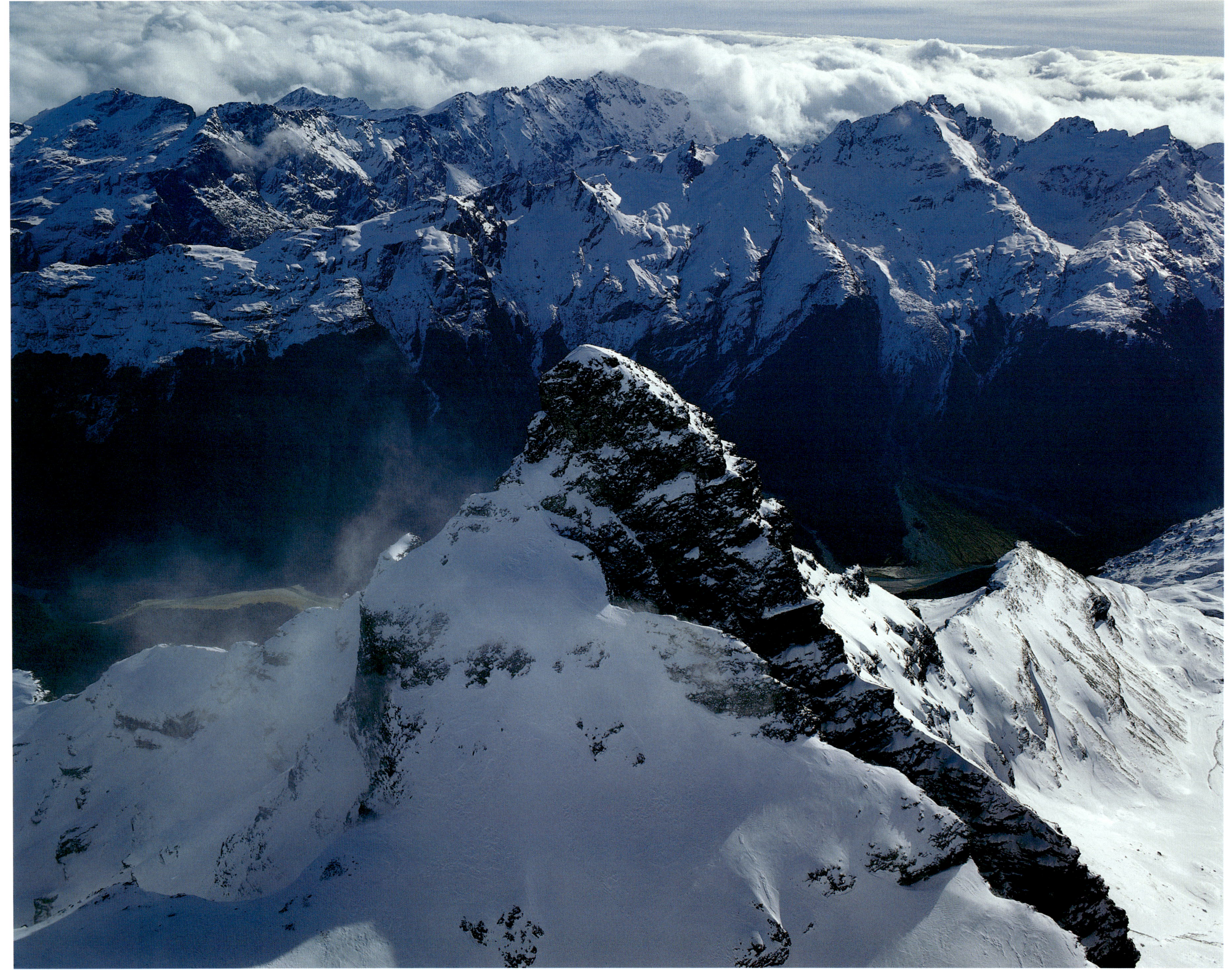

Pluto Peak

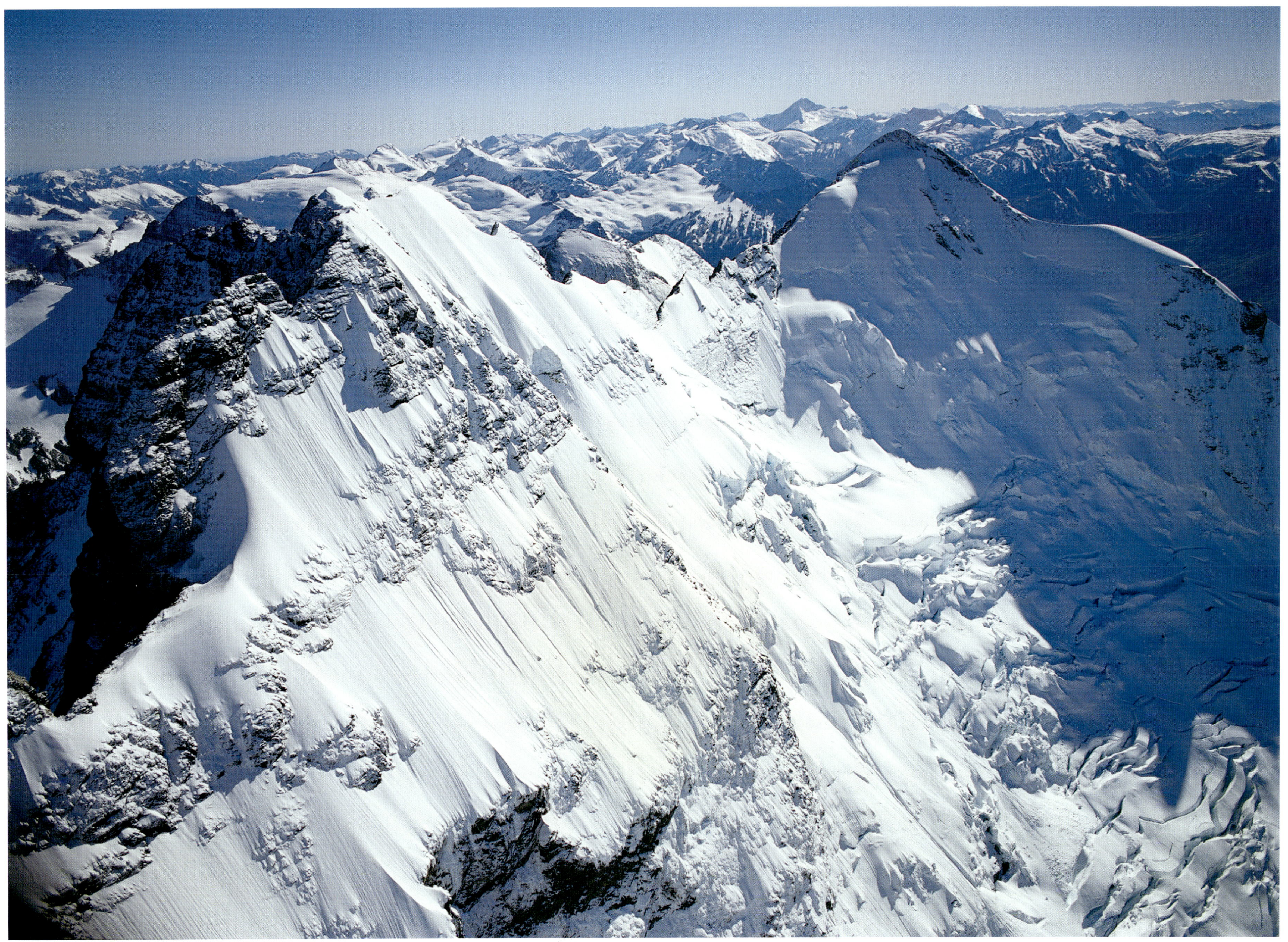

South Face of Pikirakatahi/Mt Earnslaw

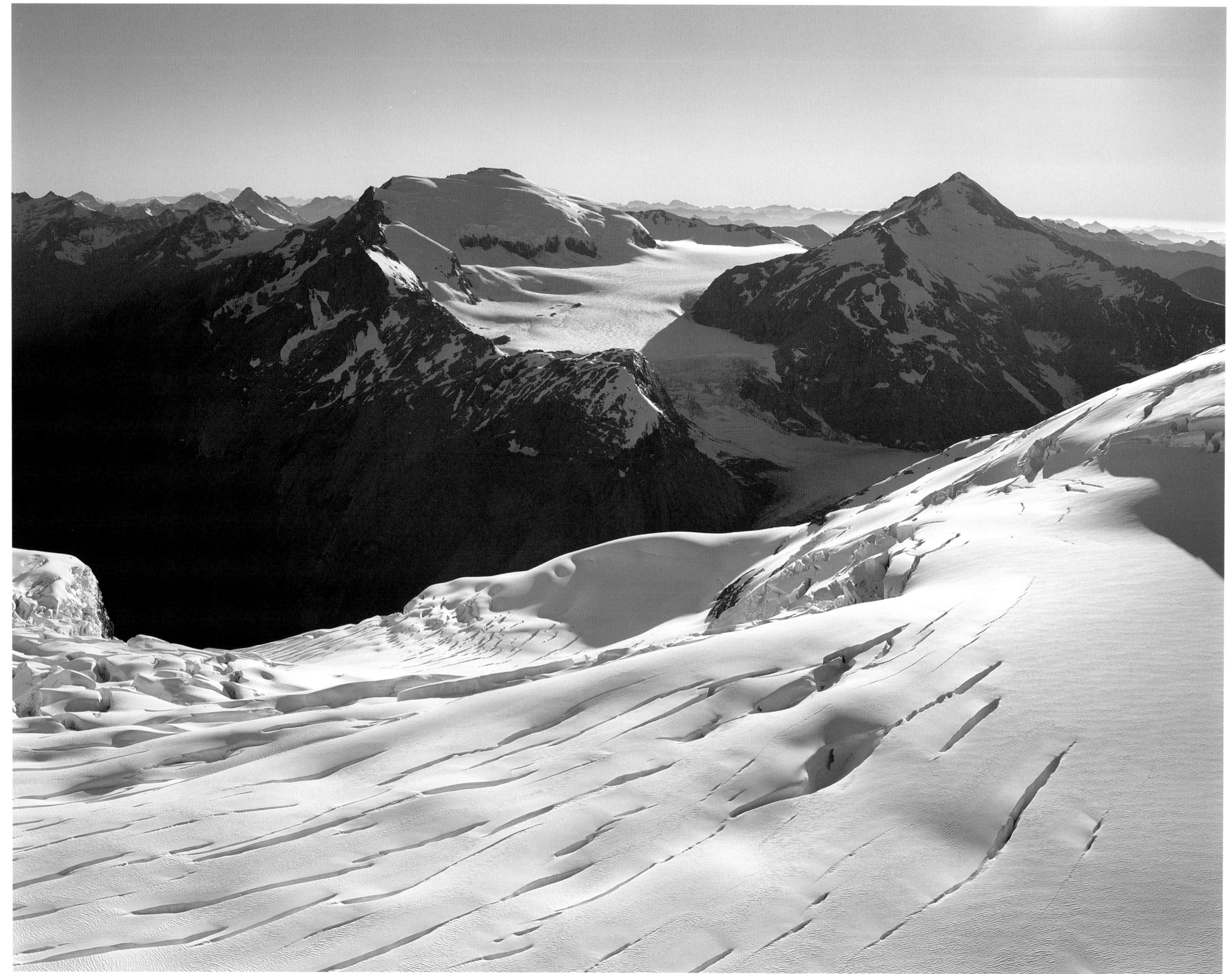

Therma and Upper Volta glaciers

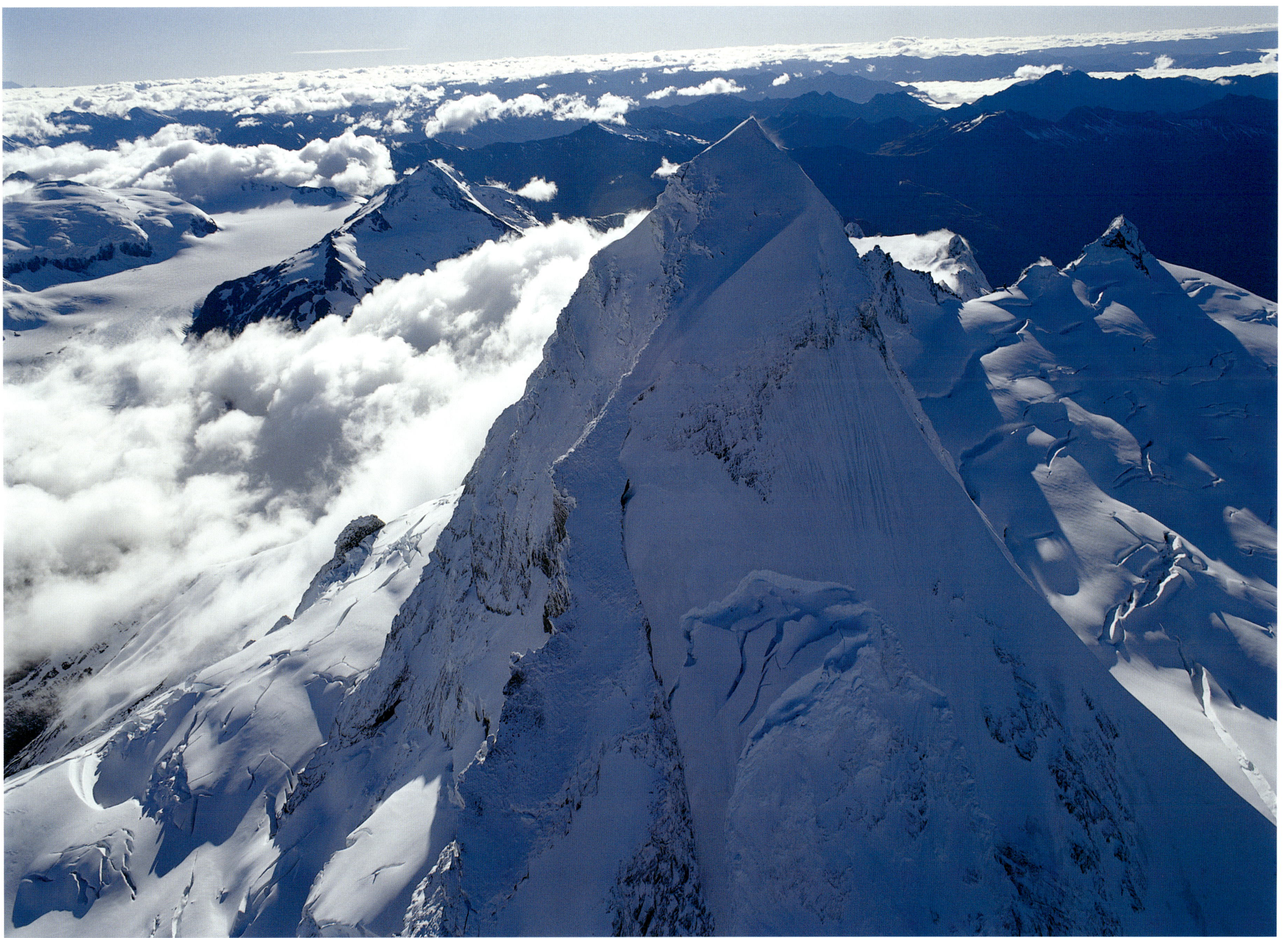

Tititea/Mt Aspiring from the west

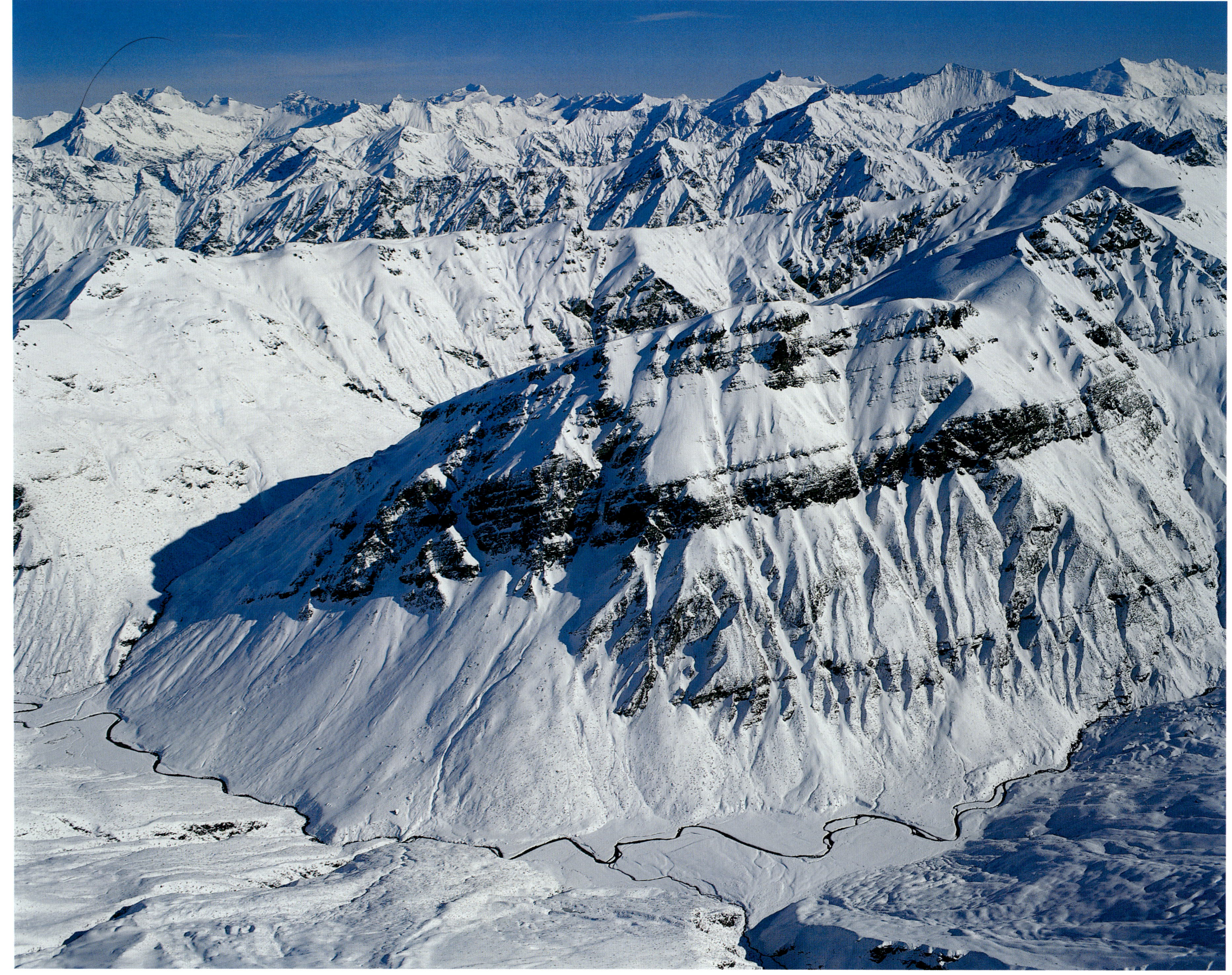

Harris Mountains

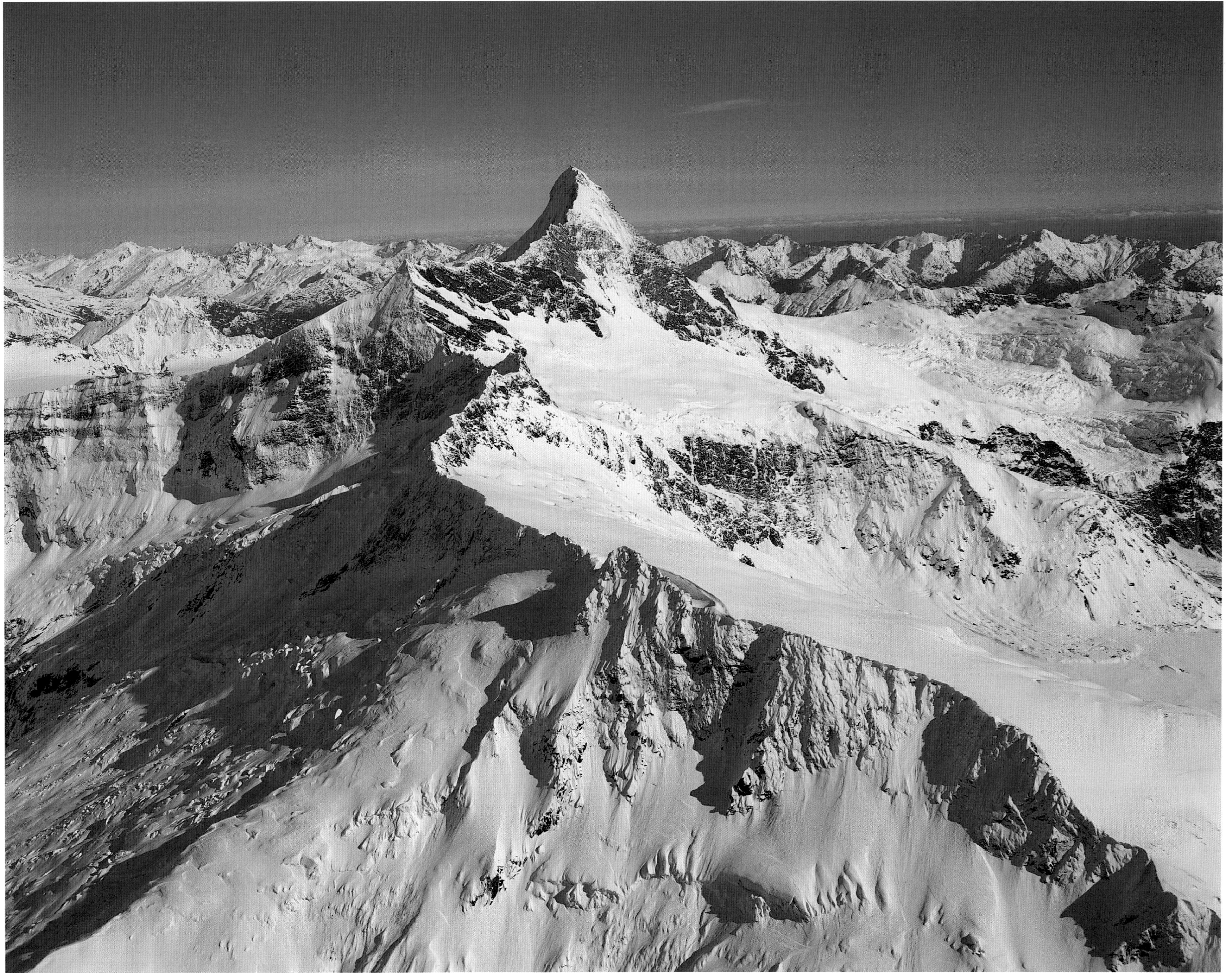

Tititea/Mt Aspiring from the east

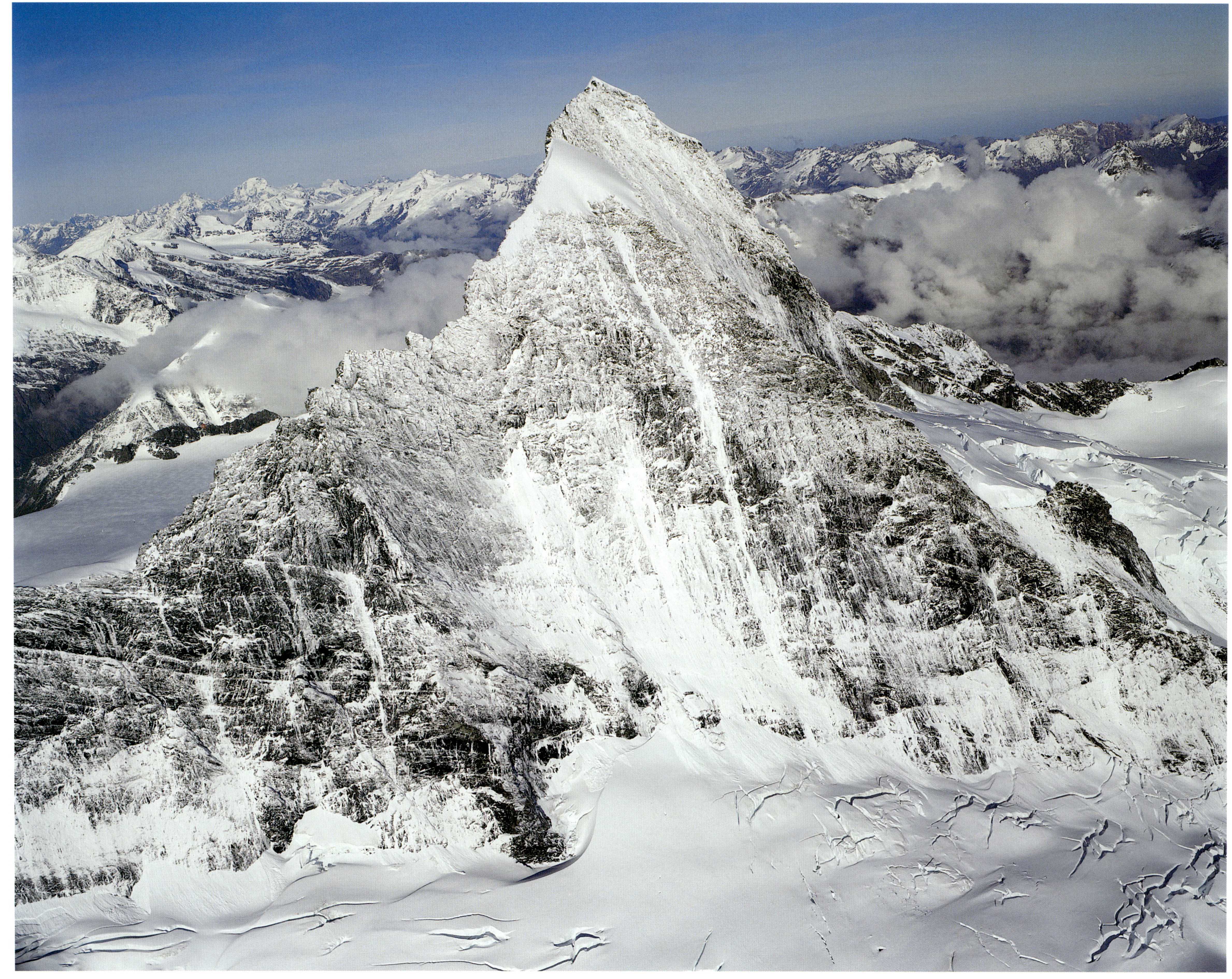

Tititea/Mt Aspiring—the Coxcomb Ridge and North East Face

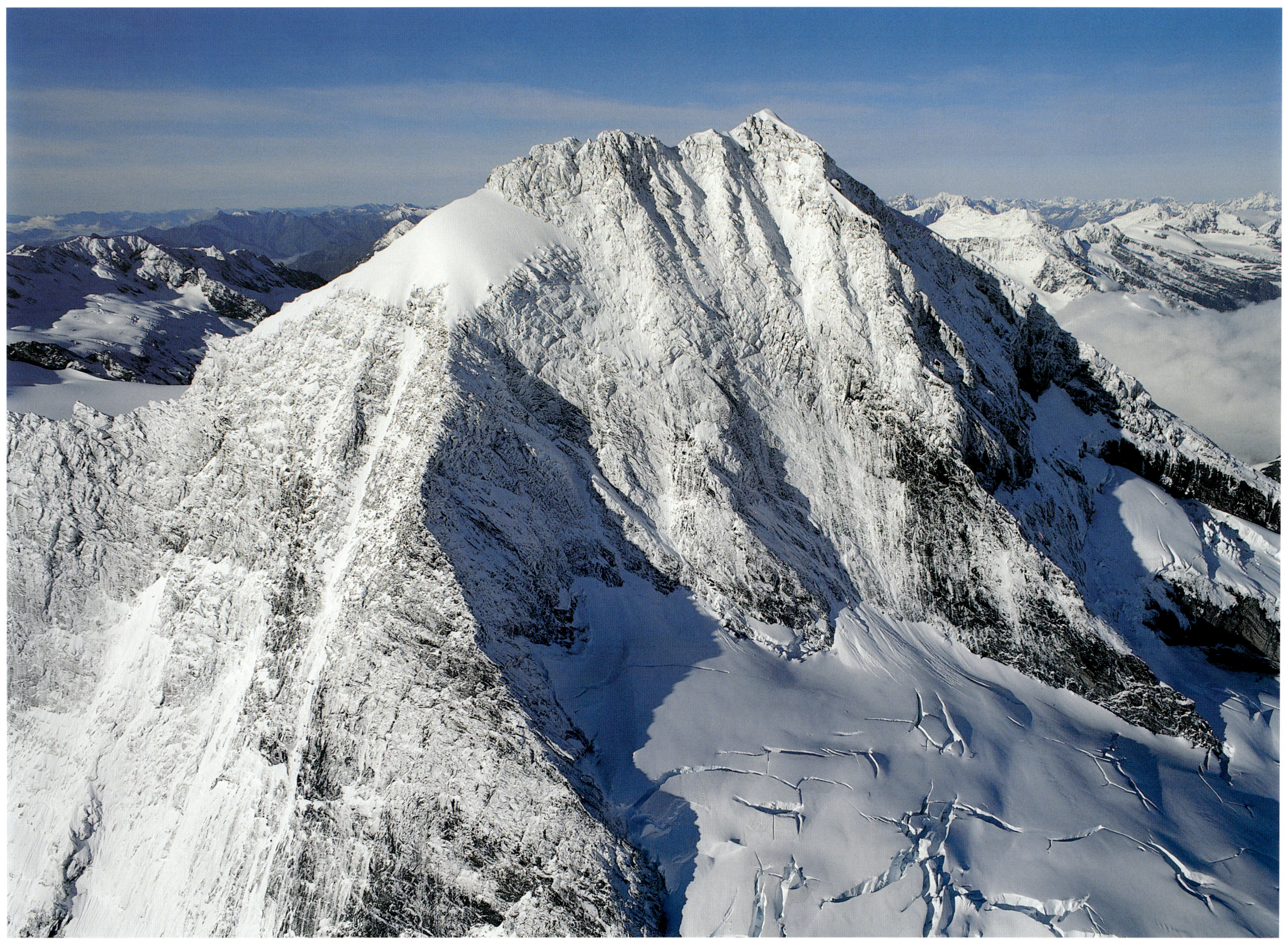

North Face, Tititea/Mt Aspiring

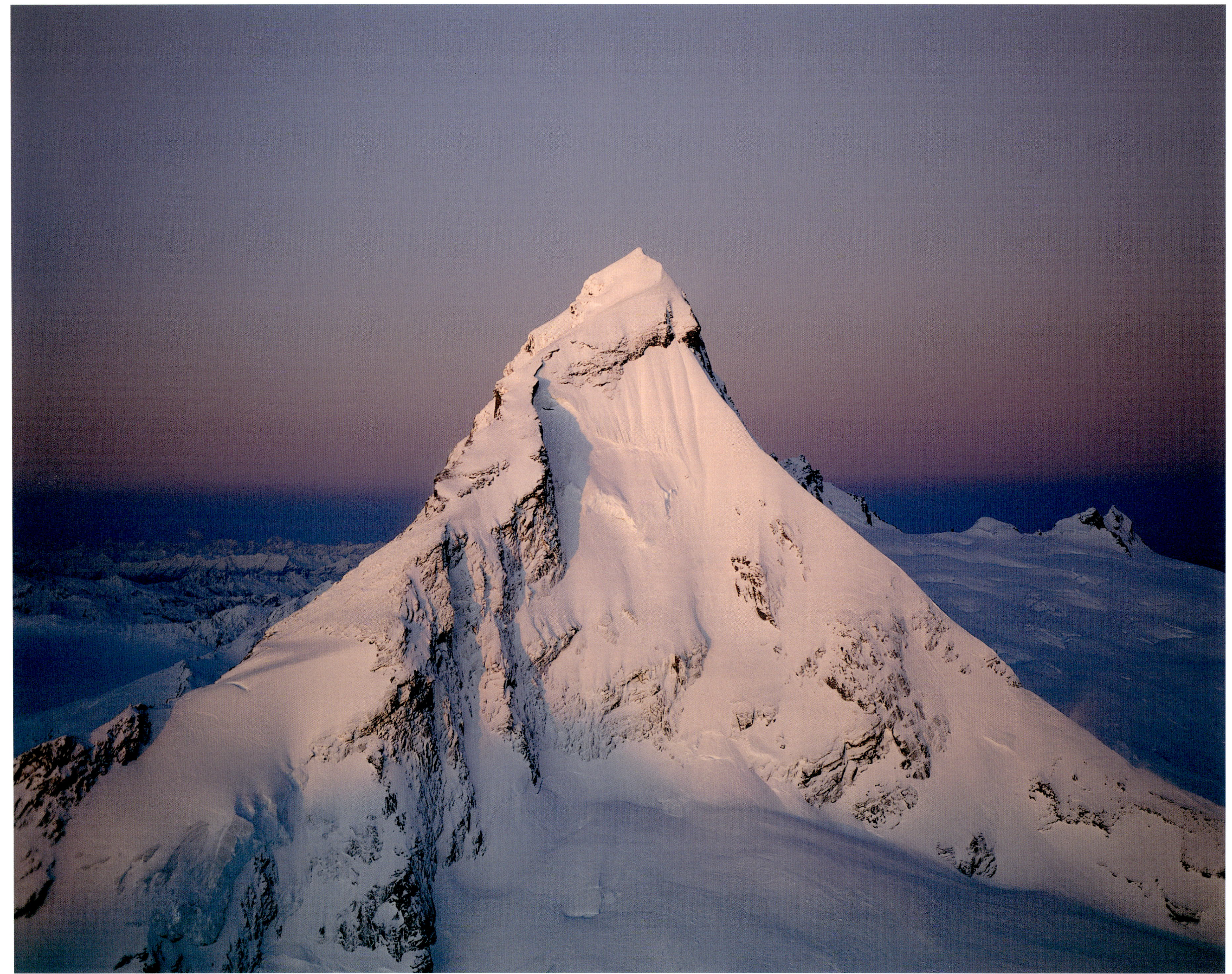

Tititea/Mt Aspiring from the west

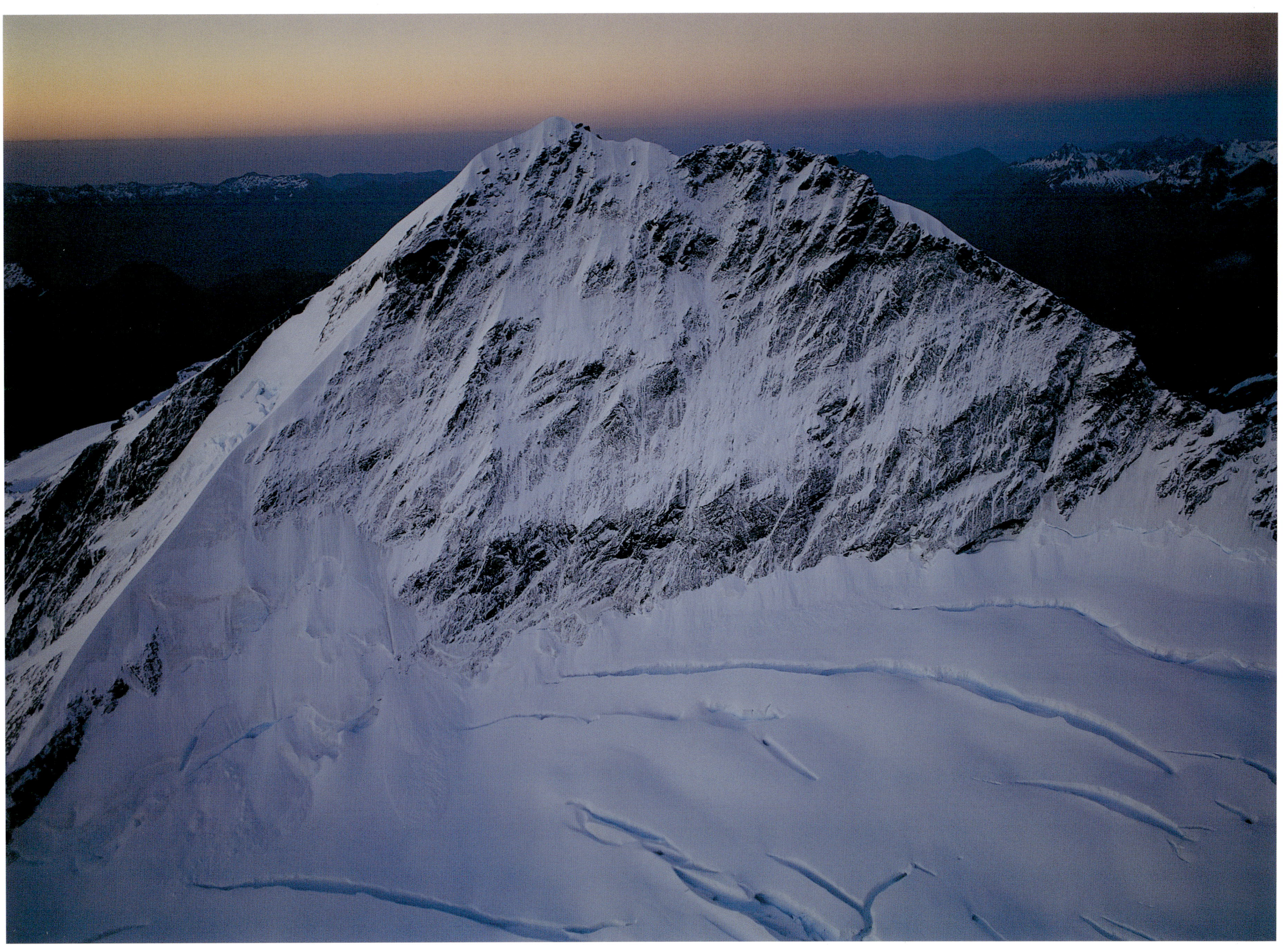

Tititea/Mt Aspiring—the South Face

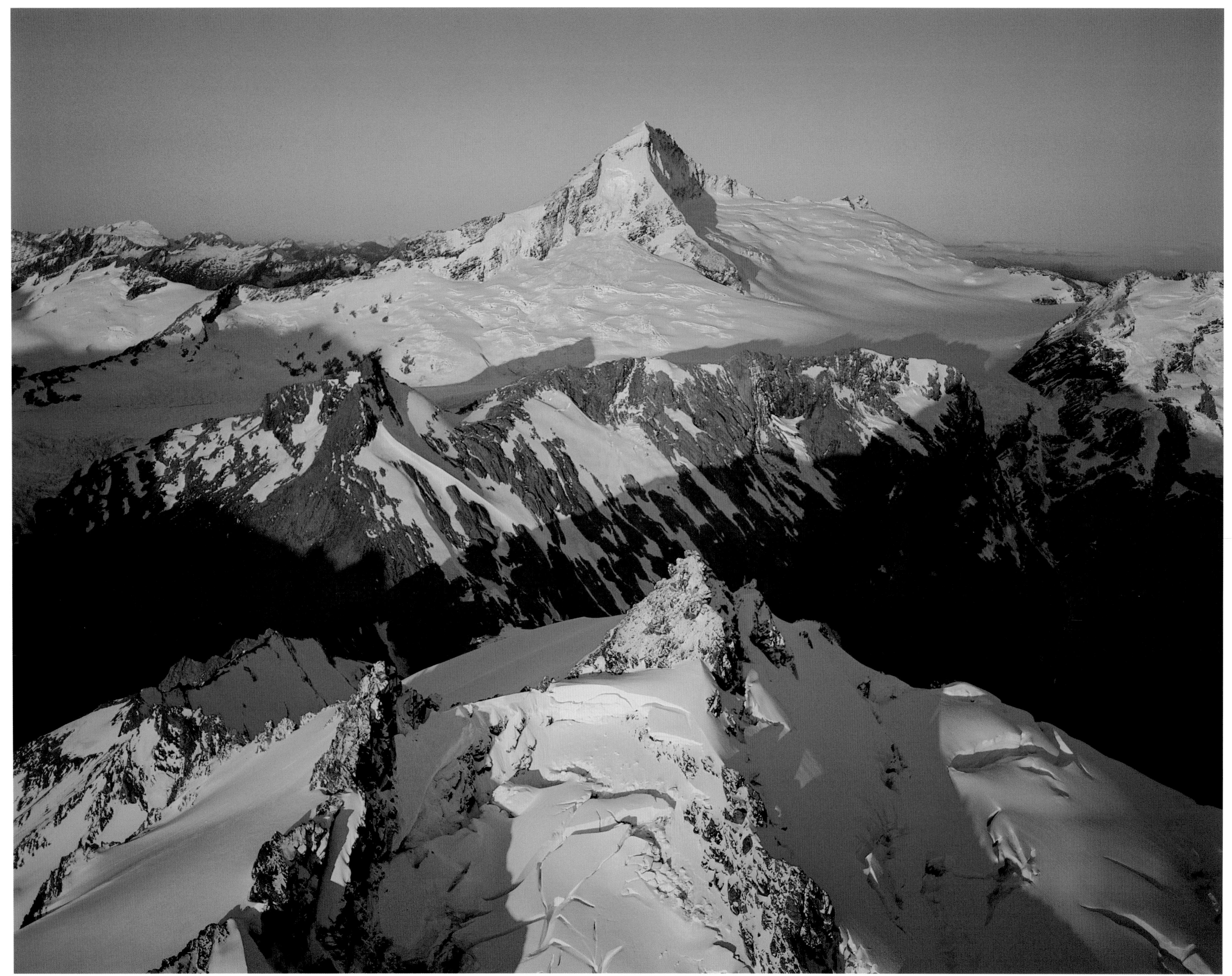

Tititea/Mt Aspiring from above the Waipara Range

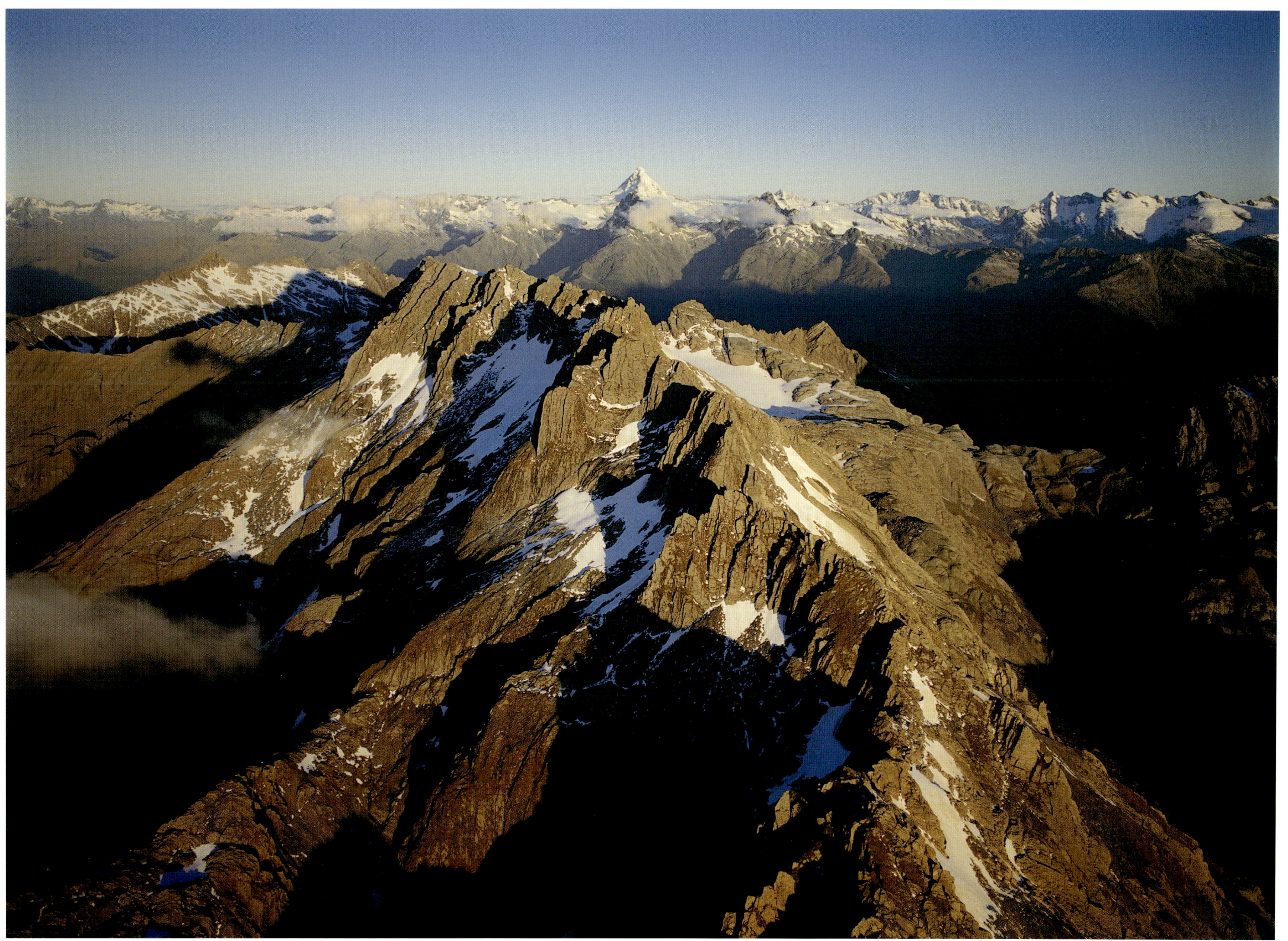

The Olivine Range with Tititea/Mt Aspiring and Main Divide peaks beyond

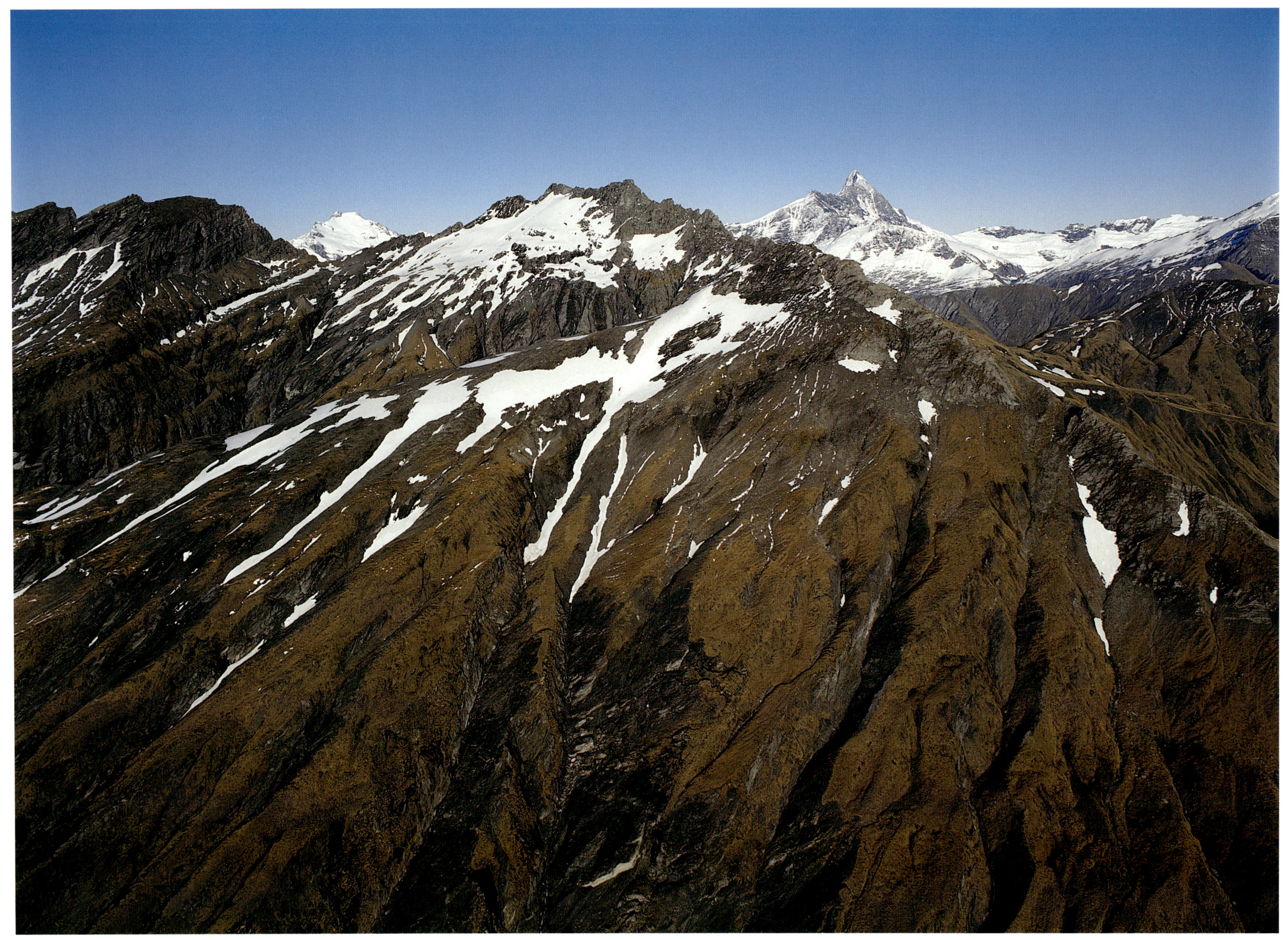

Head of the Albert Burn, Mount Aspiring National Park

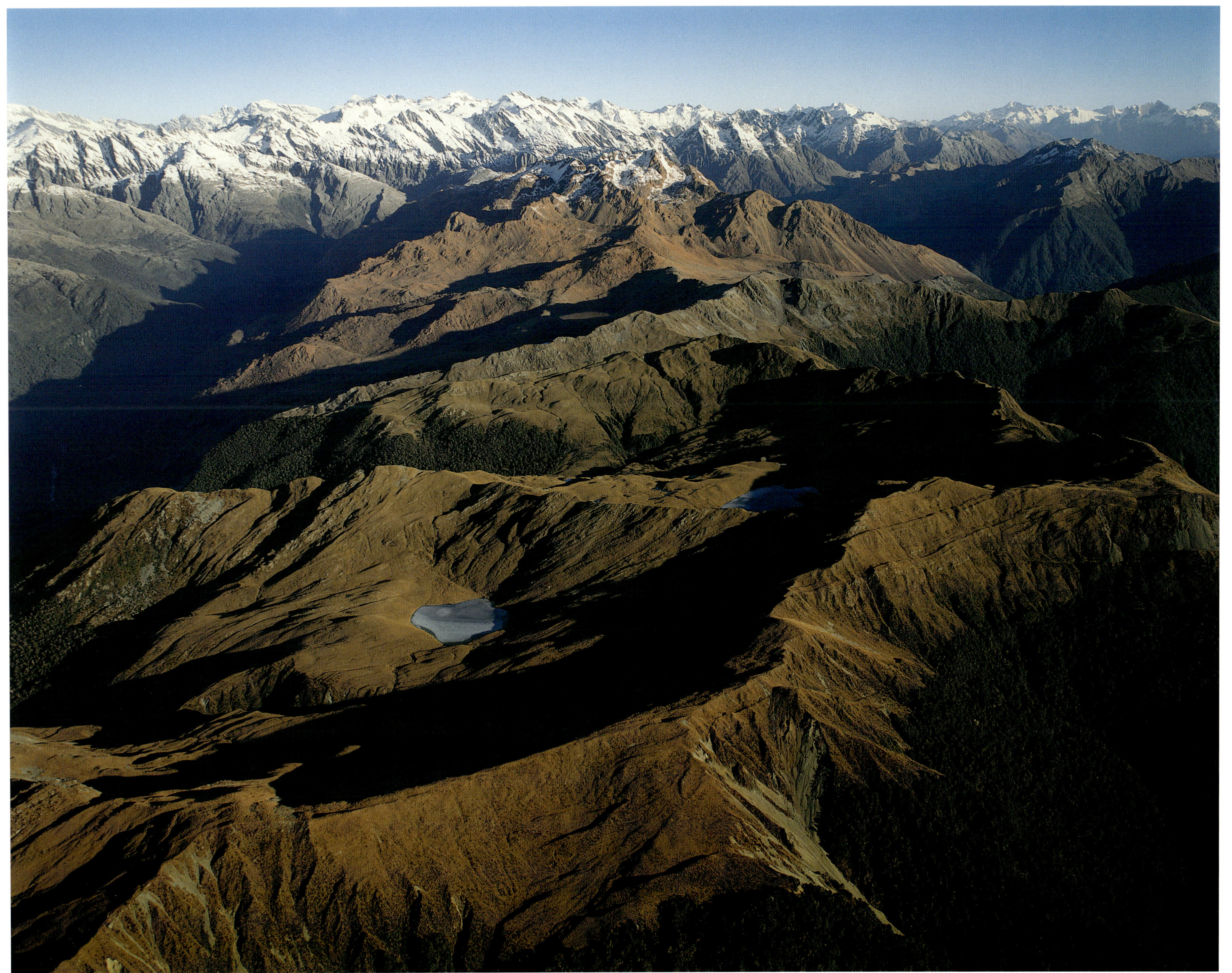

Red Hills Range, Olivine Wilderness Area

Are not the mountains, waves and skies a part of me and of my soul as I of them?

Is not the love of these deep in my heart with a pure passion?

—Lord Byron

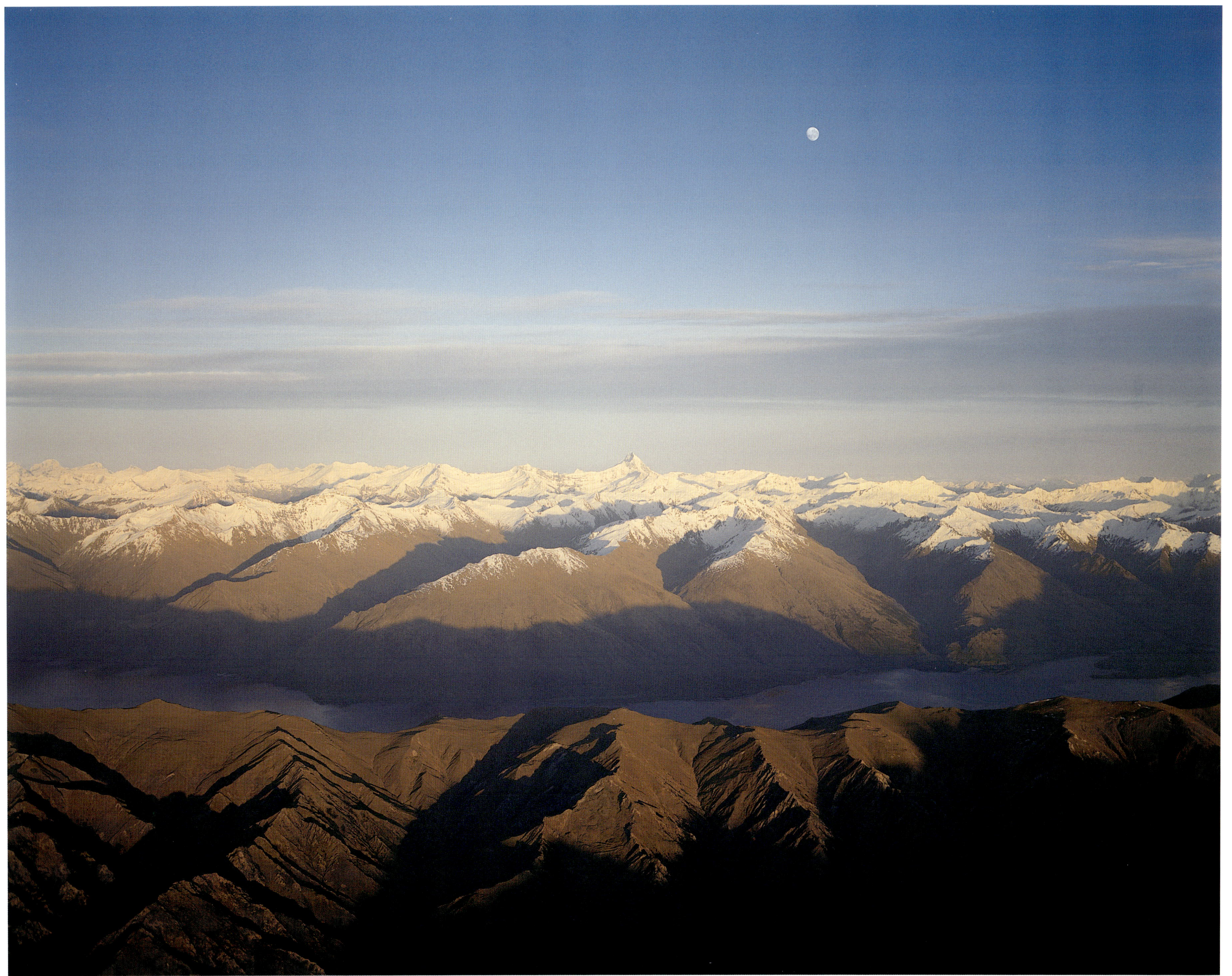

Lake Wanaka and Tititea/Mt Aspiring

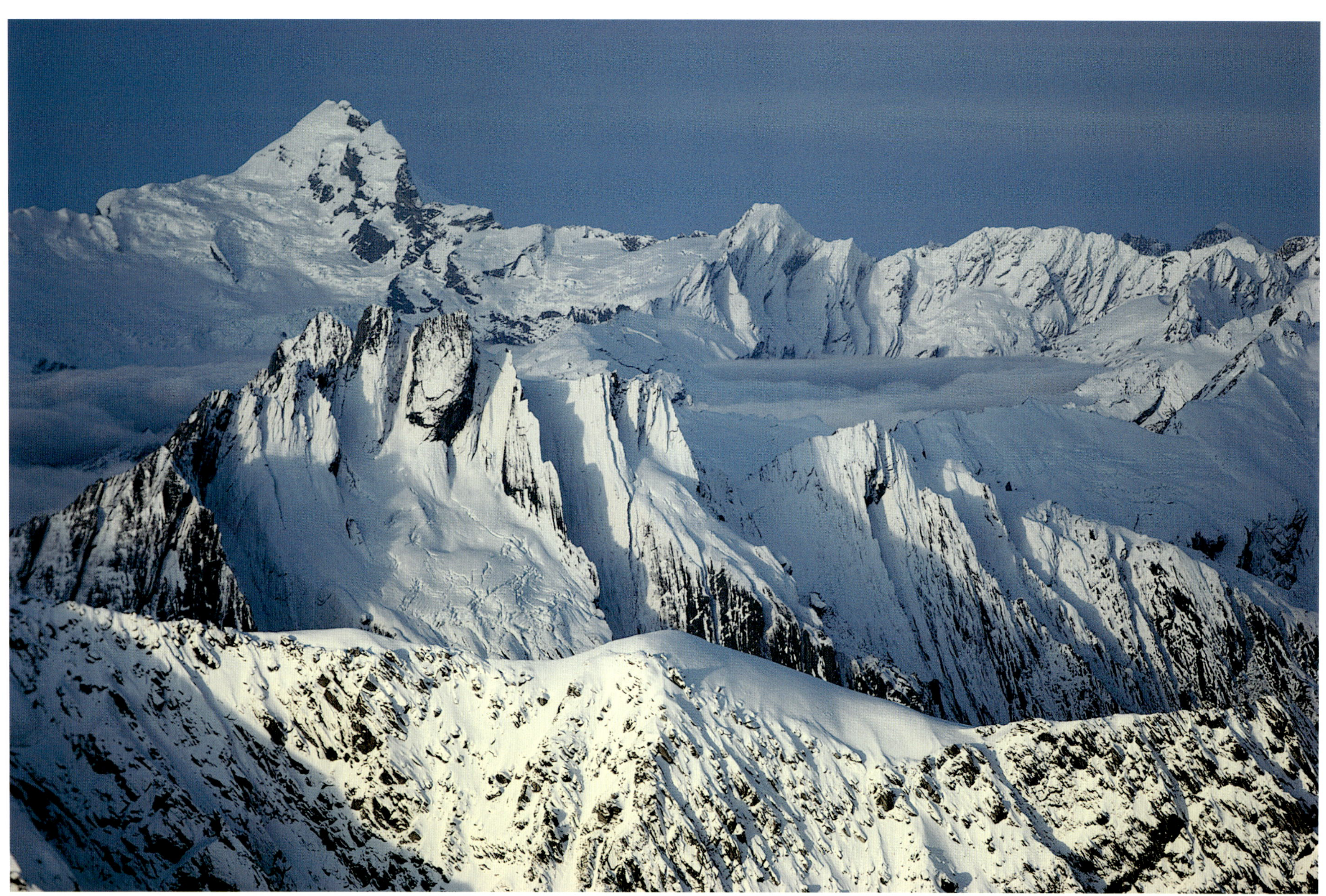

Mt Sefton, Westland/Tai Poutini National Park

South Westland and Aoraki/Mount Cook

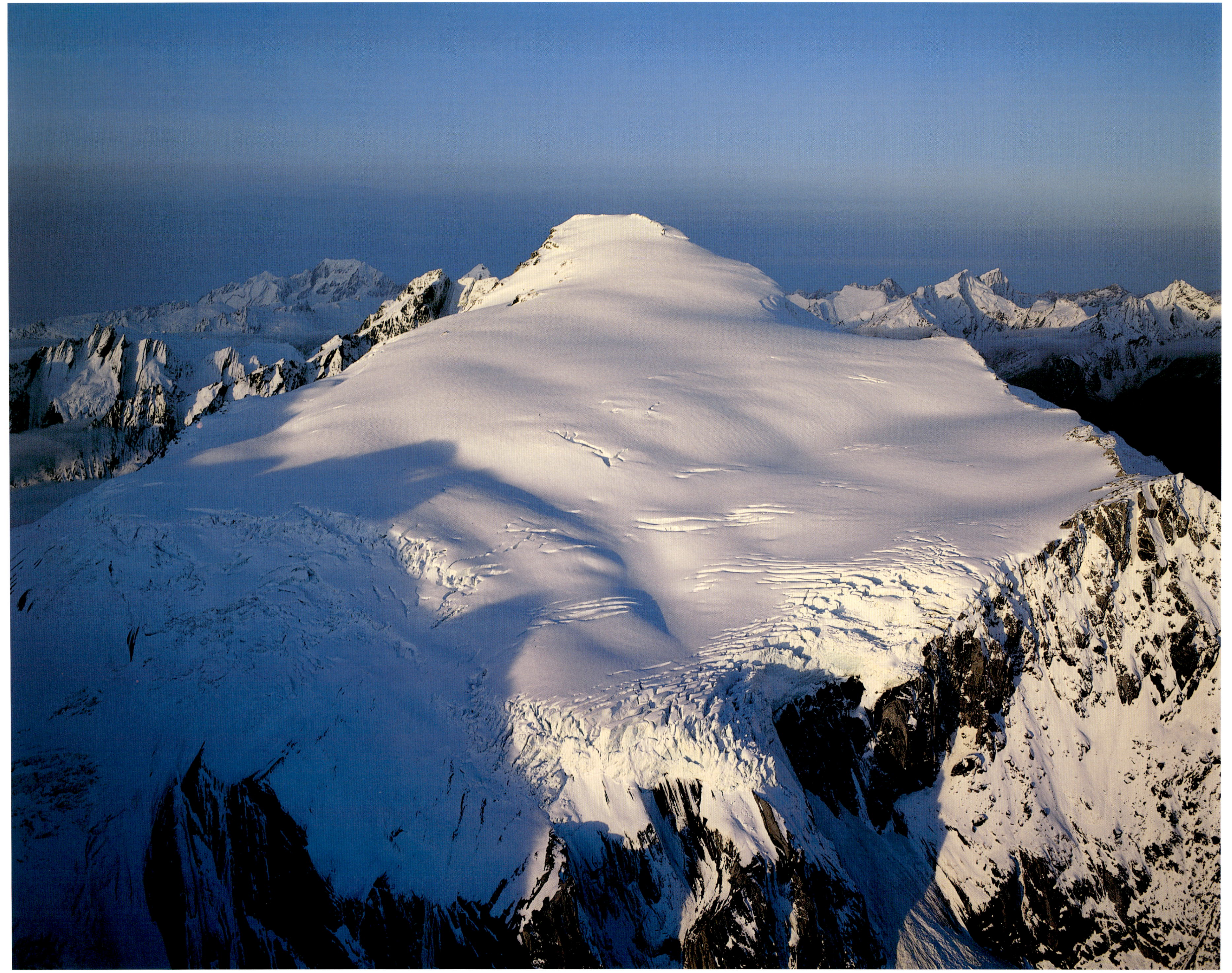

Mt Dechen, Hooker Range

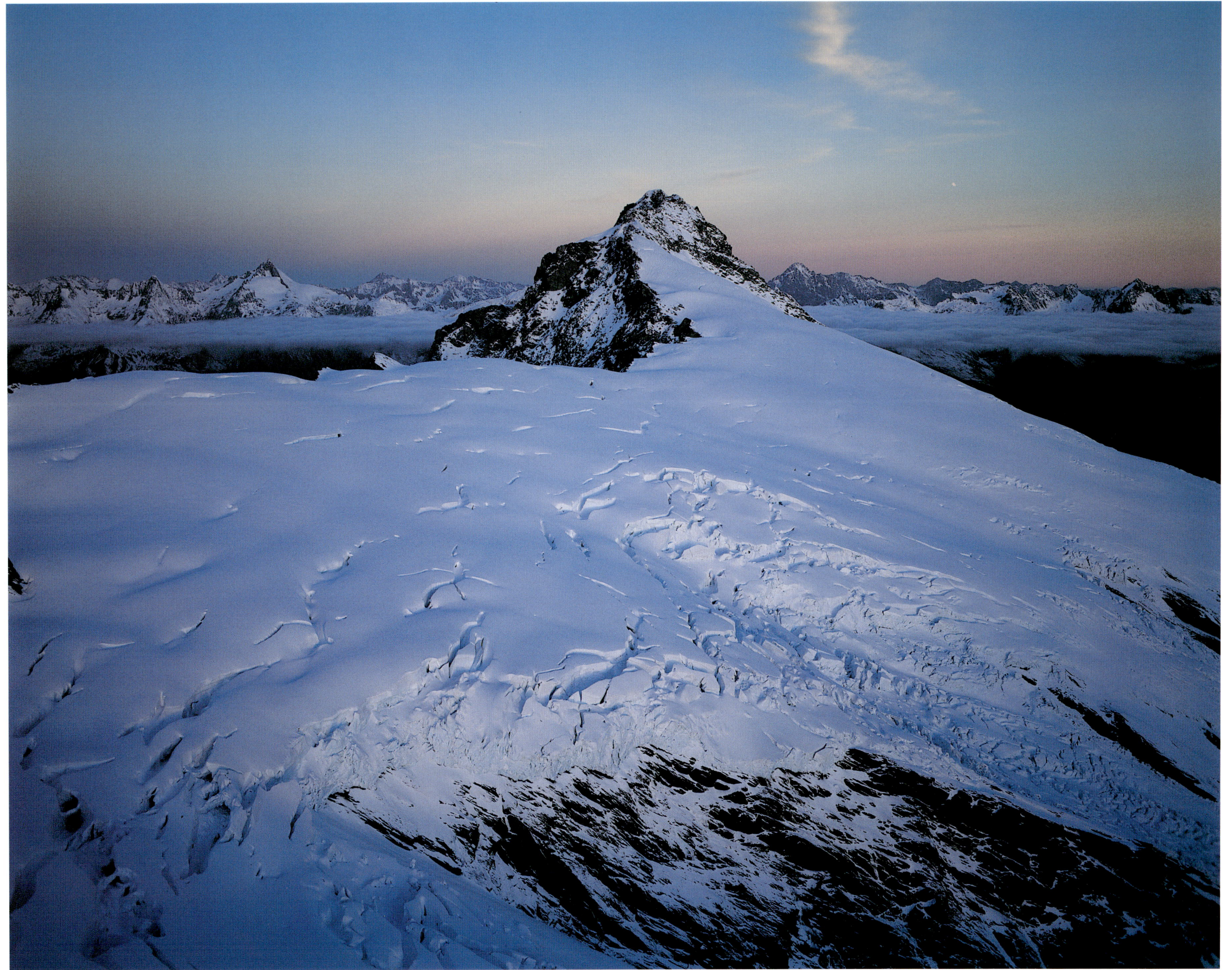

Mt Hooker and the Hooker Glacier

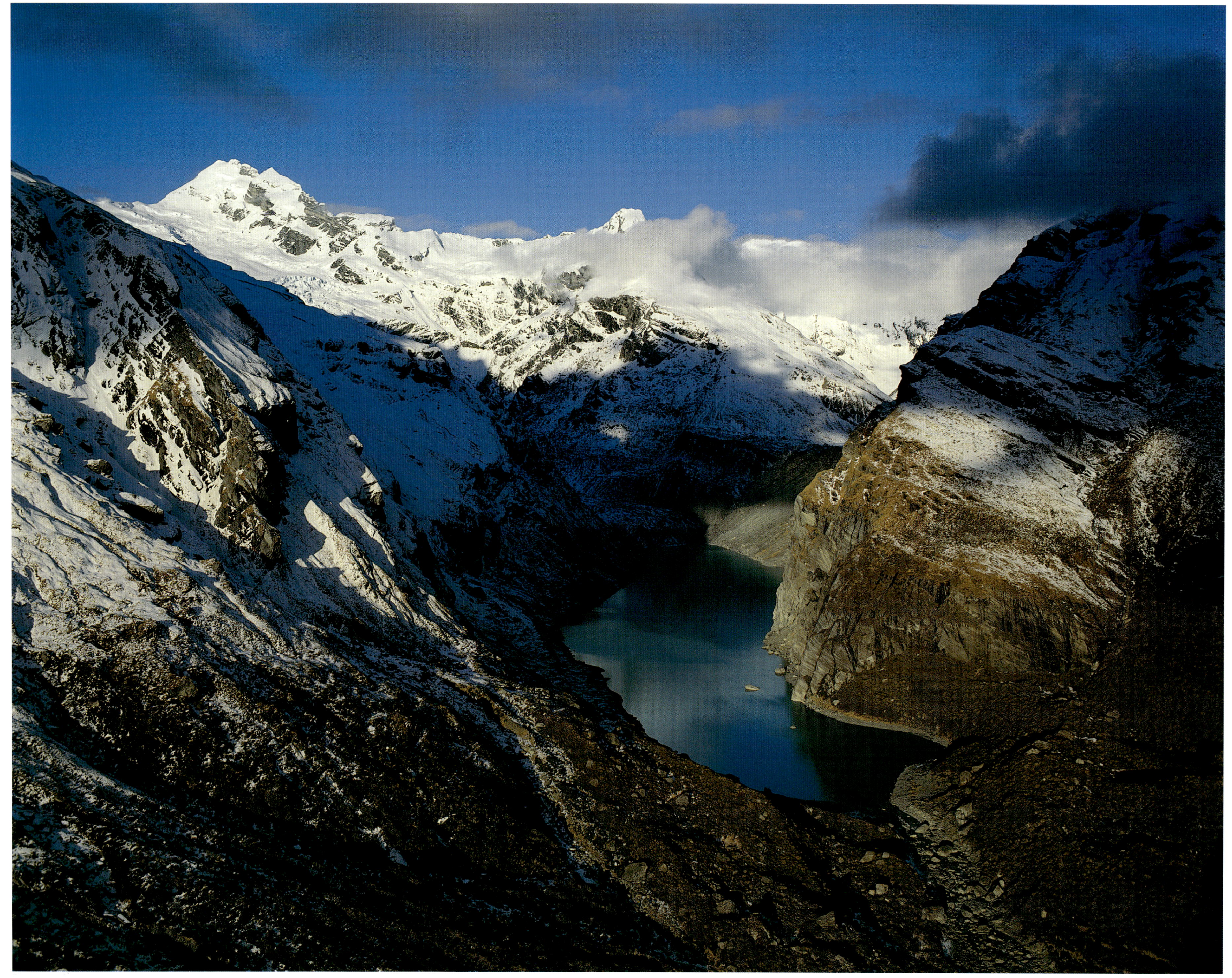

Mt Sefton and the terminal lake of the Douglas Glacier

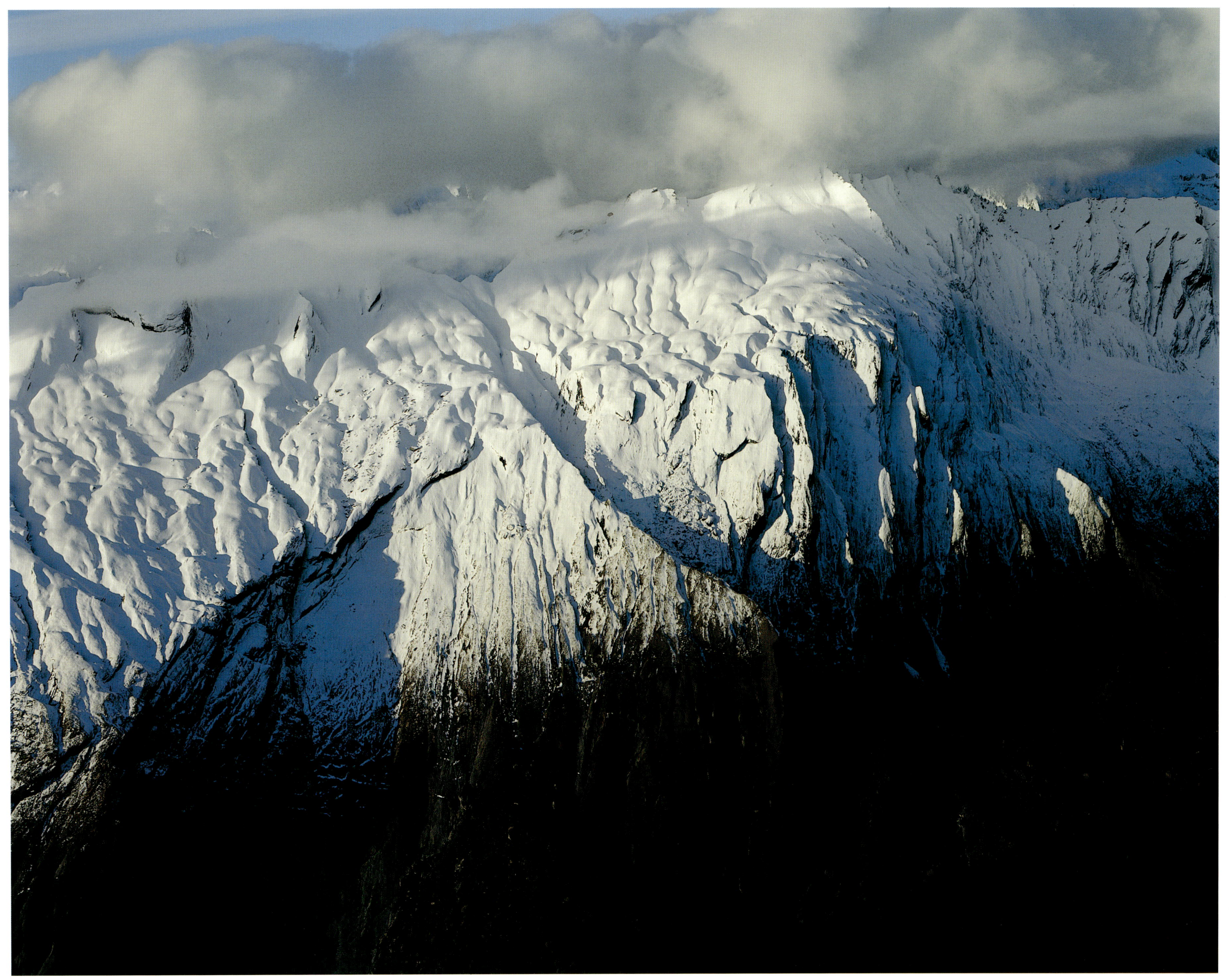

Ridge west of the Landsborough Valley, South Westland

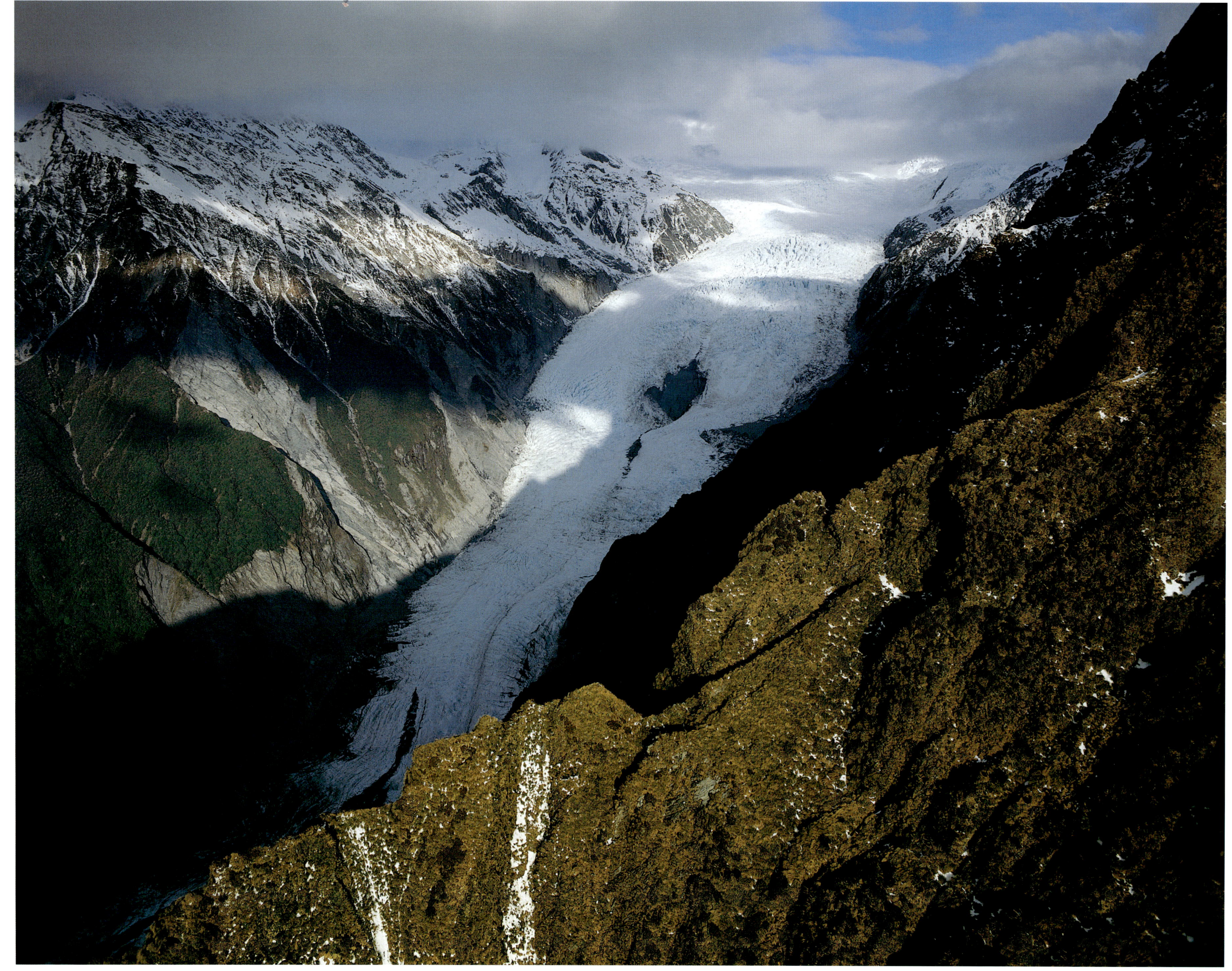

Franz Josef Glacier

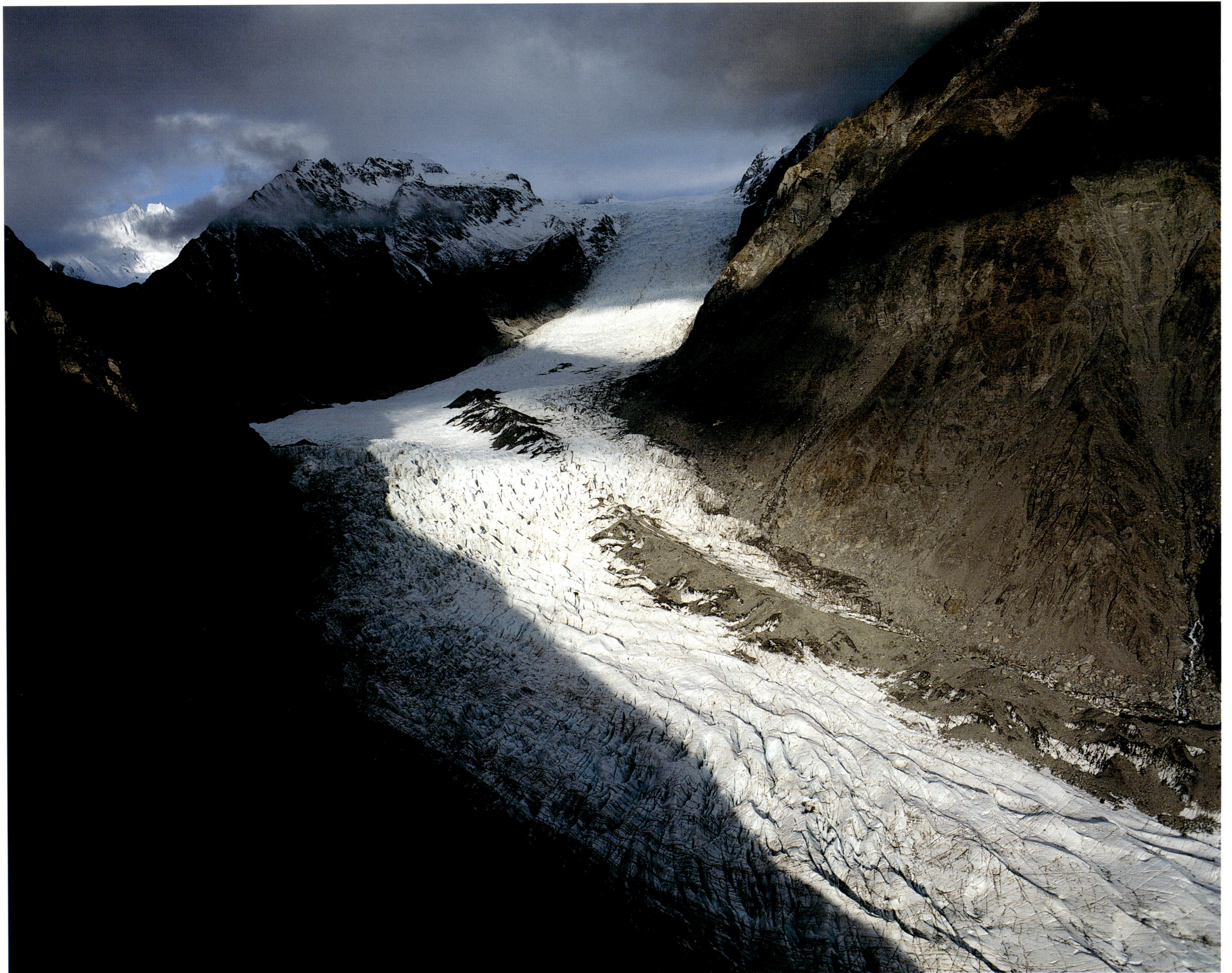

Fox Glacier

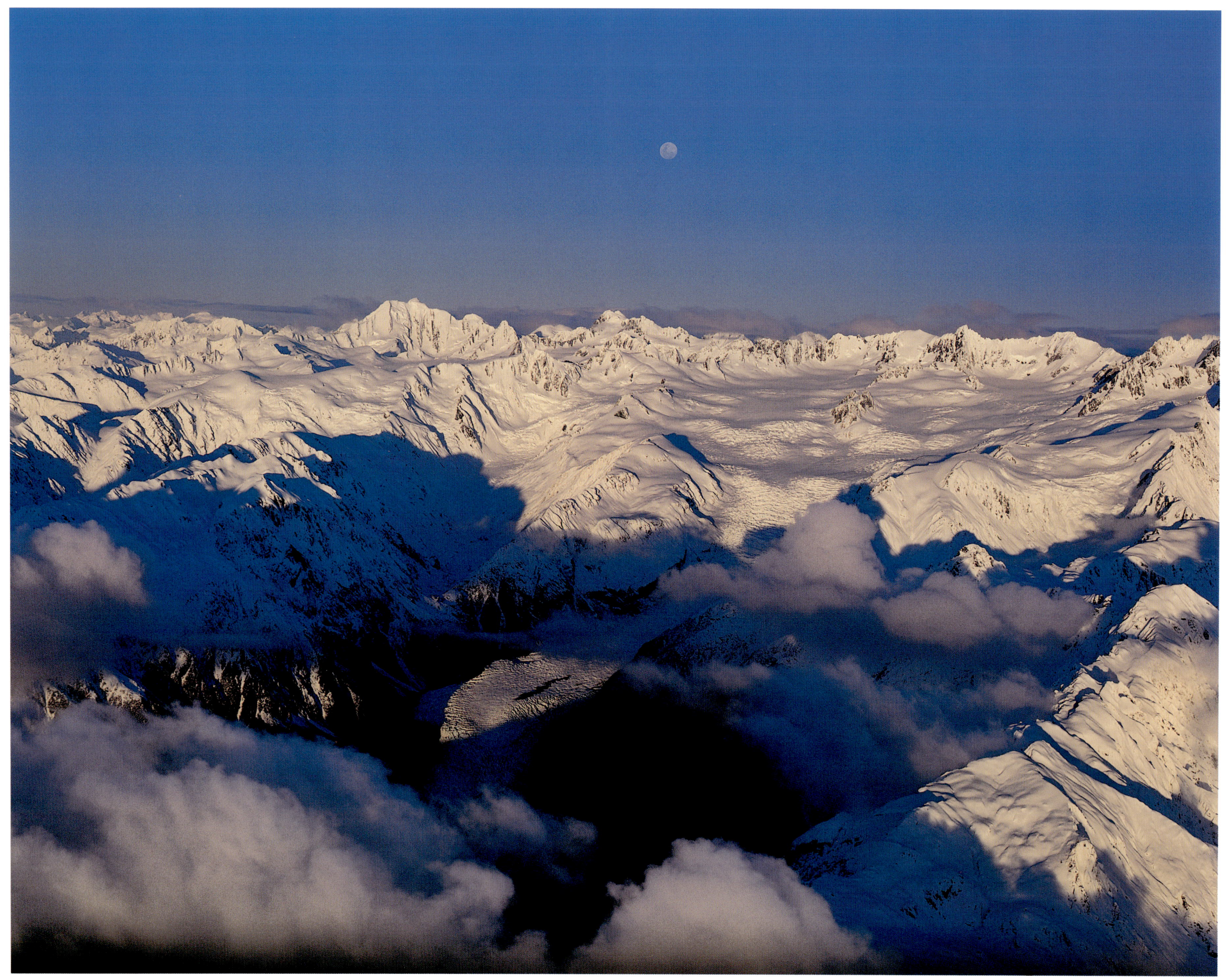

Fox Glacier and névé below the Main Divide

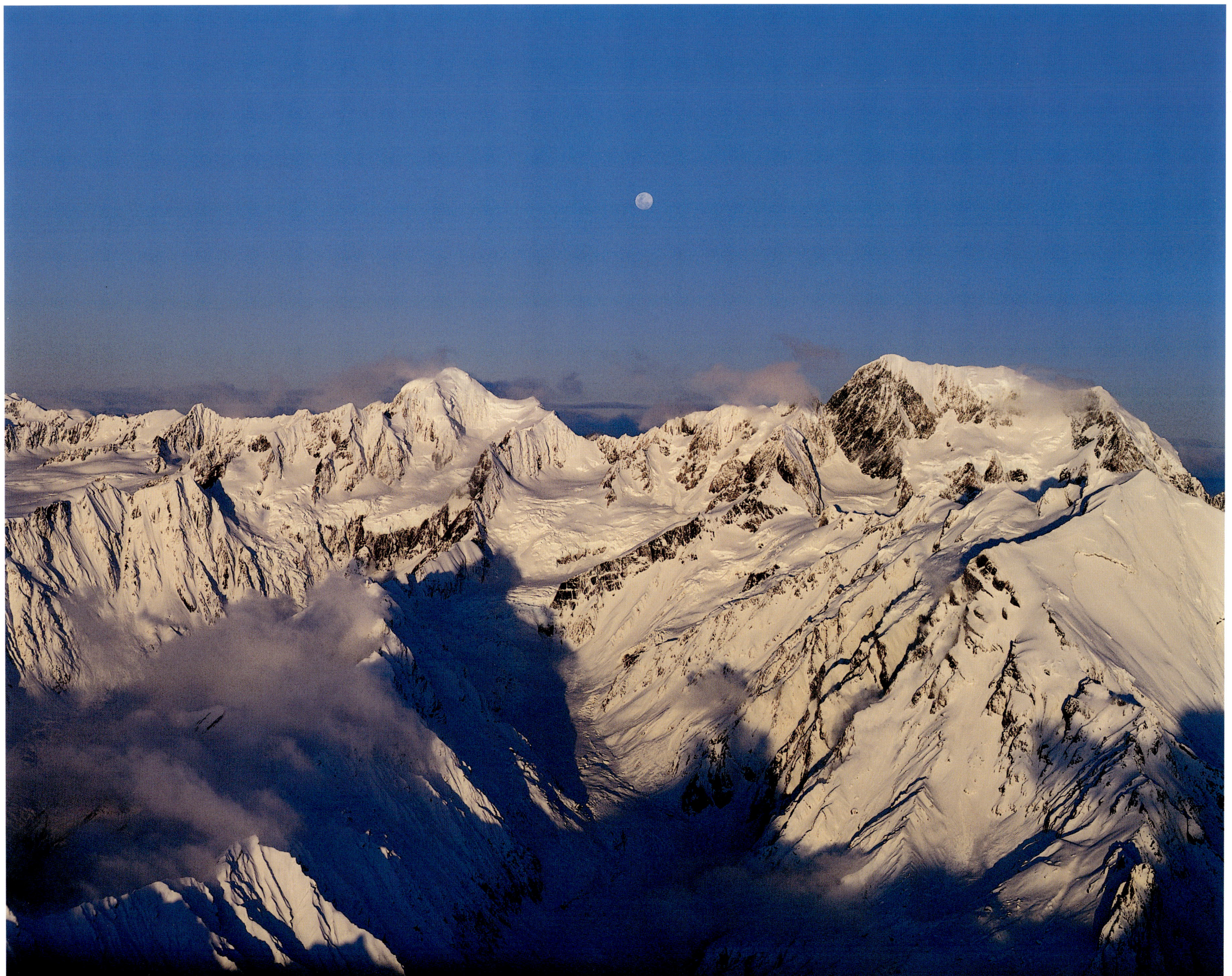

Mt Tasman and Aoraki/Mt Cook above the Upper La Perouse Valley

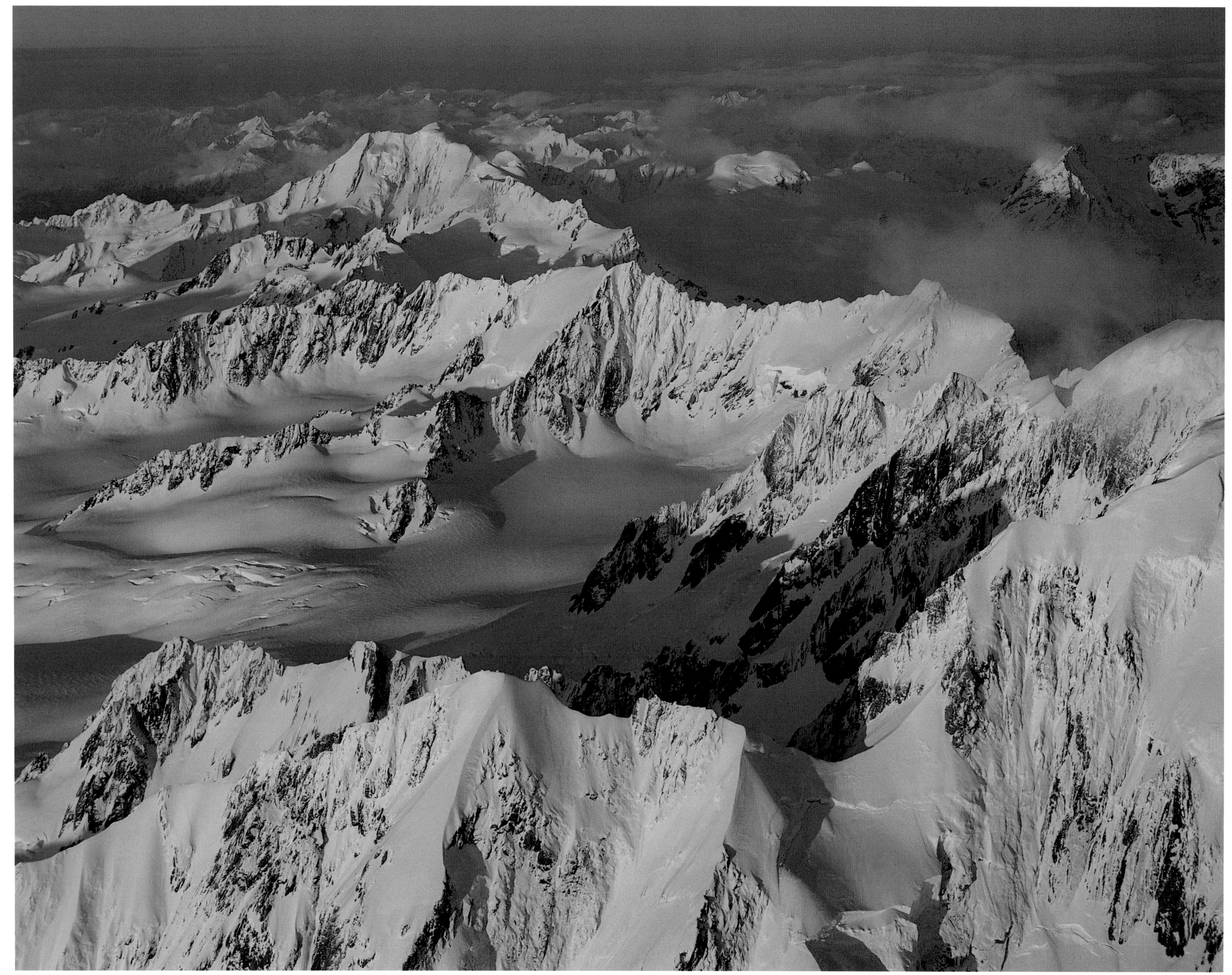

Upper Fox and Franz Josef névés

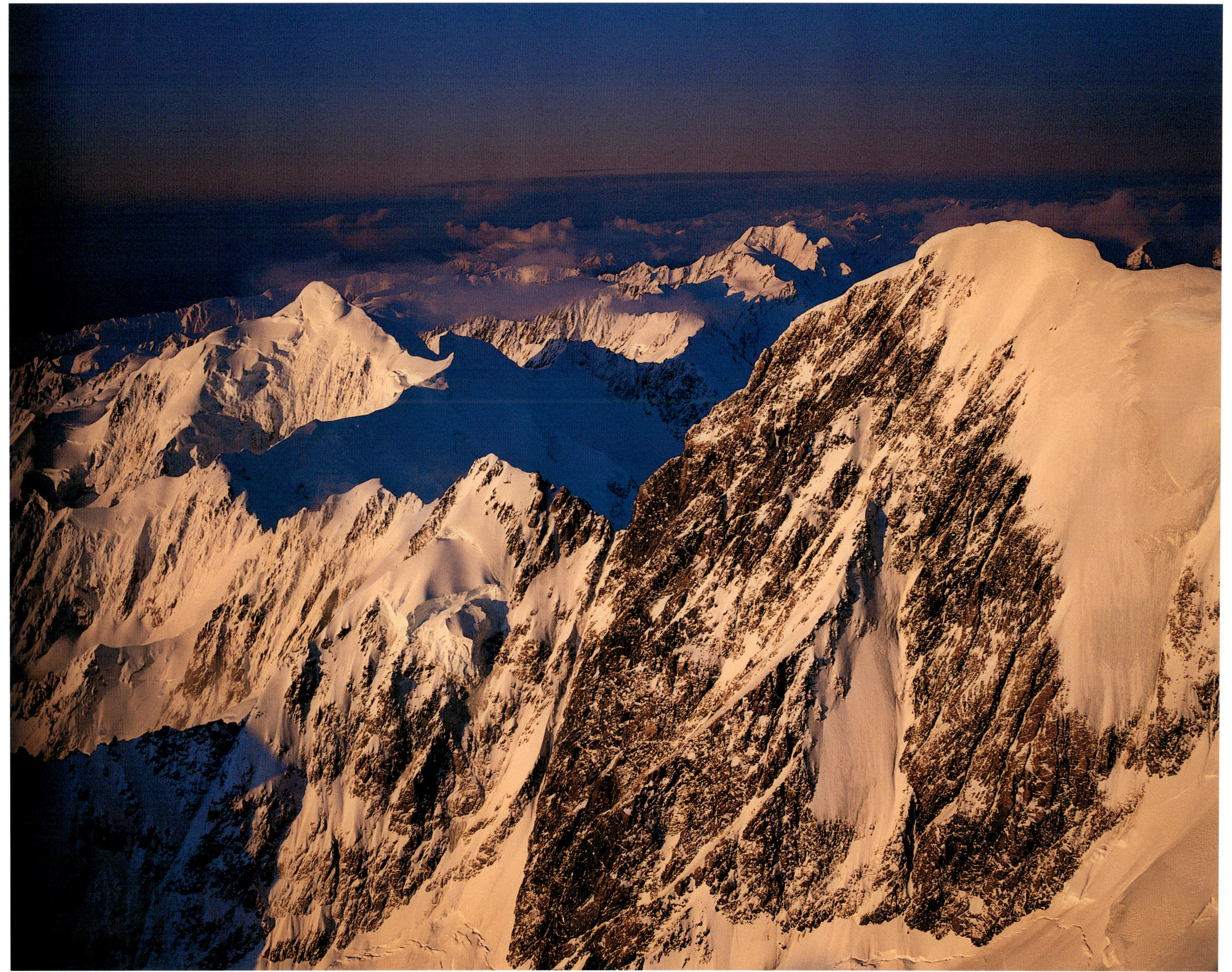

Aoraki/Mt Cook: Sheila and Hooker faces

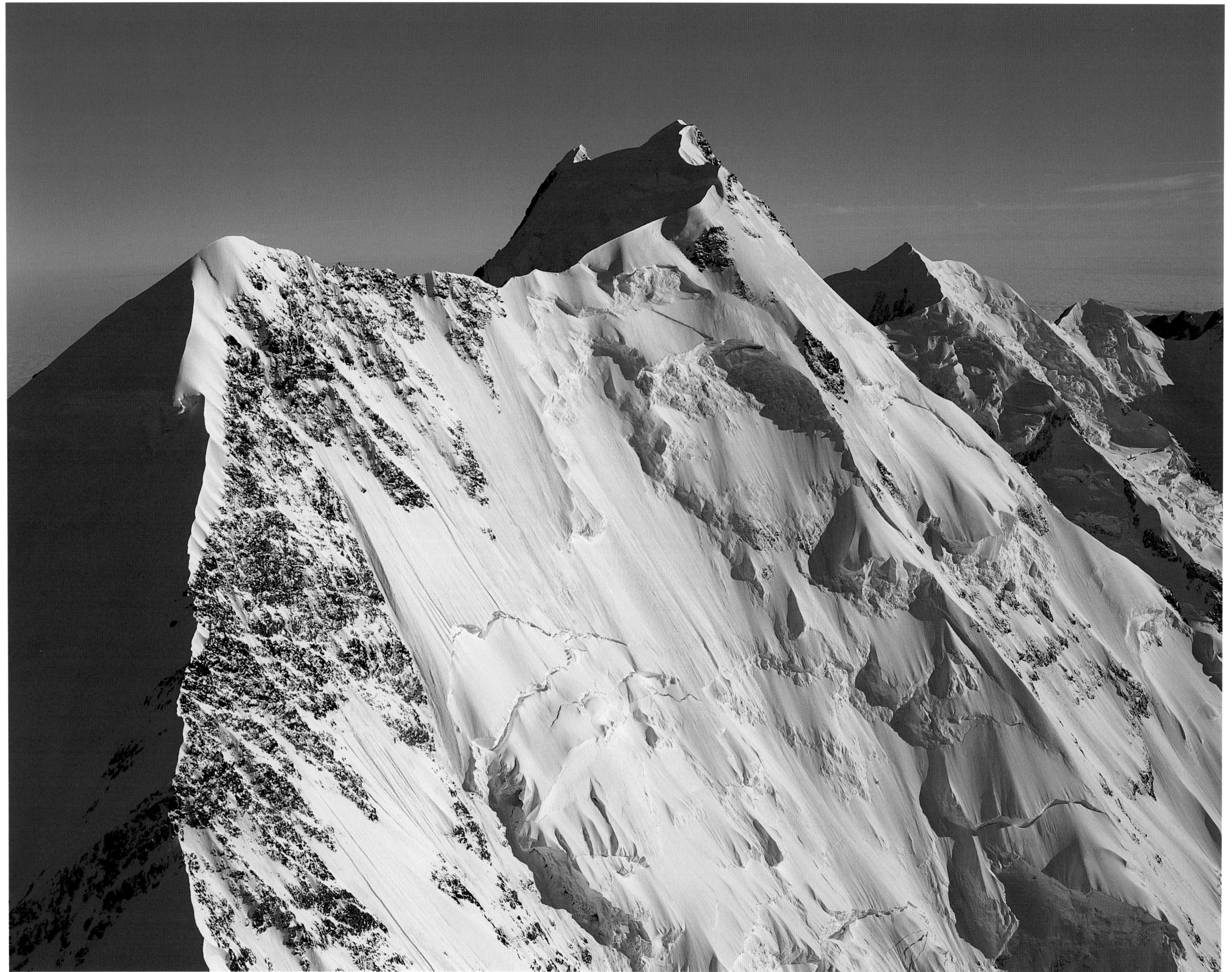

Aoraki/Mt Cook and Mt Tasman

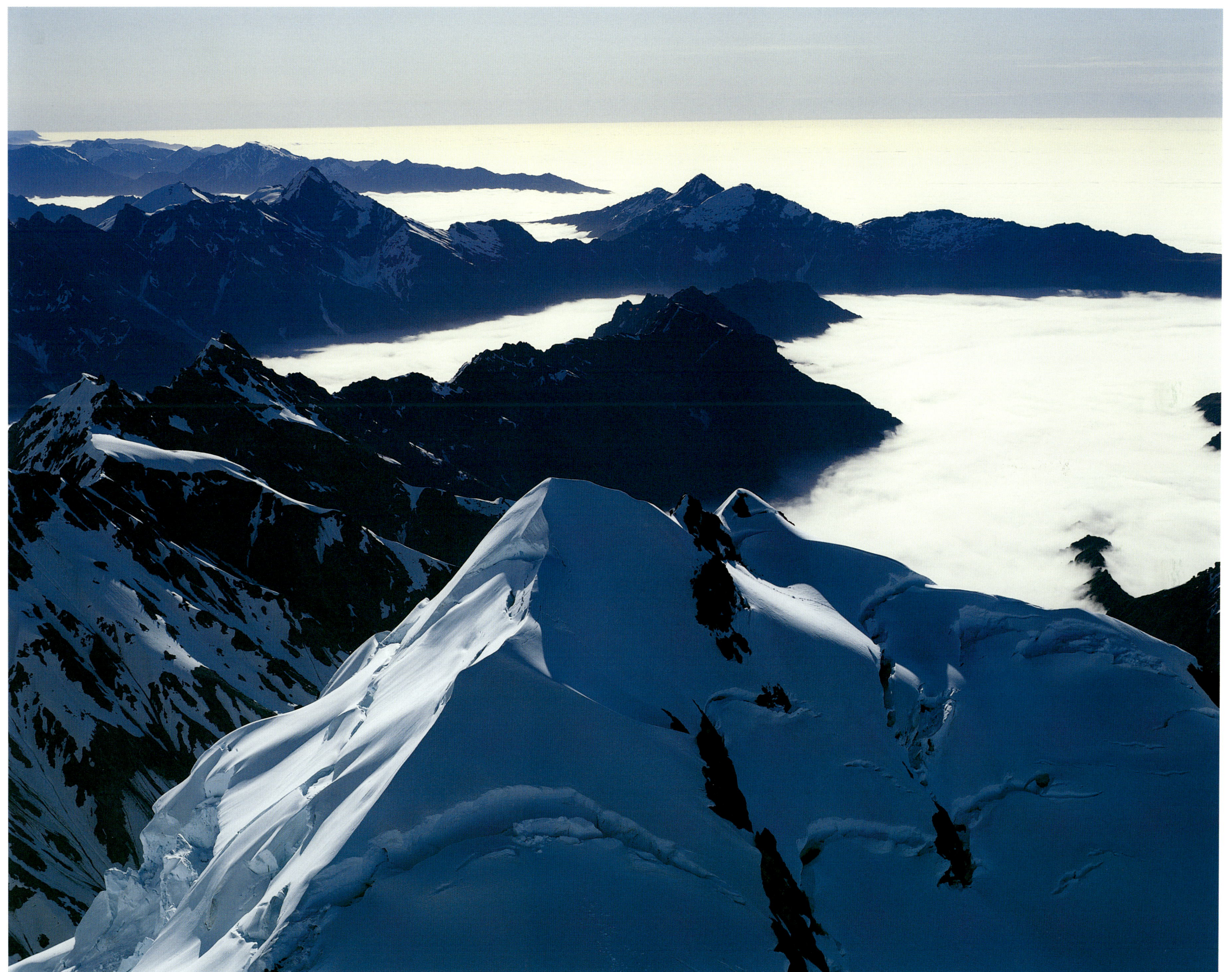

Torres Peak west of Mt Tasman, Westland/Tai Poutini National Park

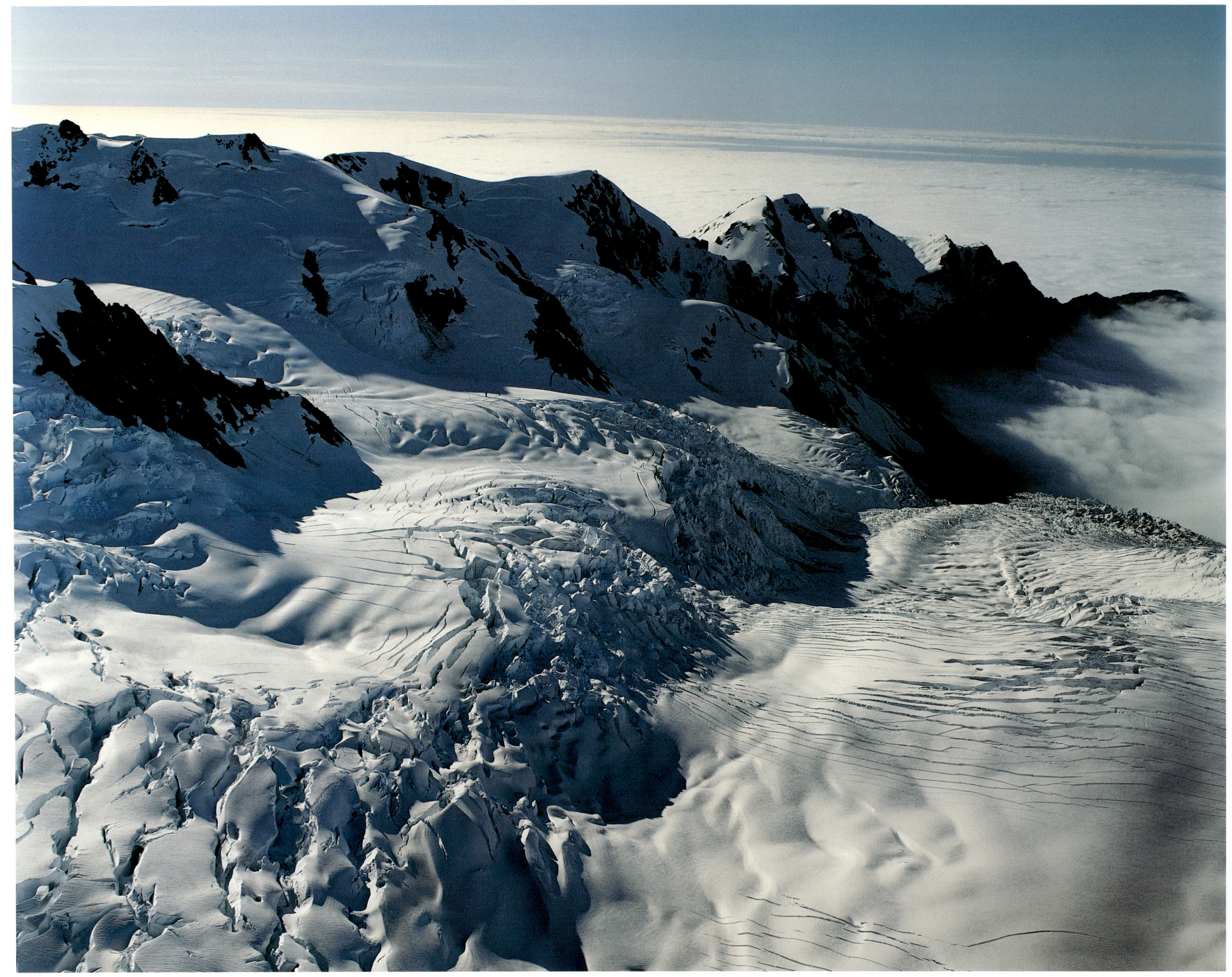

Albert Glacier above the Fox Glacier

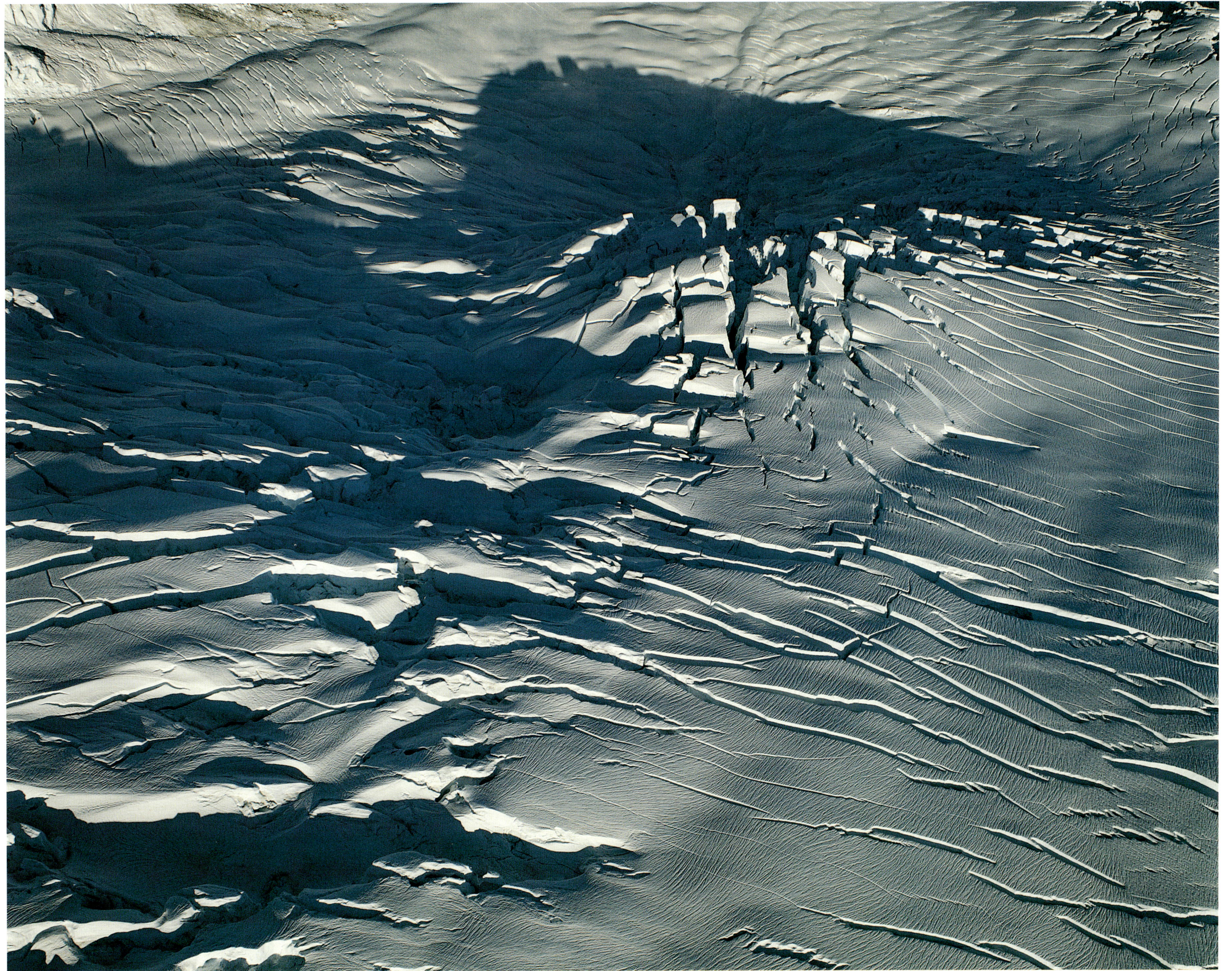

Albert Glacier detail

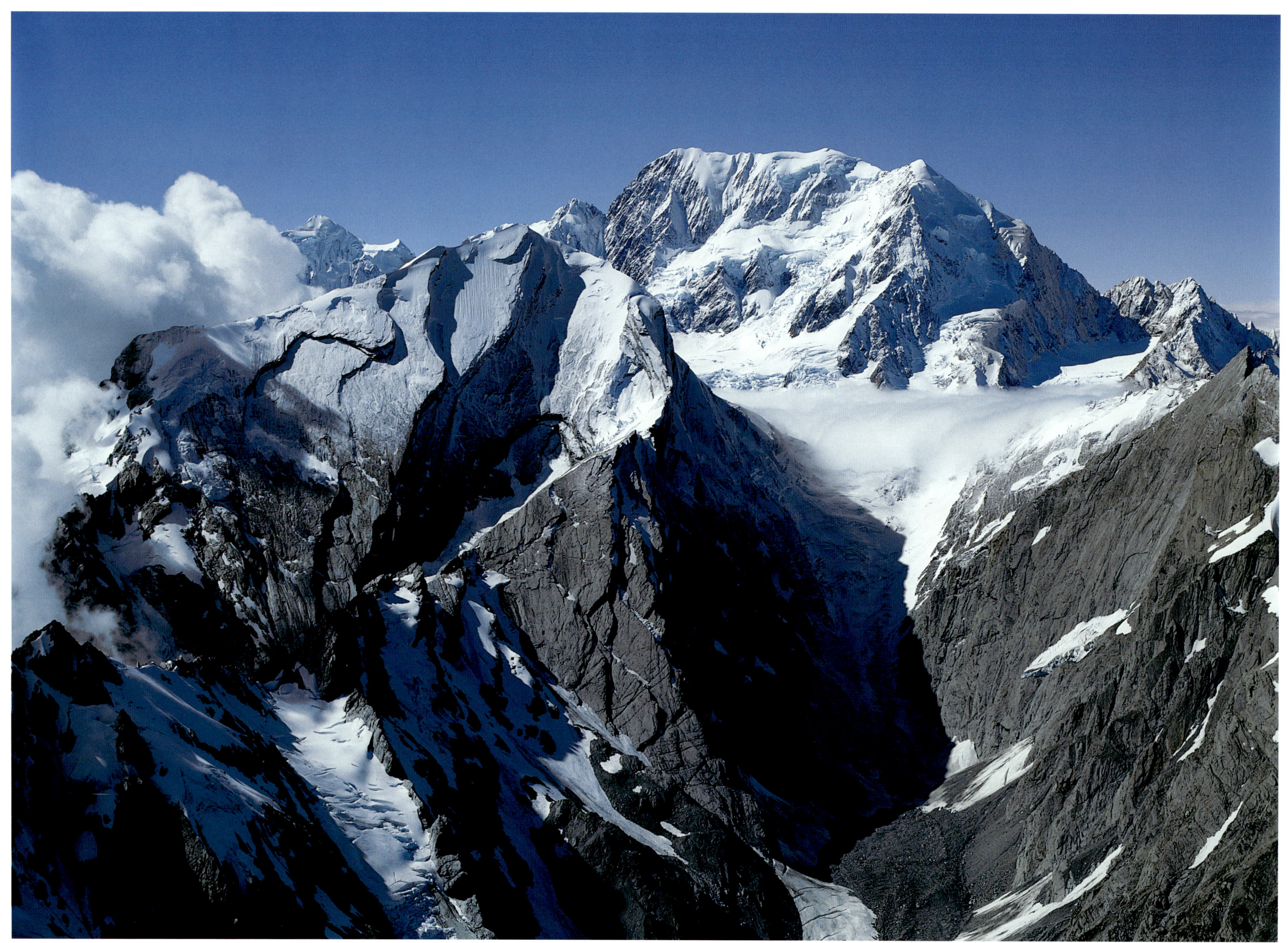

Rock slabs on the Gulch Face of La Perouse and Aoraki/Mt Cook

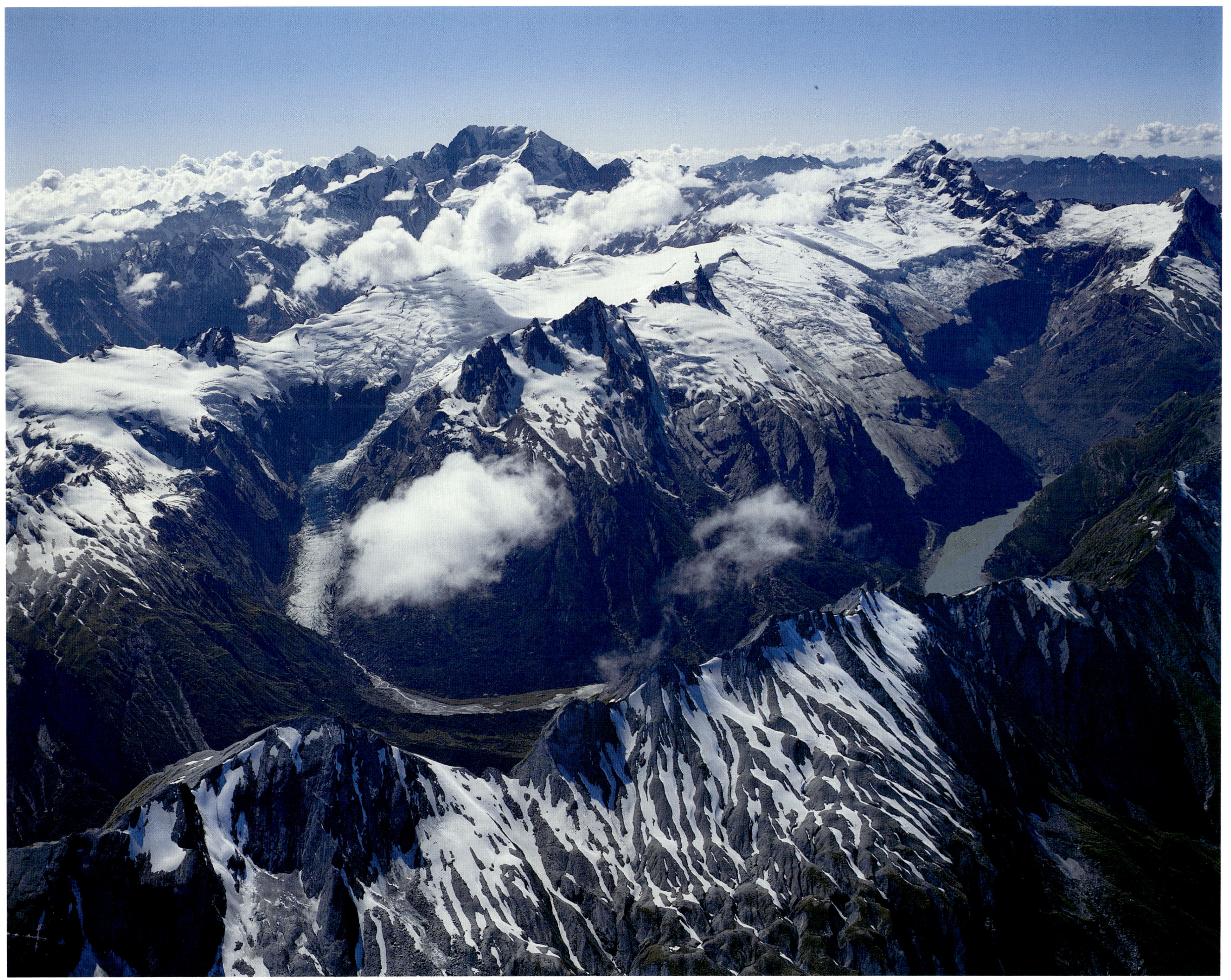

Mt Sefton with Aoraki/Mt Cook beyond, from above the Karangarua Valley

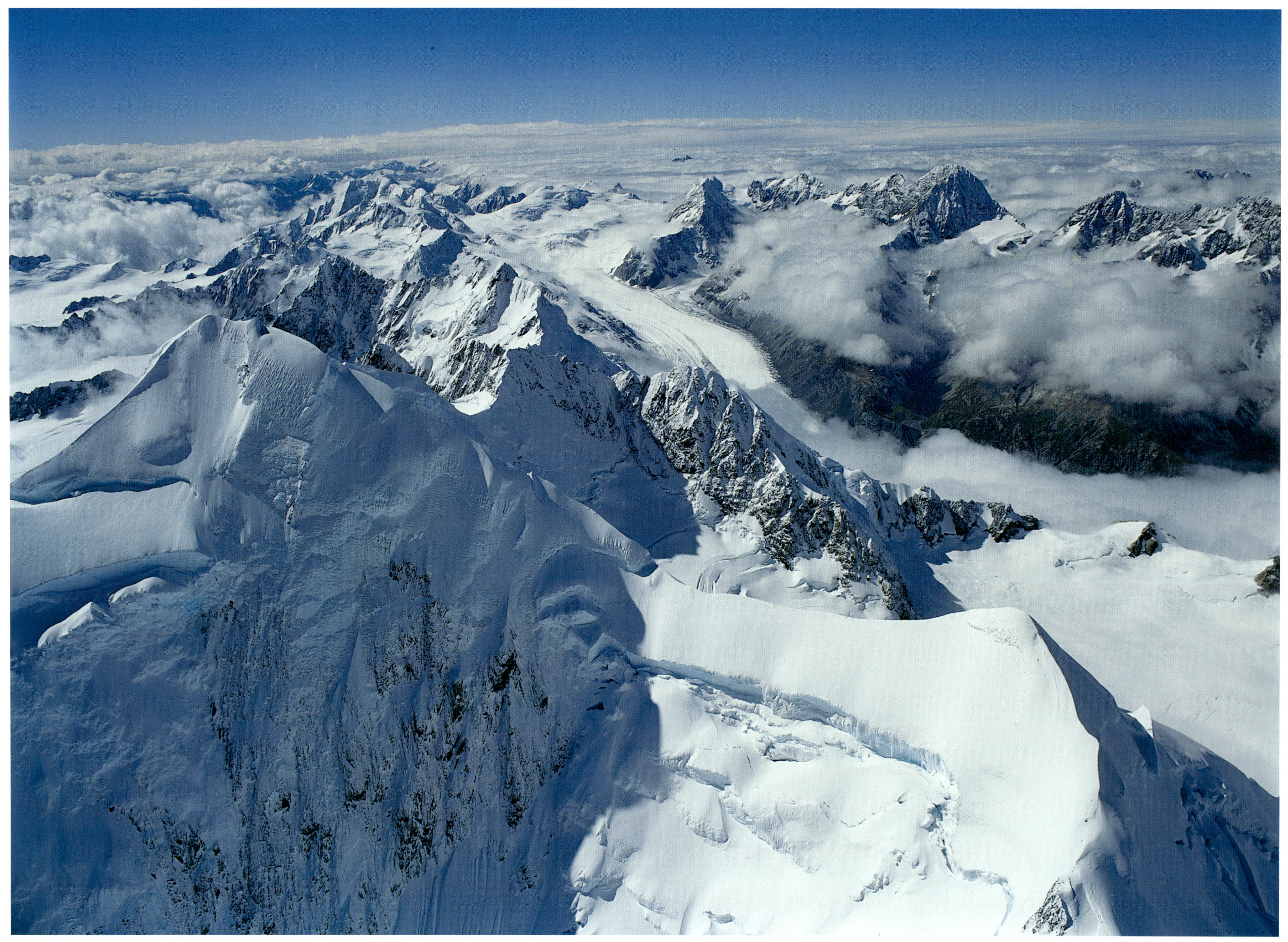

Mt Tasman, Balfour Face

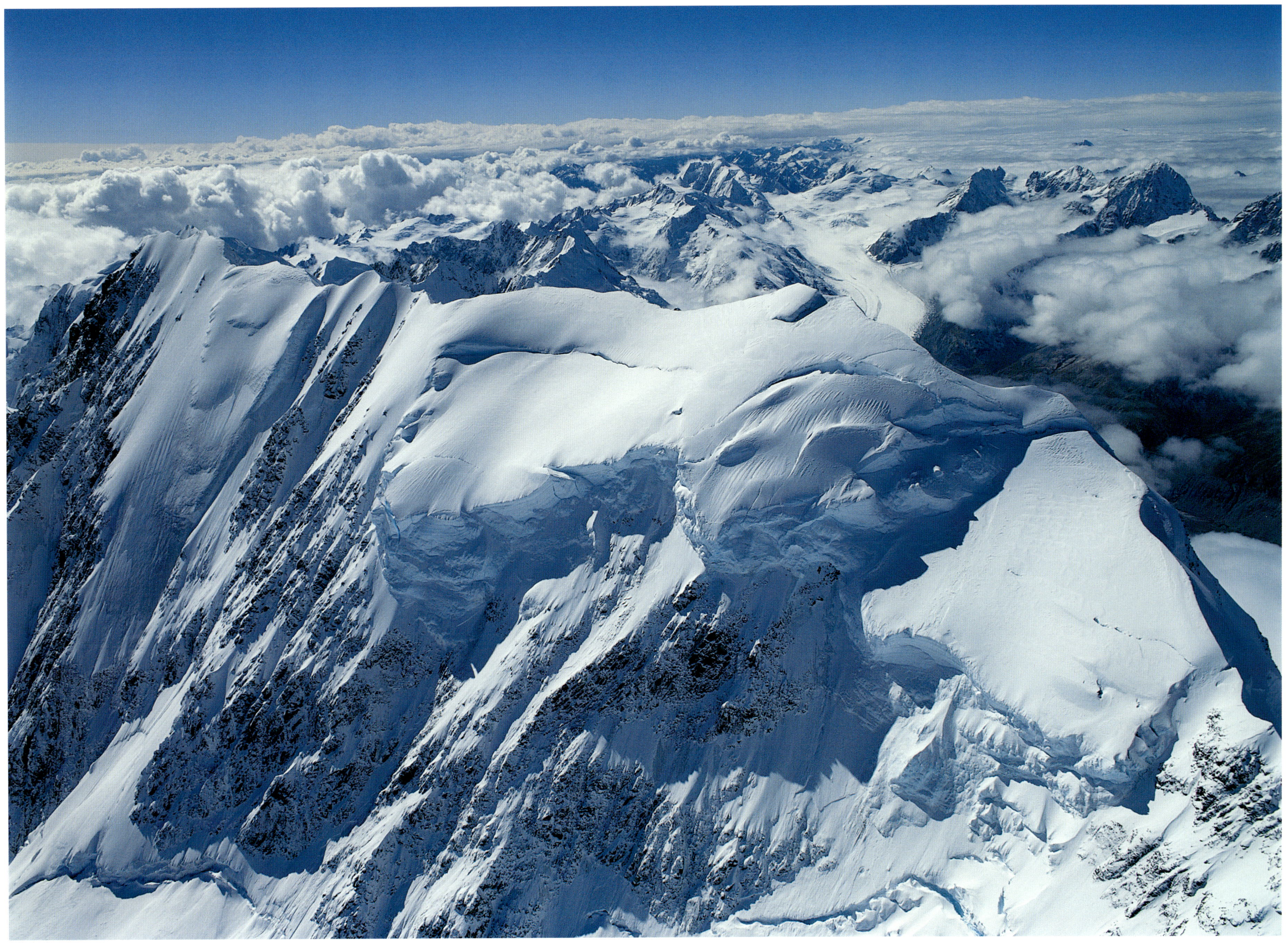

Hooker Face, Aoraki/Mt Cook

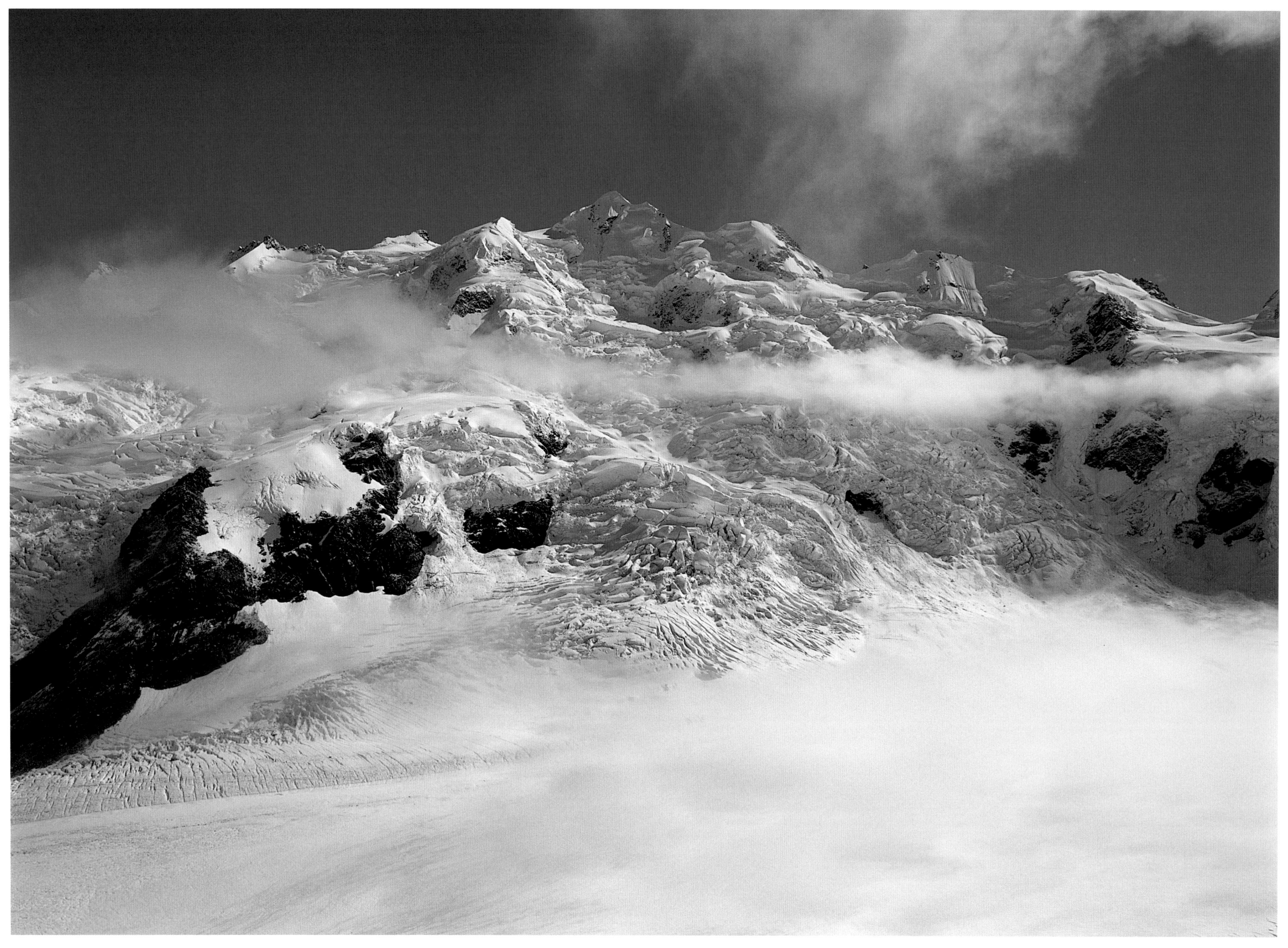

The Minarets from the Tasman Glacier

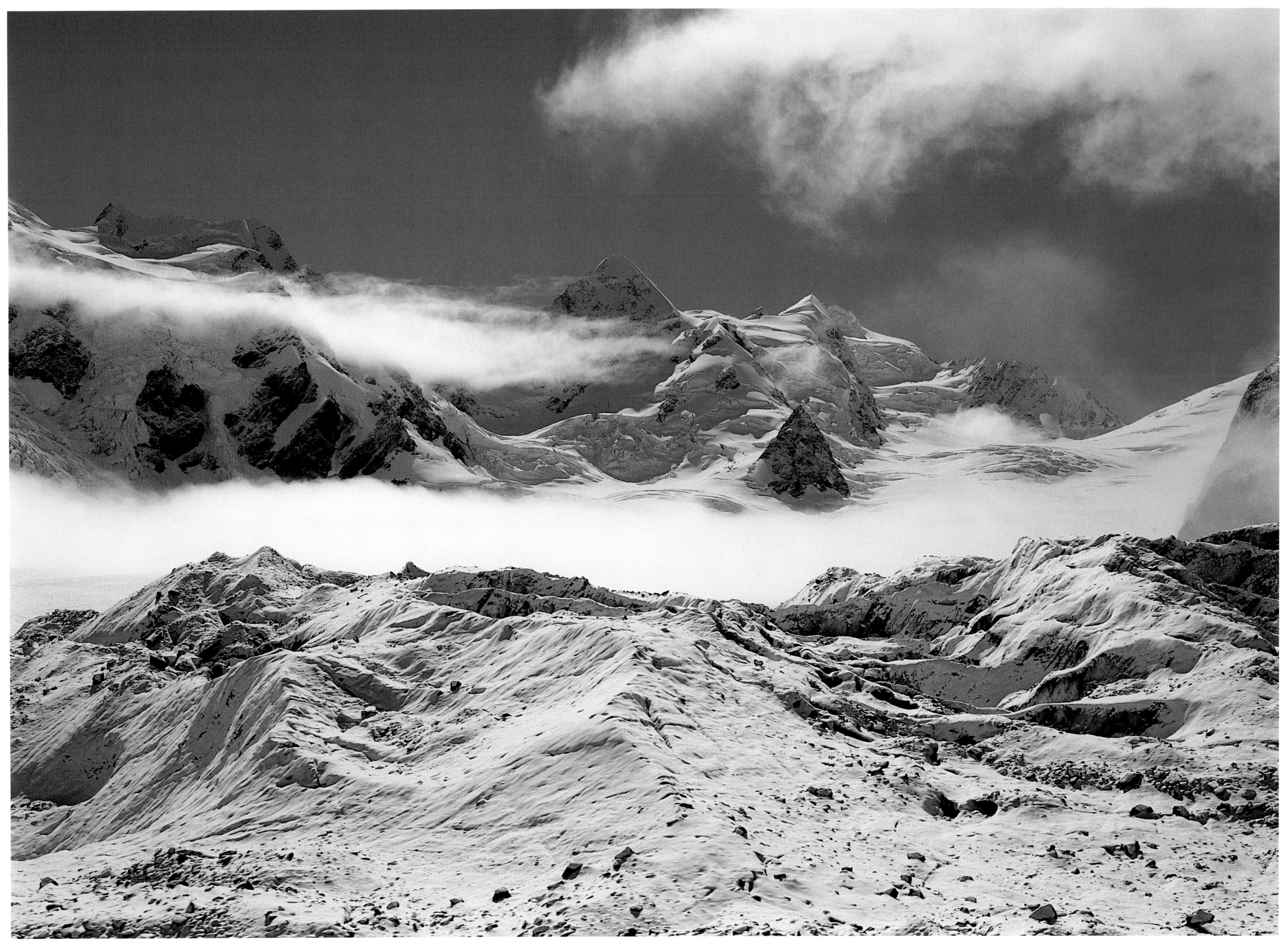

Mt Green and Mt Walter from the Tasman Glacier

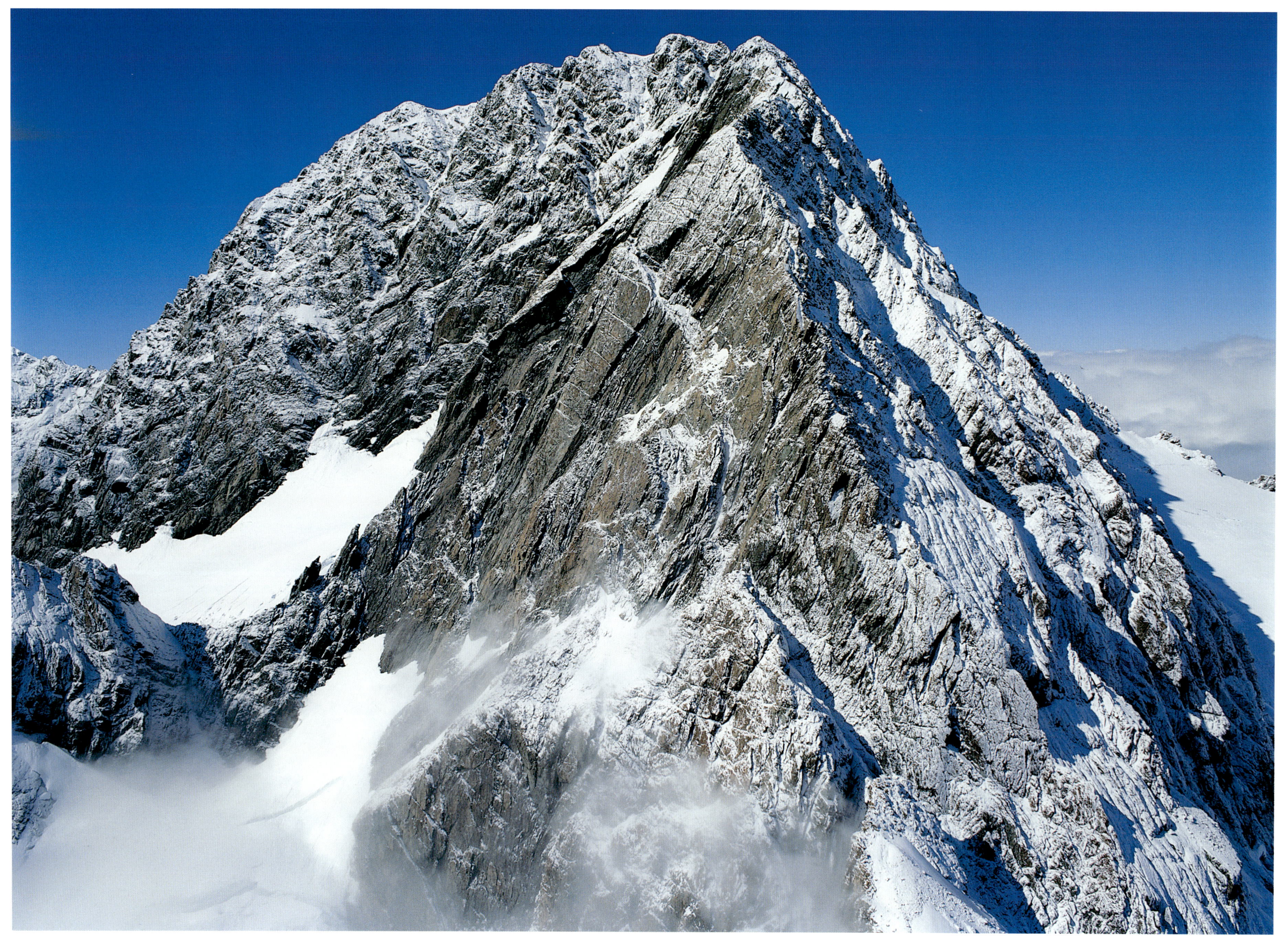

The West Ridge and the North West Face of Malte Brun

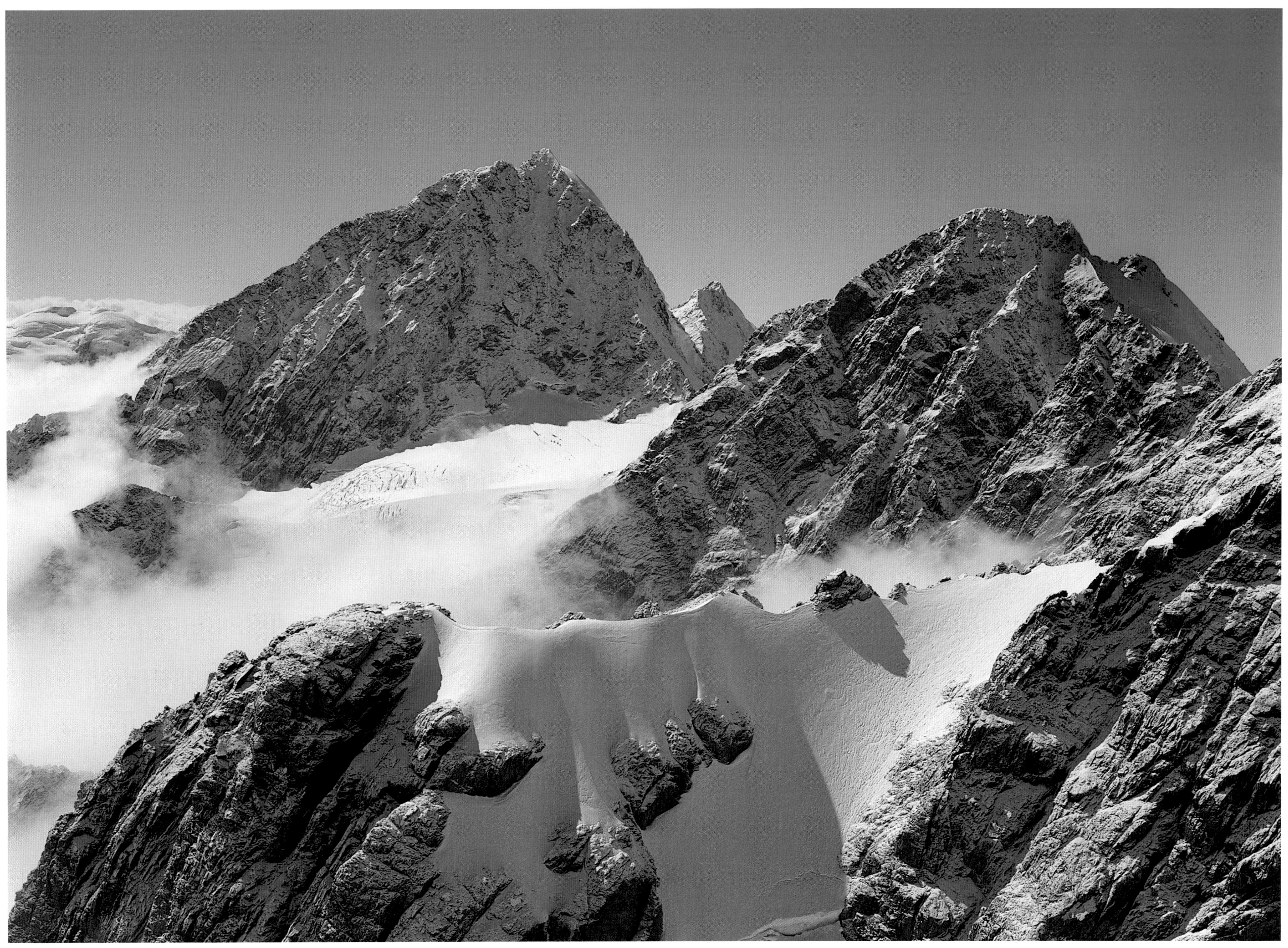

Aiguille Rouge with the South Face of Malte Brun beyond

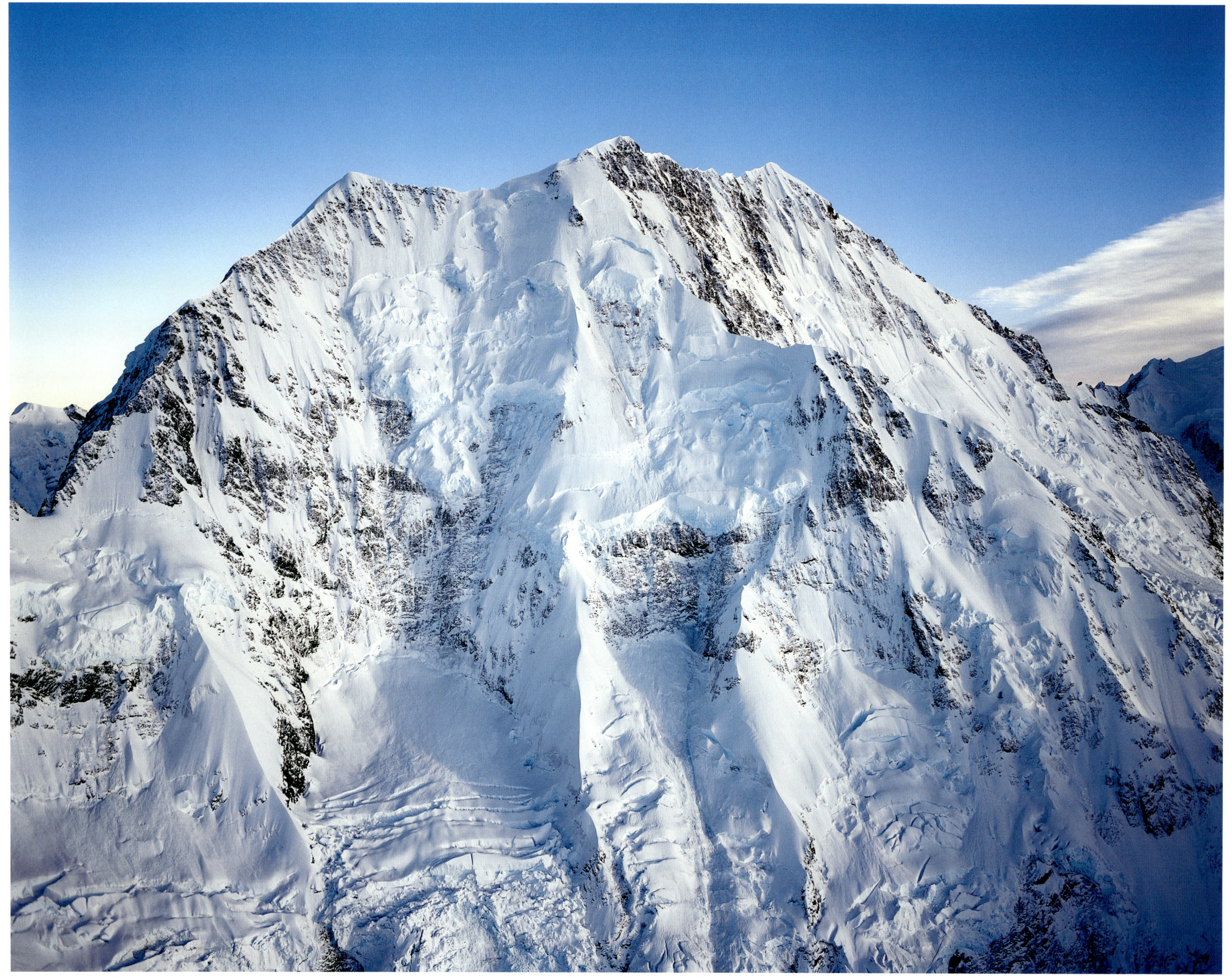

Caroline Face, Aoraki/Mt Cook

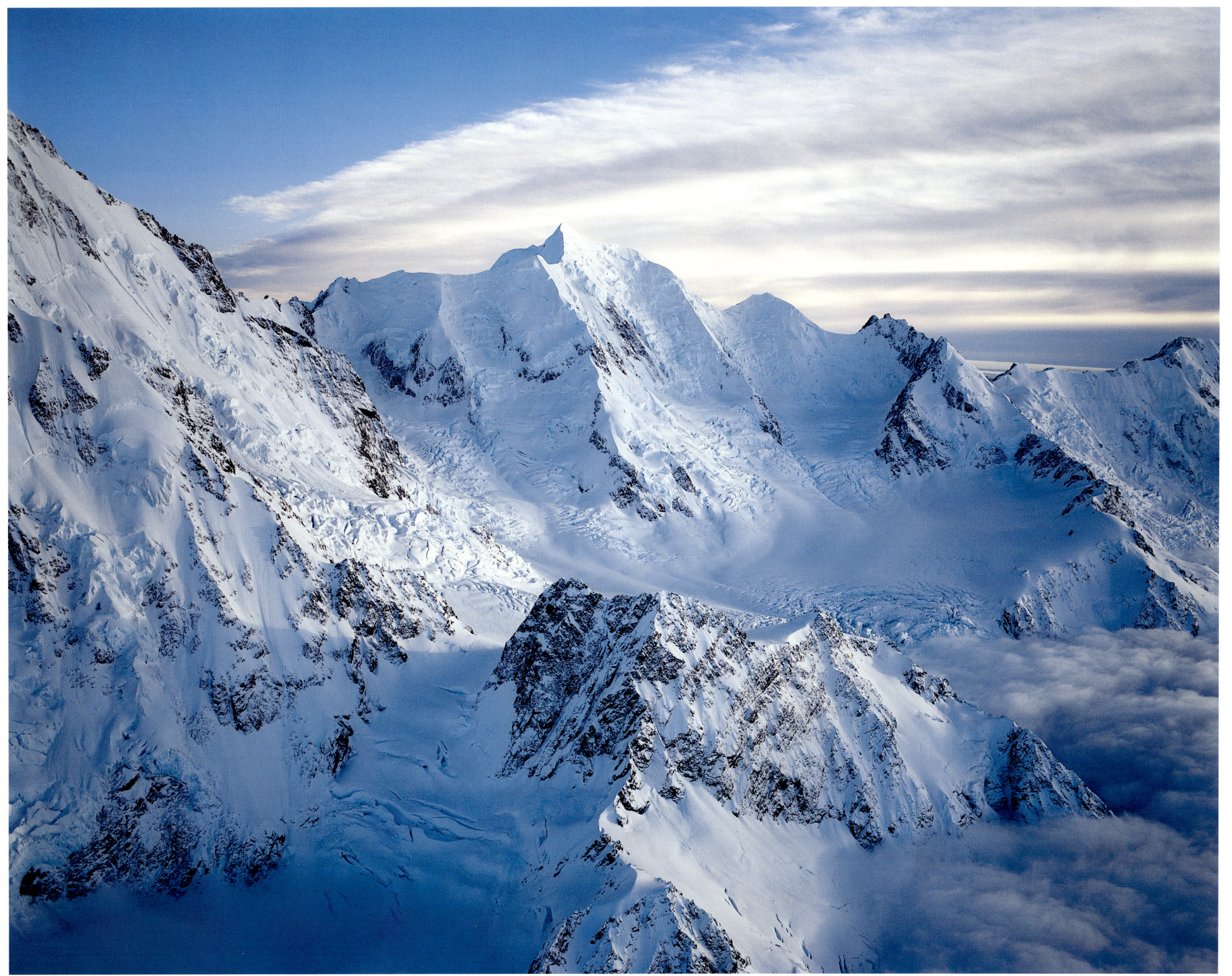

Mt Tasman and the Grand Plateau from the south

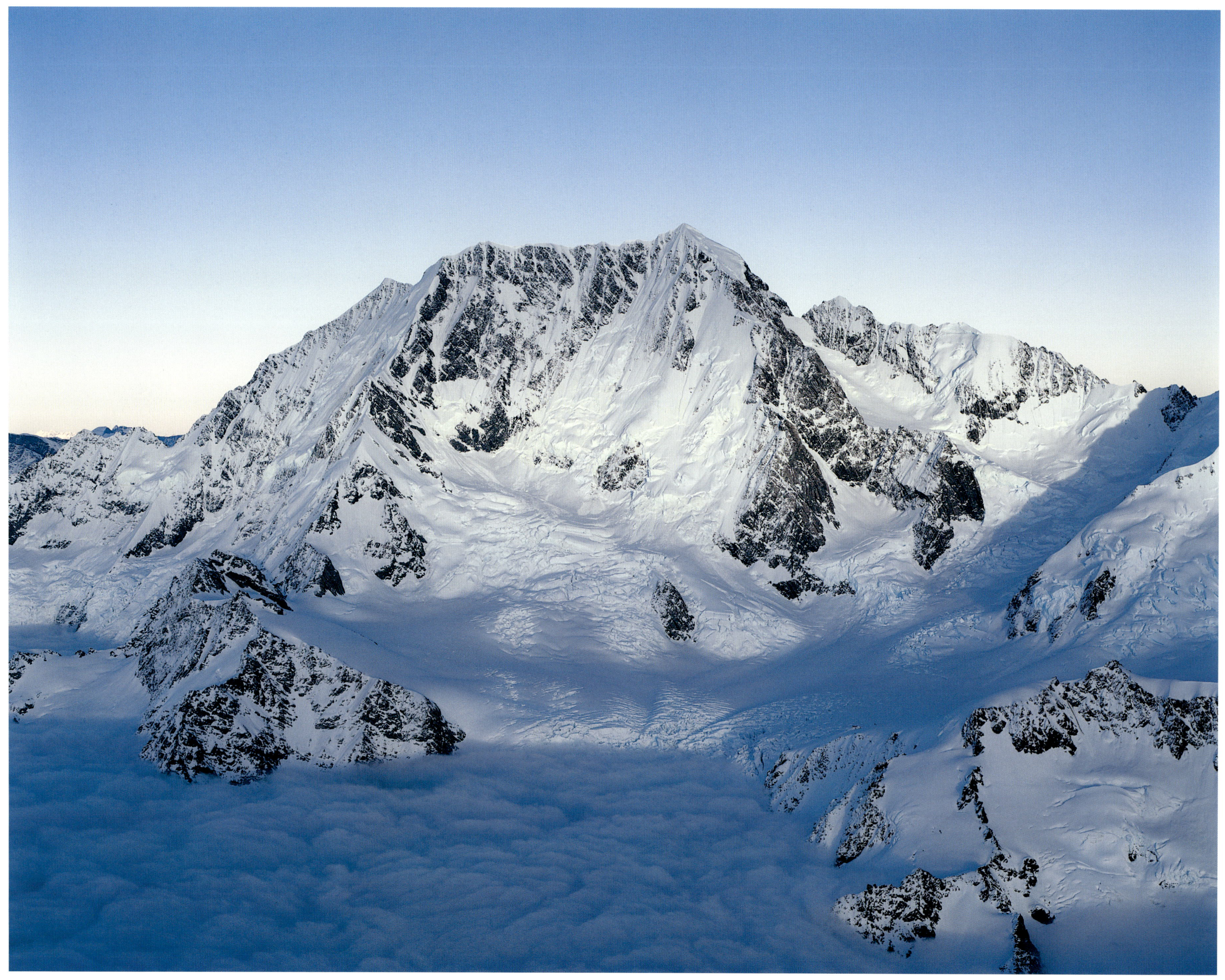

The East Face of Aoraki/Mt Cook and the Grand Plateau

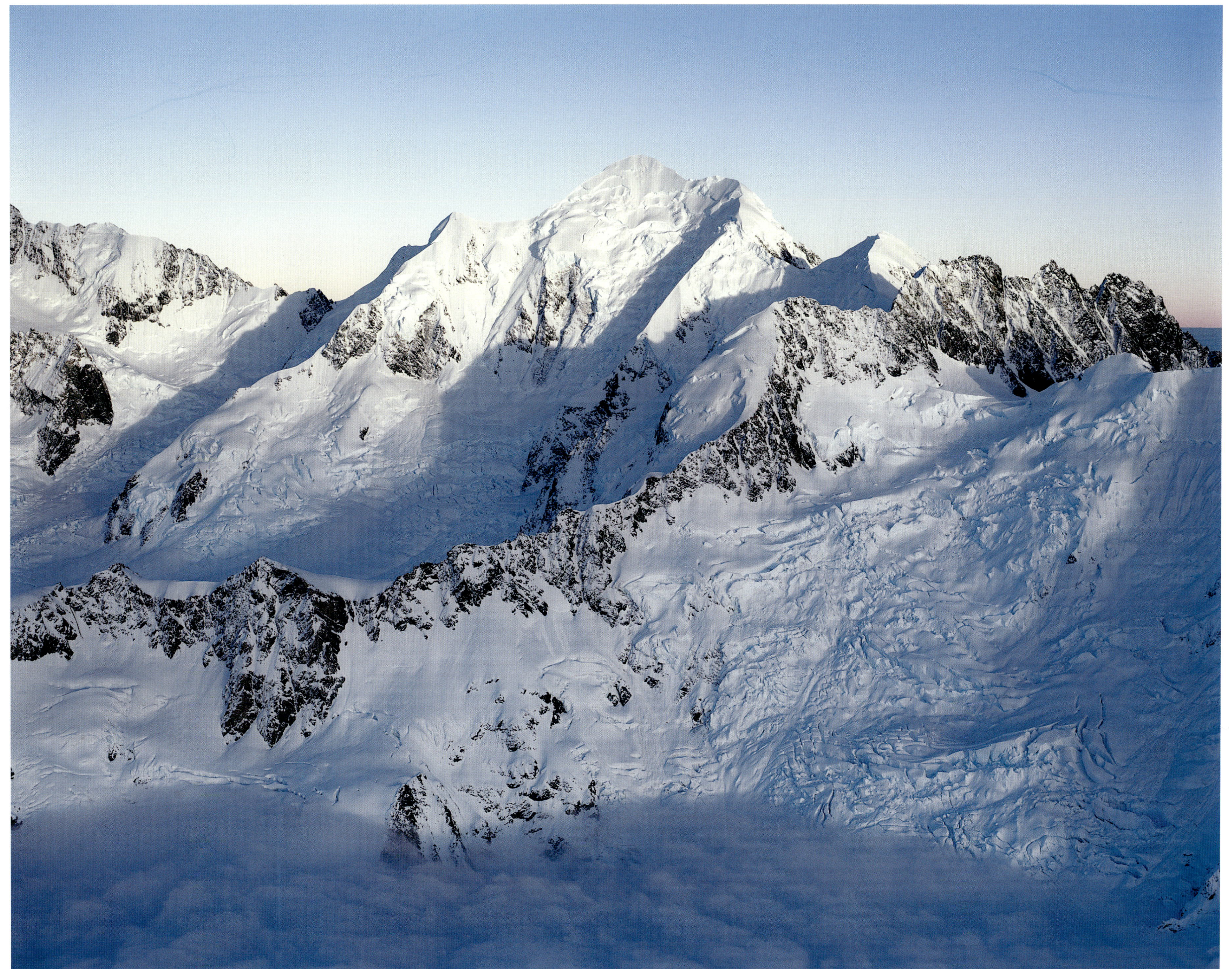

Mt Tasman from the north-east

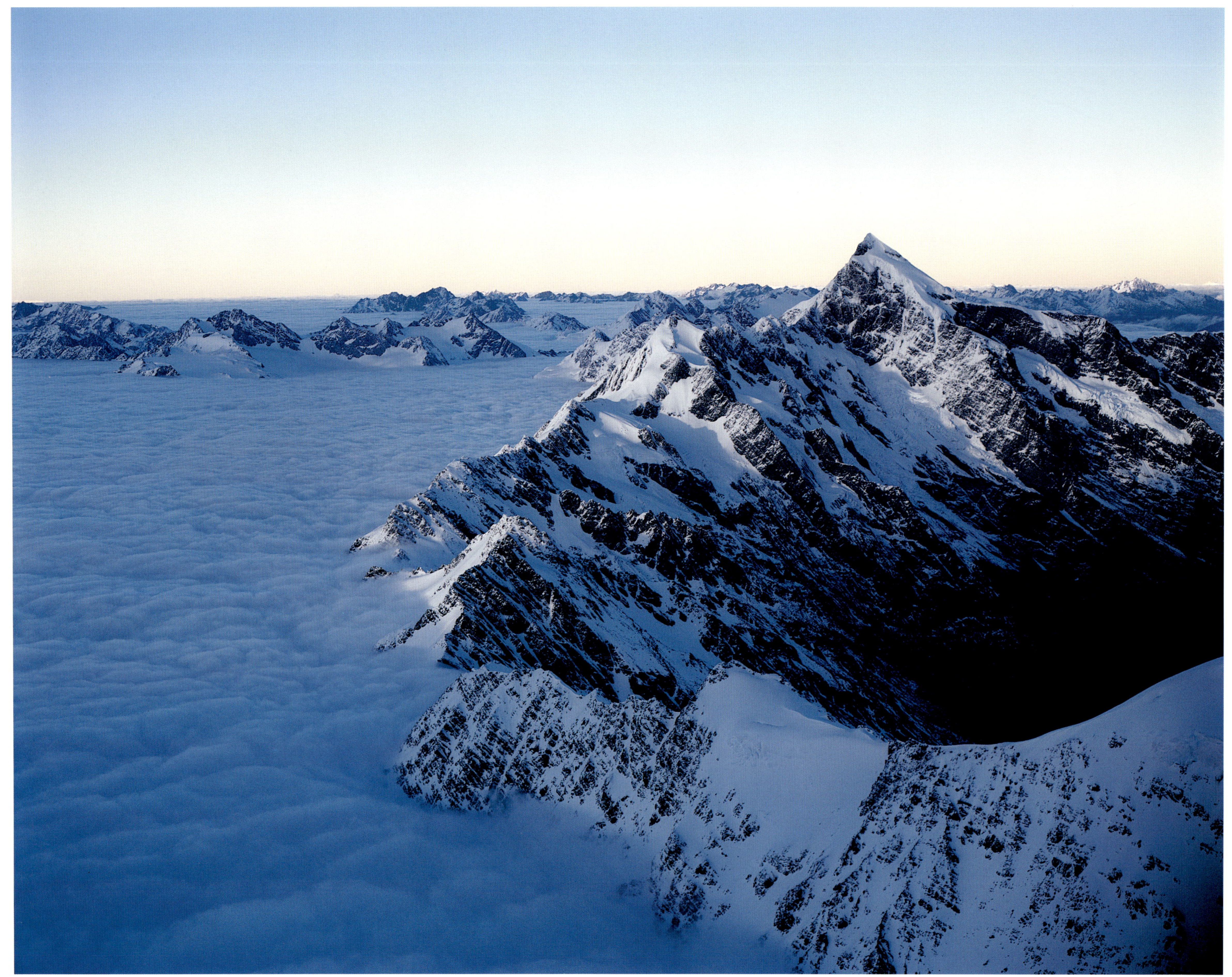

Mt Sefton from above the Hooker Valley

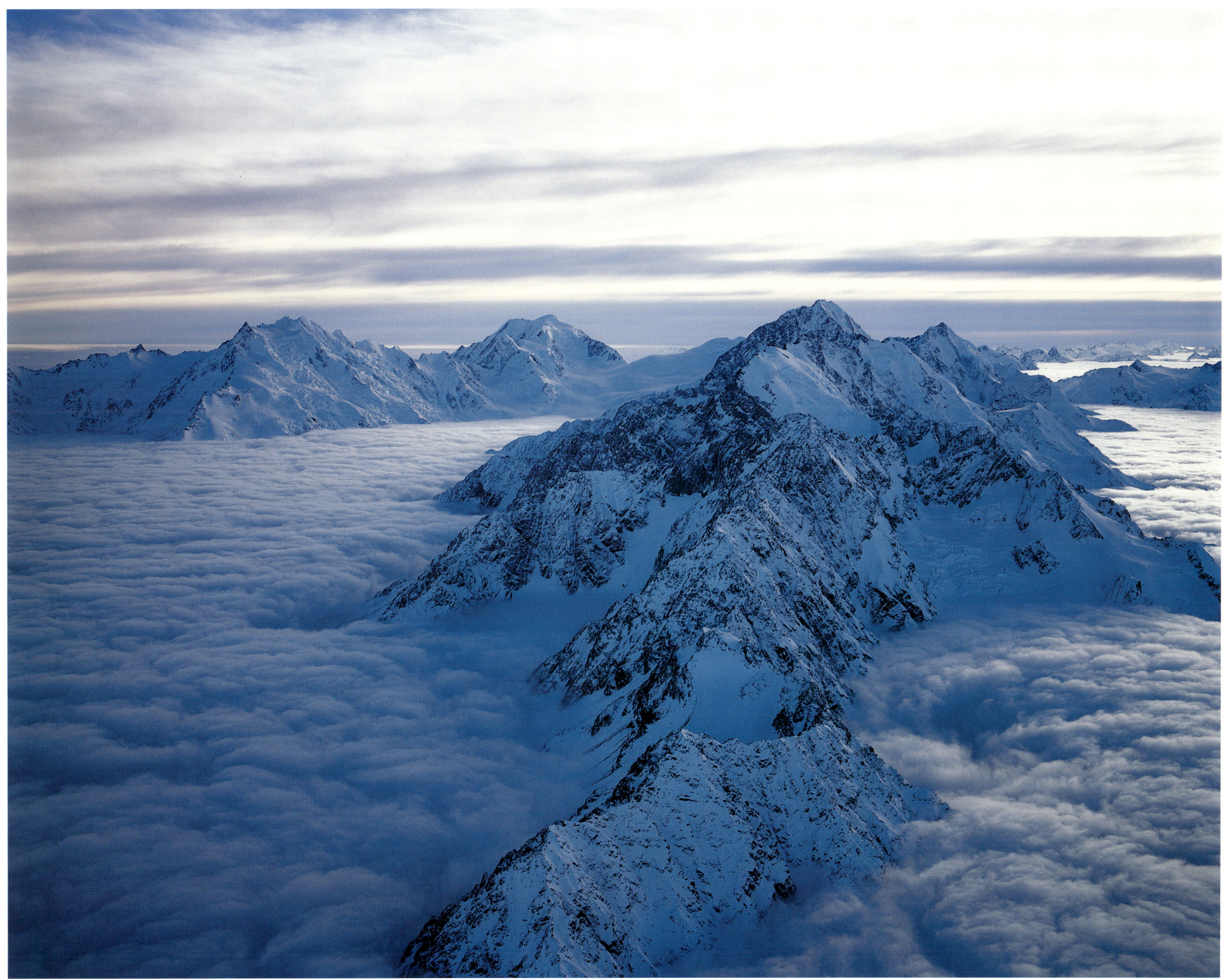

Malte Brun Range with the Minarets and Elie de Beaumont beyond

If you want to cleanse the rust from
the mirror of your mind,
Look into the depth of the pure sky
And meditate in quiet mountains.

—Milarepa

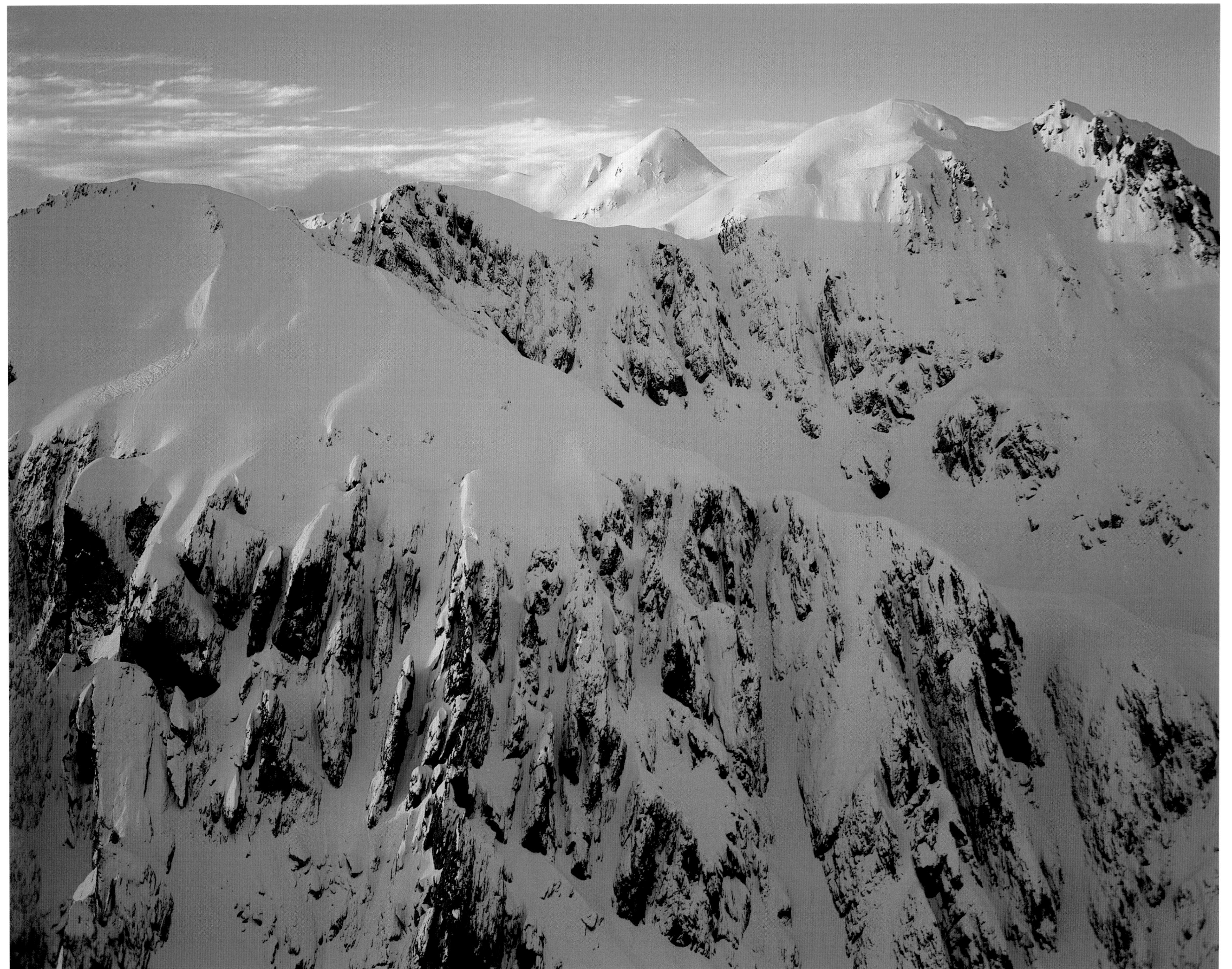

Ridge north of Franz Josef Glacier

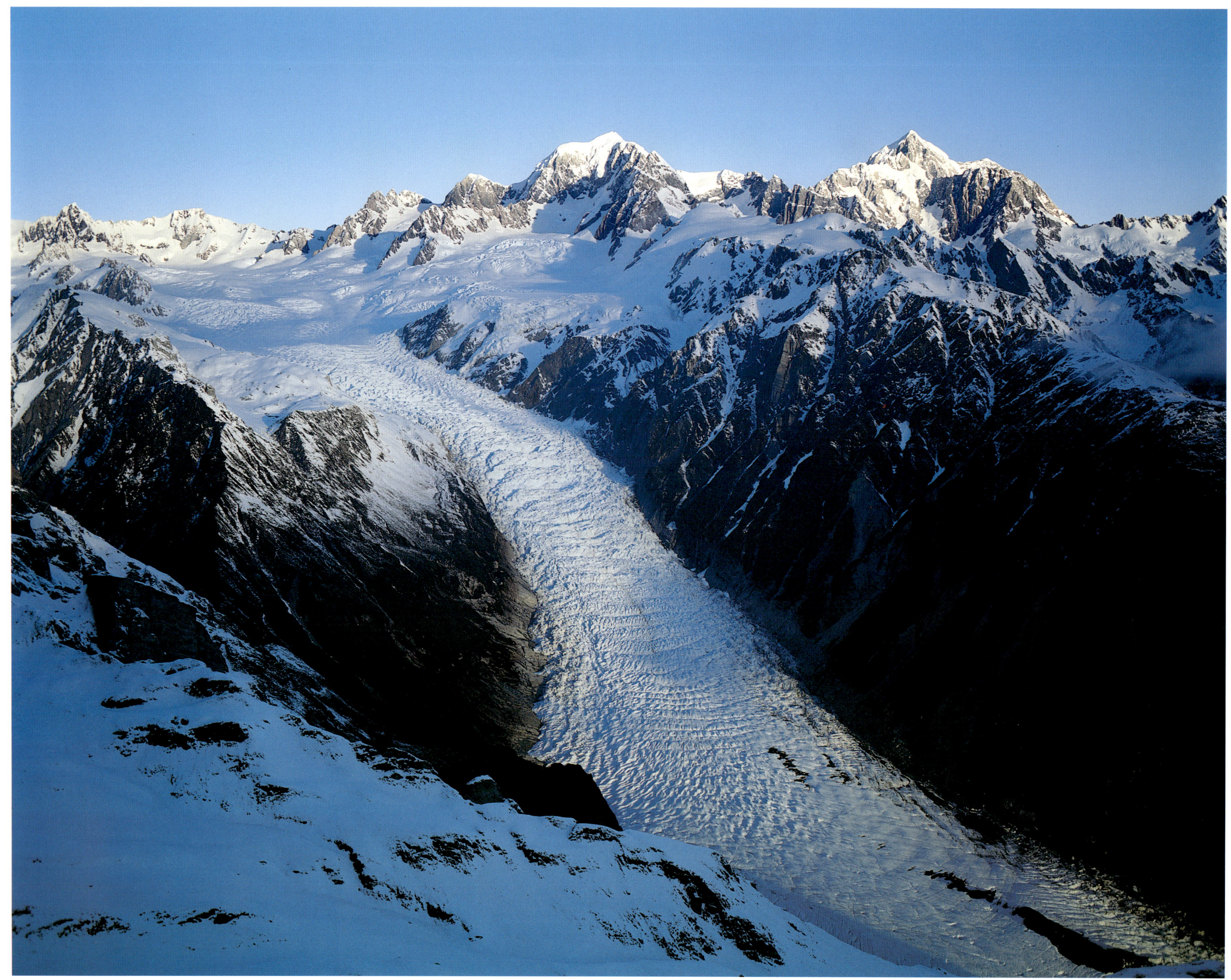

Fox Glacier with Mt Tasman and Aoraki/Mt Cook beyond

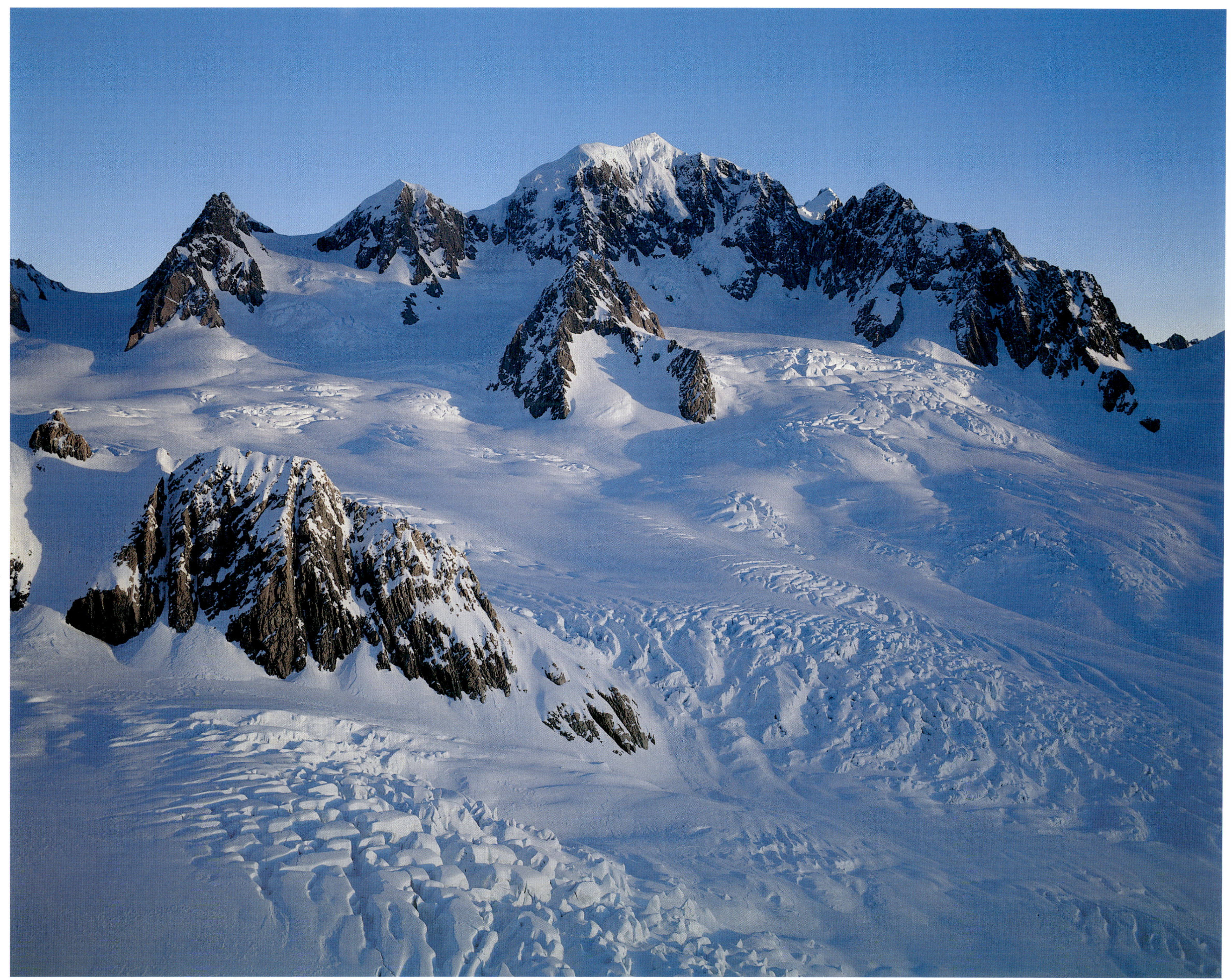

Mt Tasman and surrounding peaks above the Albert Glacier

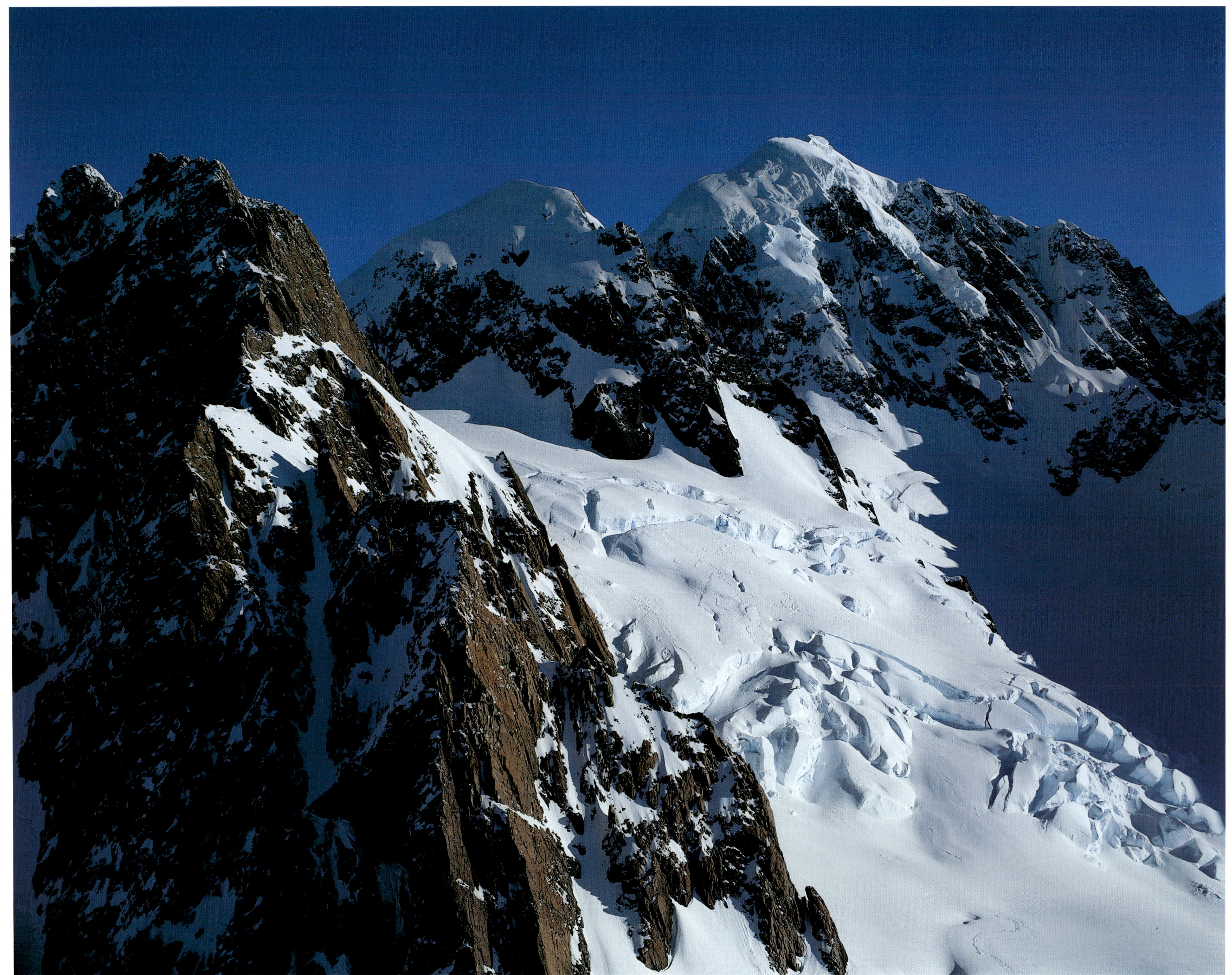

Mt Haast, Lendenfeld Peak and Mt Tasman

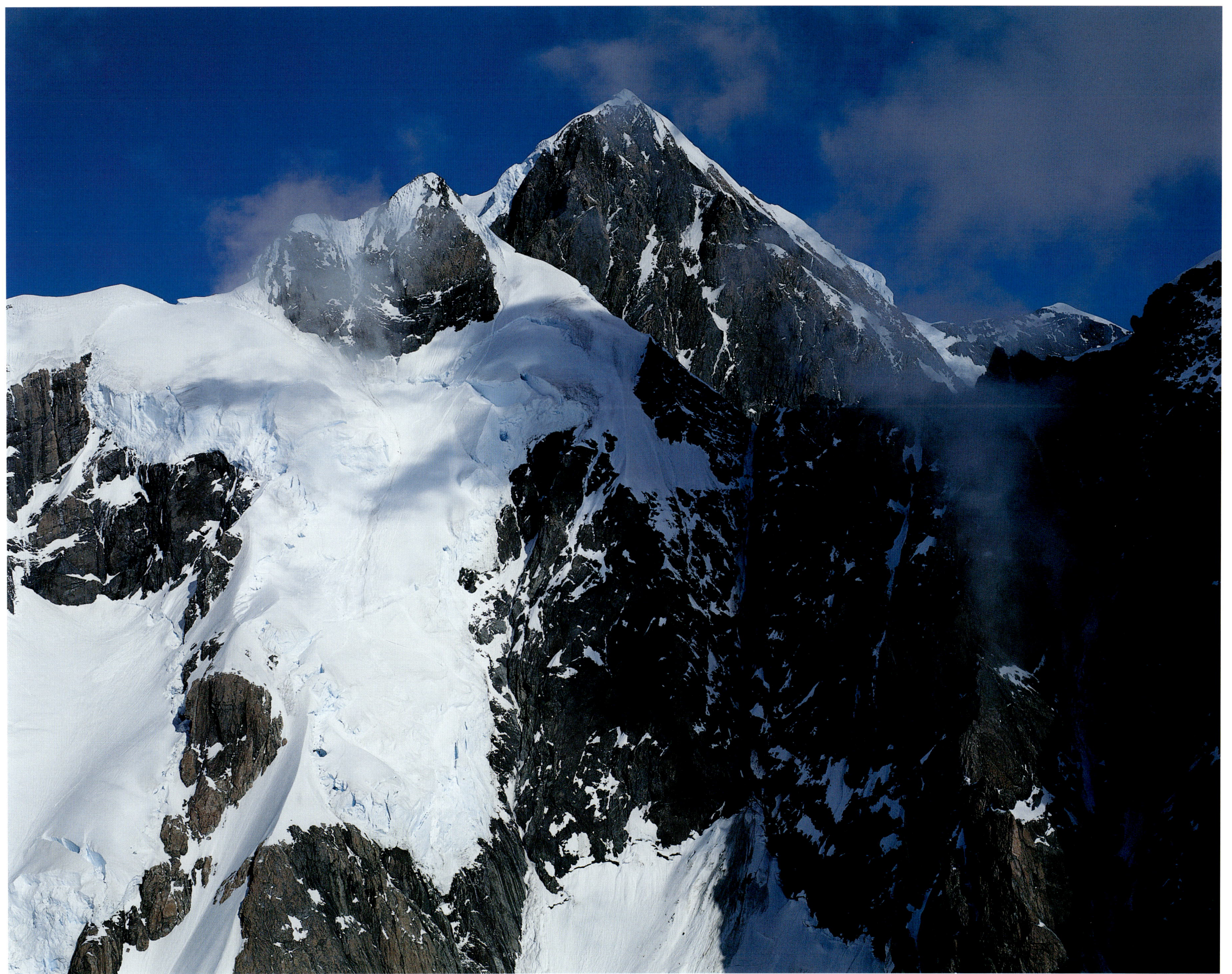

Sheila Face of Aoraki/Mt Cook above the Dampier-Hicks Ridge

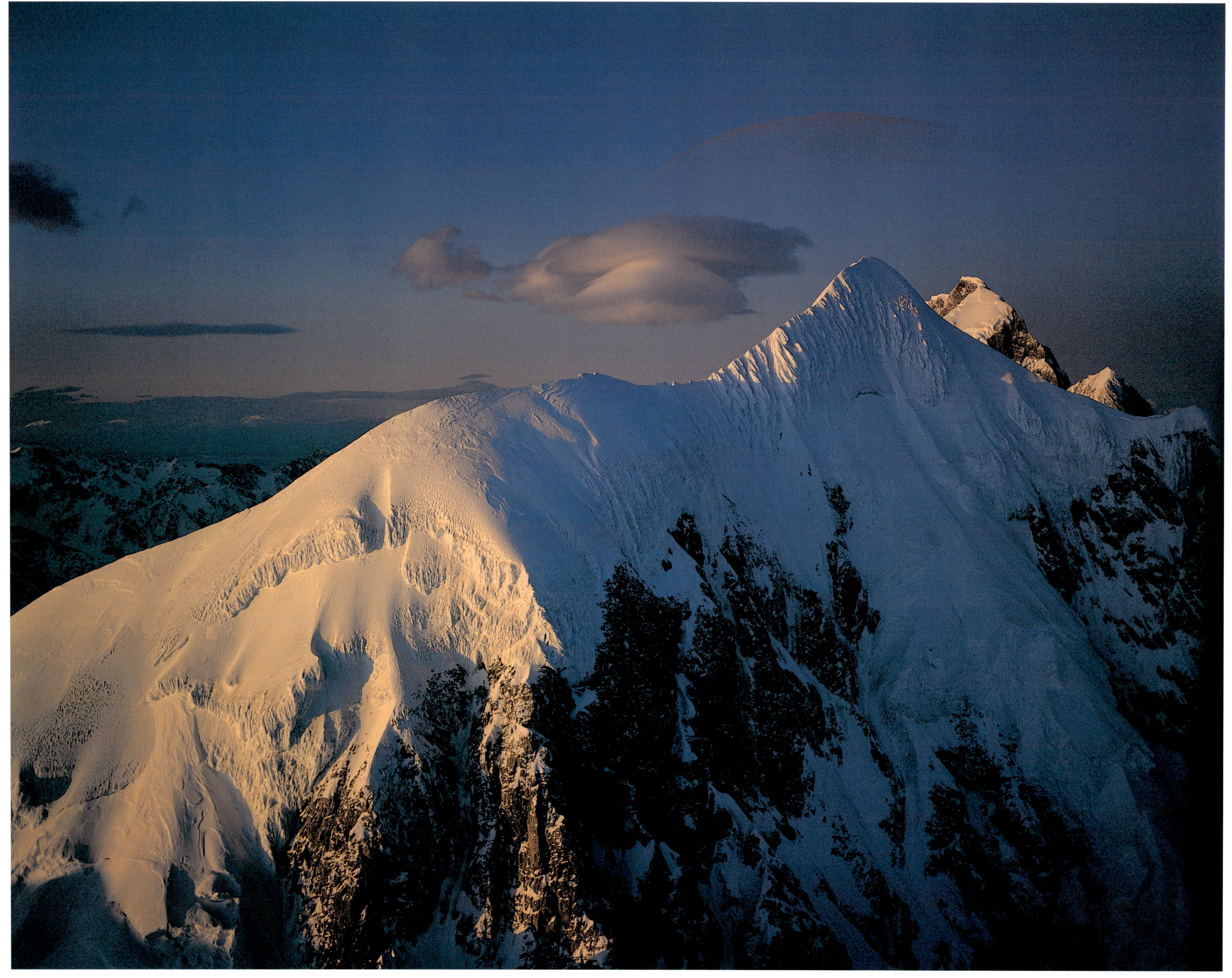

North Shoulder, Mt Tasman

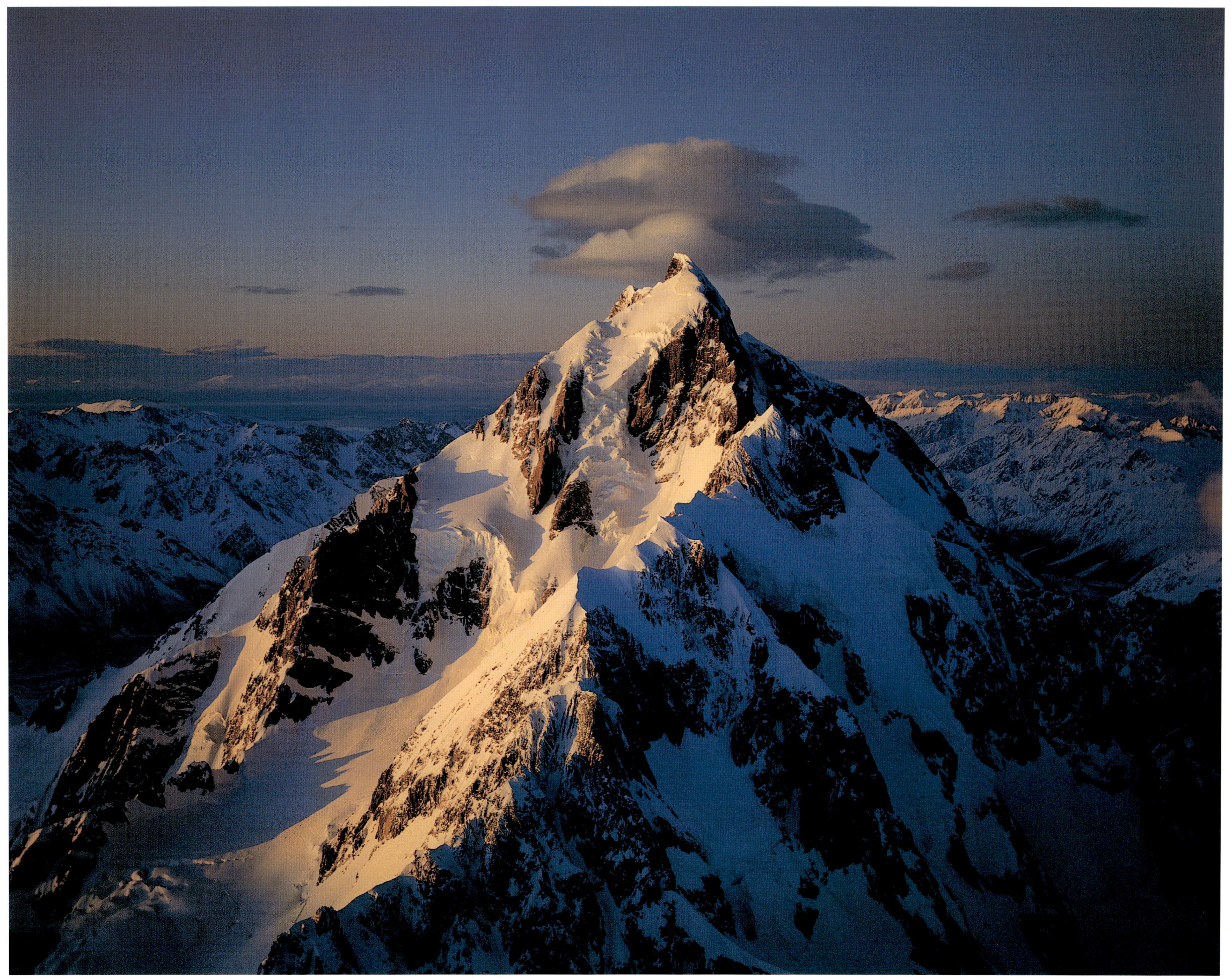

Aoraki/Mt Cook from the north

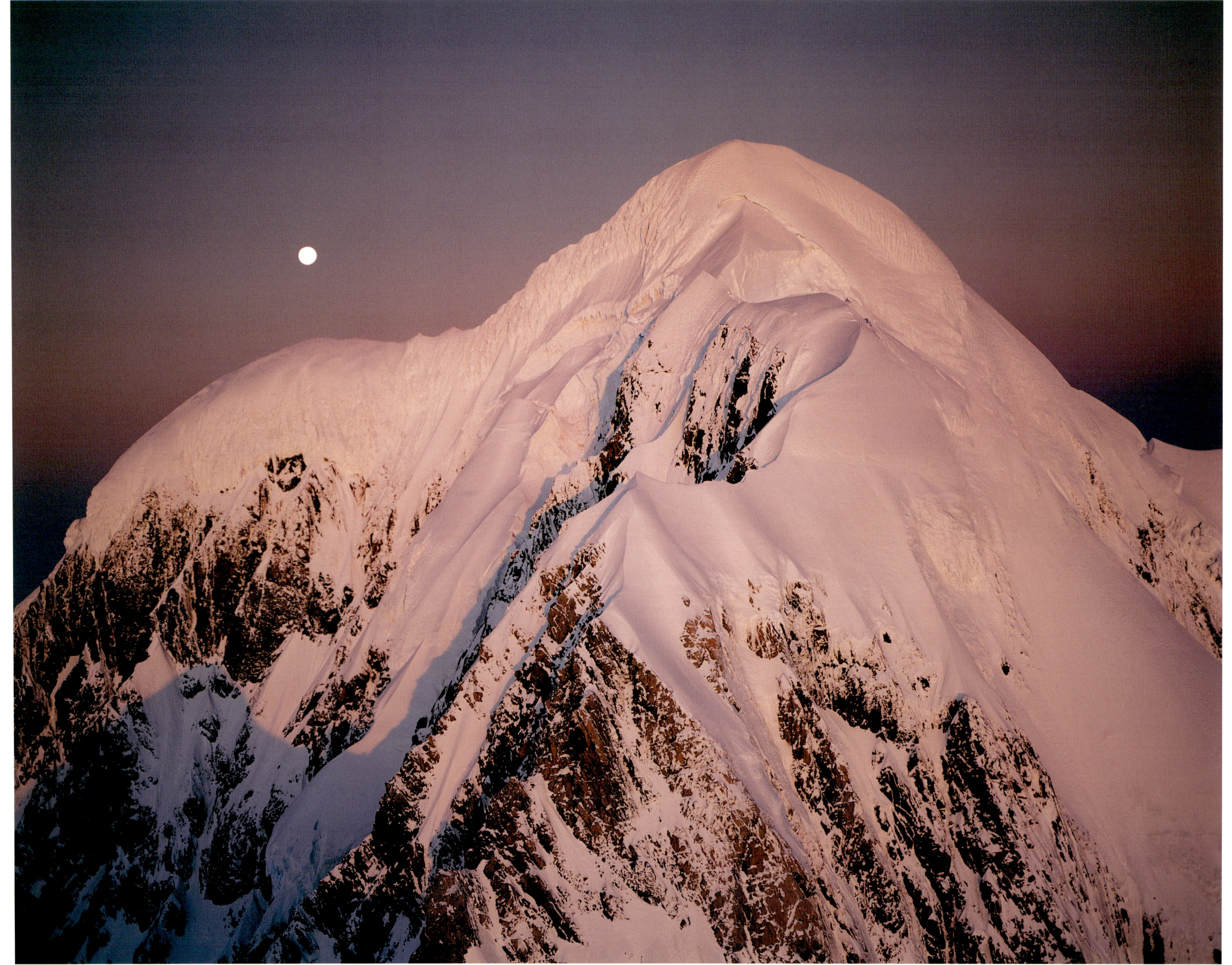

Mt Tasman

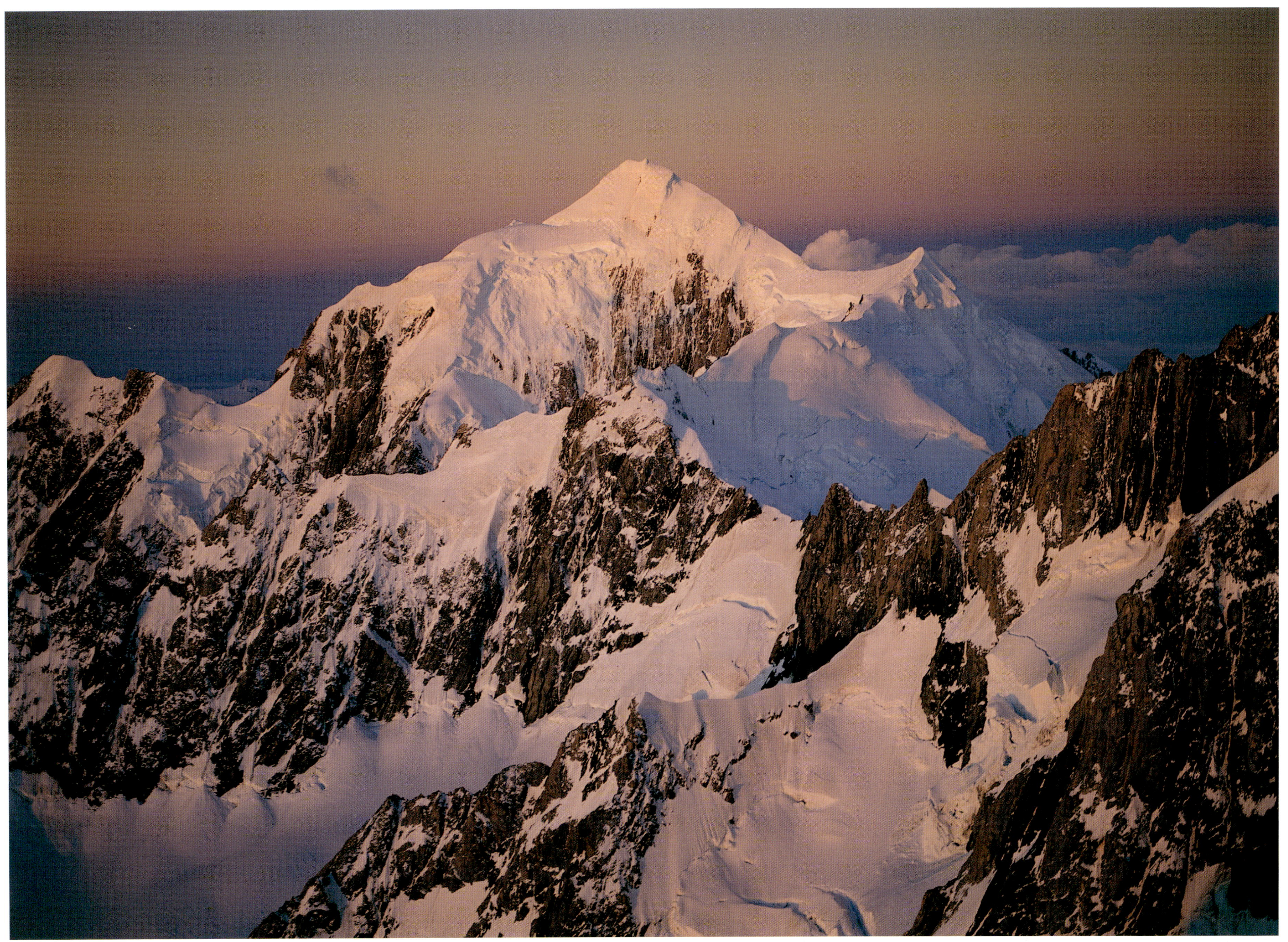

The Main Divide, looking north towards the Balfour Face of Mt Tasman

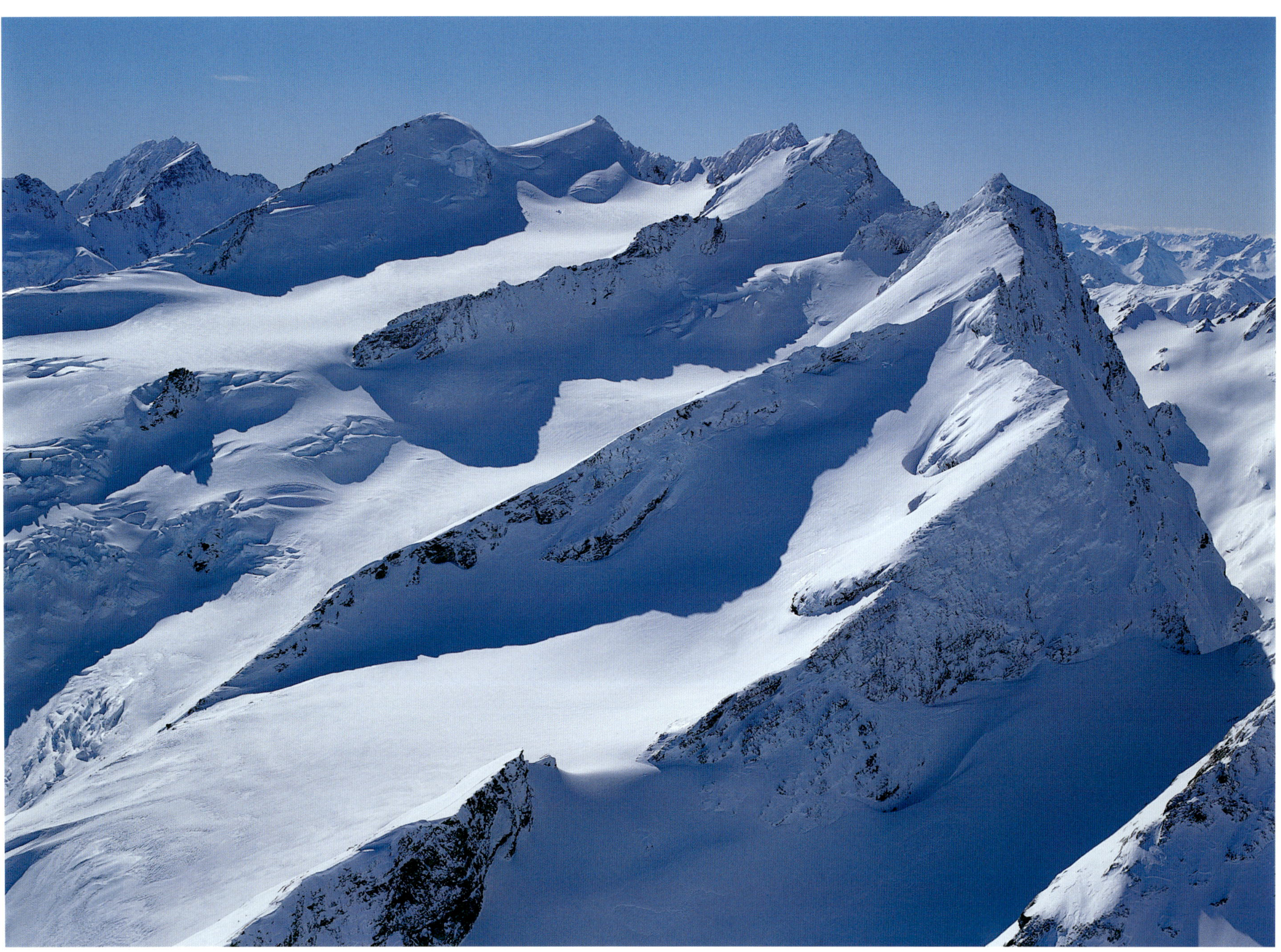

Western flanks of Mt Whitcombe

Central Alps and north to Nelson Lakes

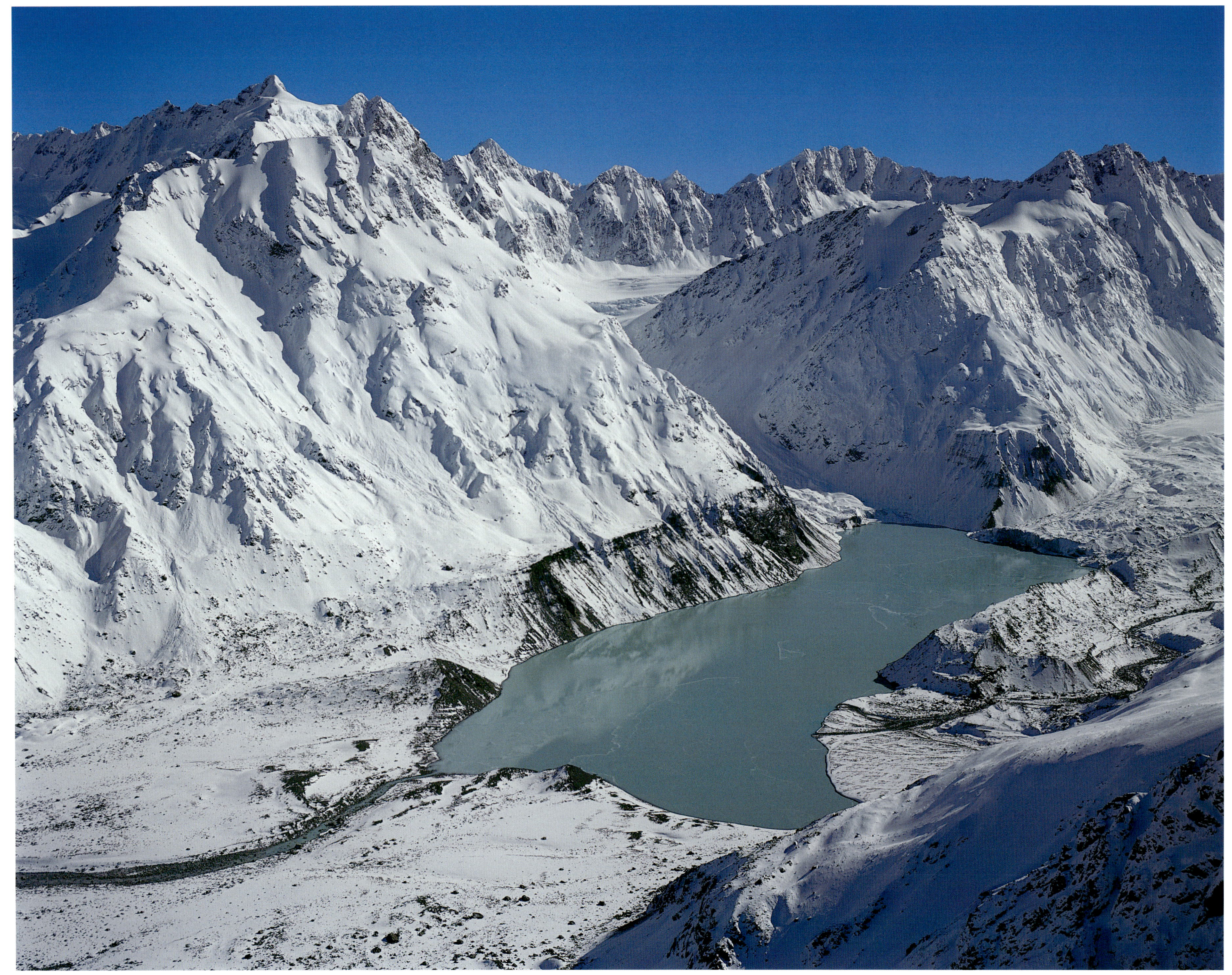

Terminal lake, Grey and Maud glaciers with the Main Divide beyond, Godley Valley

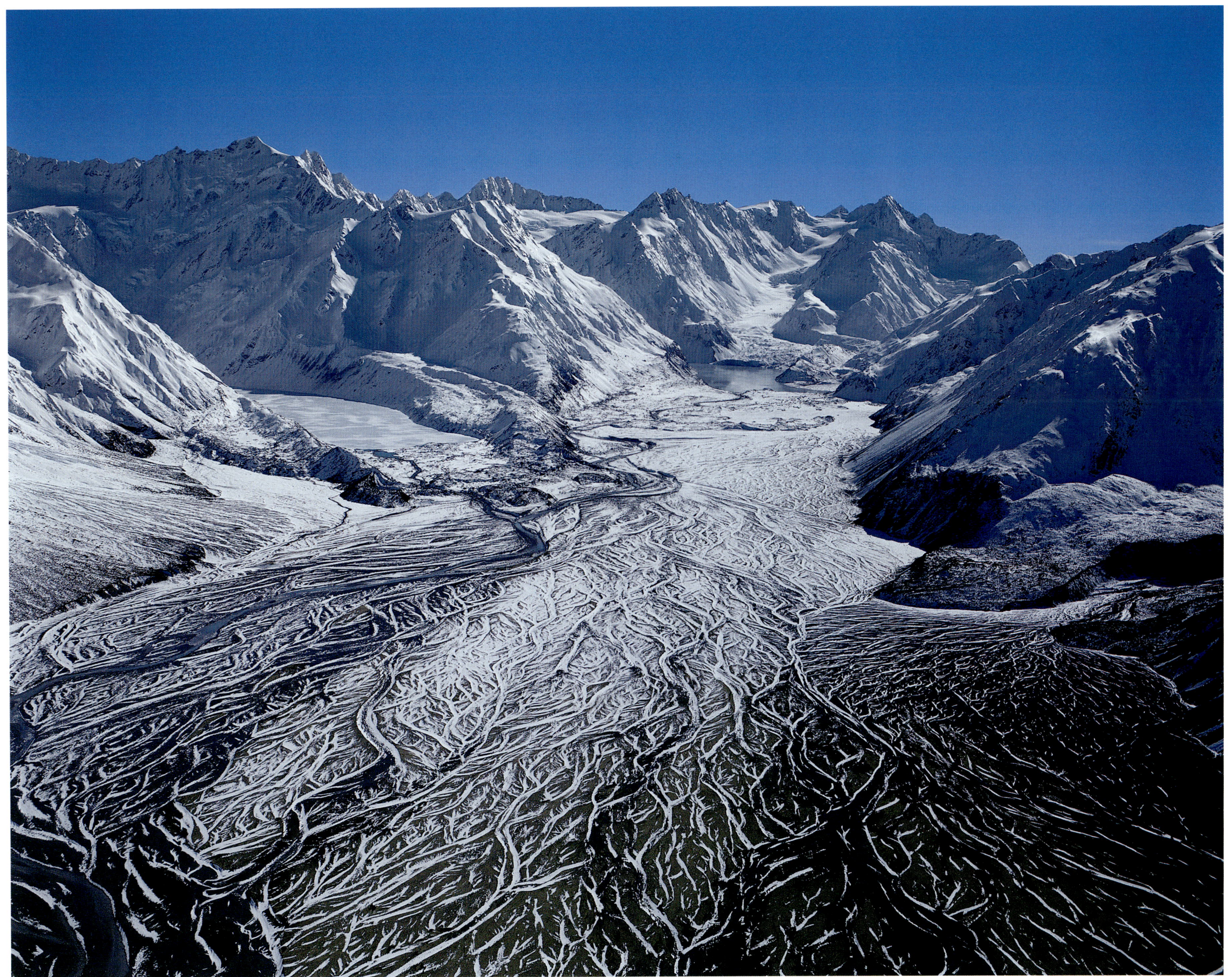

Head of the Godley Valley

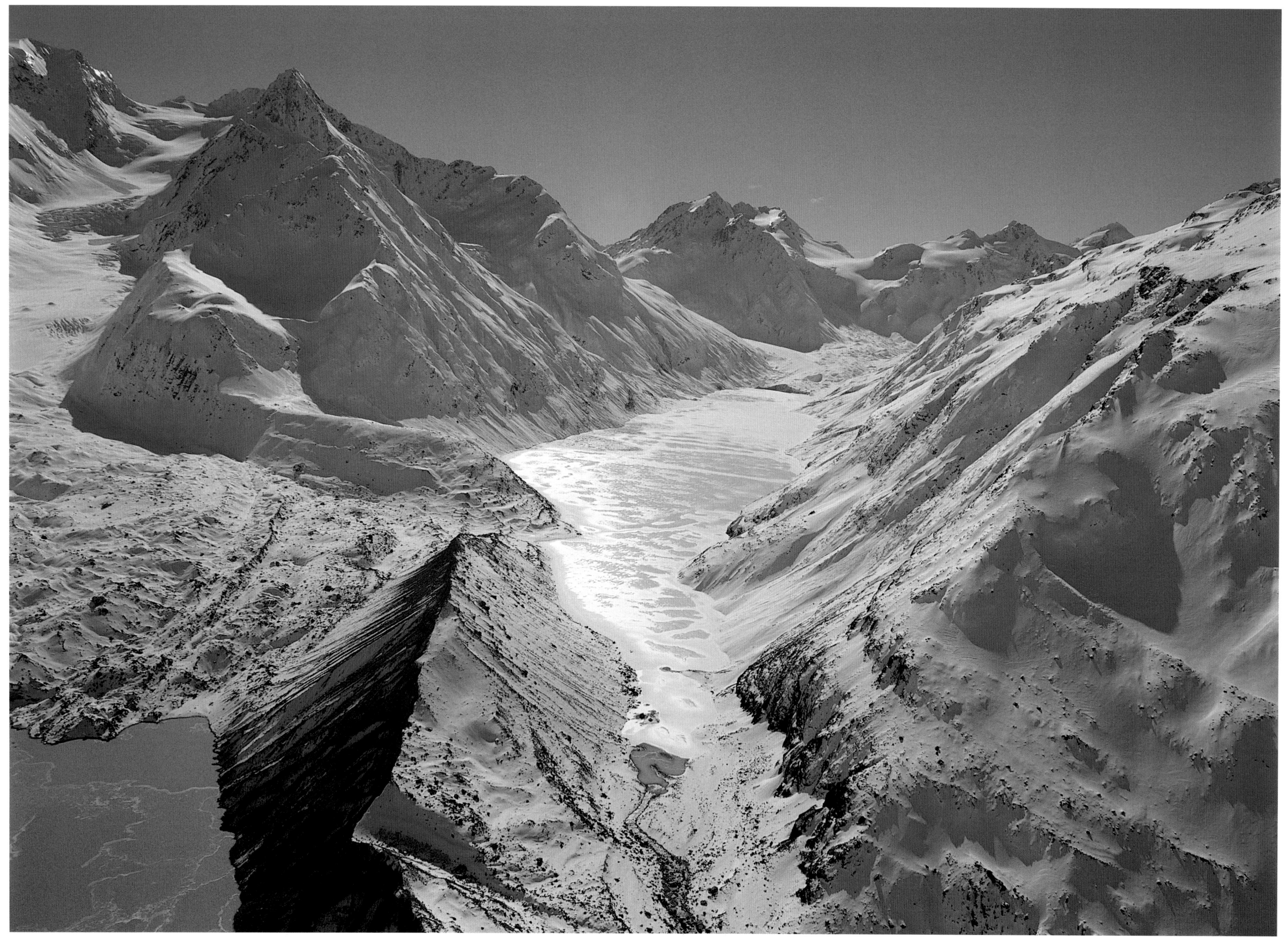

Godley Glacier terminal lake

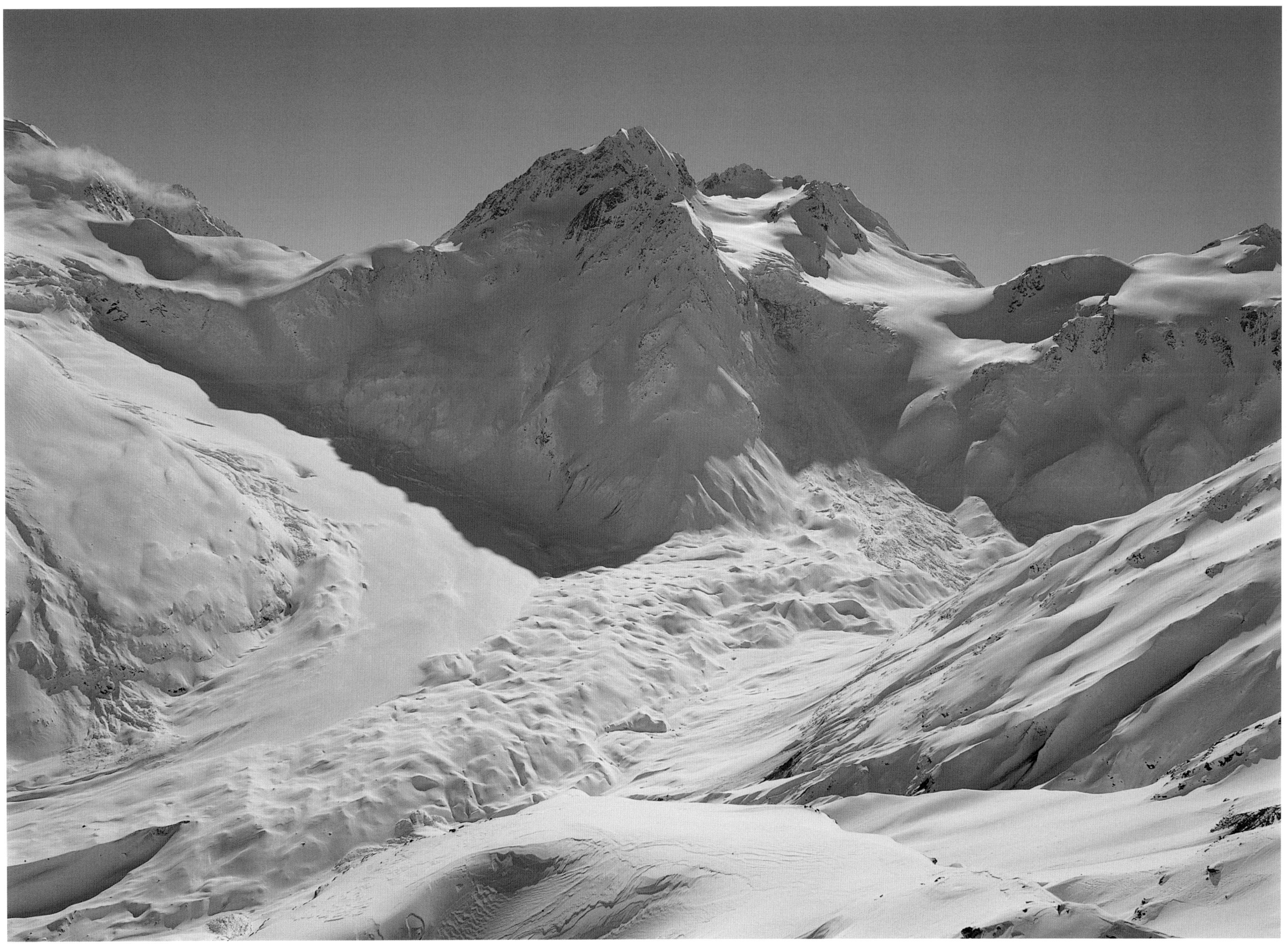

Sealy Pass and Mt Shyness, Upper Godley Valley

Who can leap the world's ties
And sit with me among the white clouds
I gaze afar towards the southern mountains.

—Han Shan, *Cold Mountain*

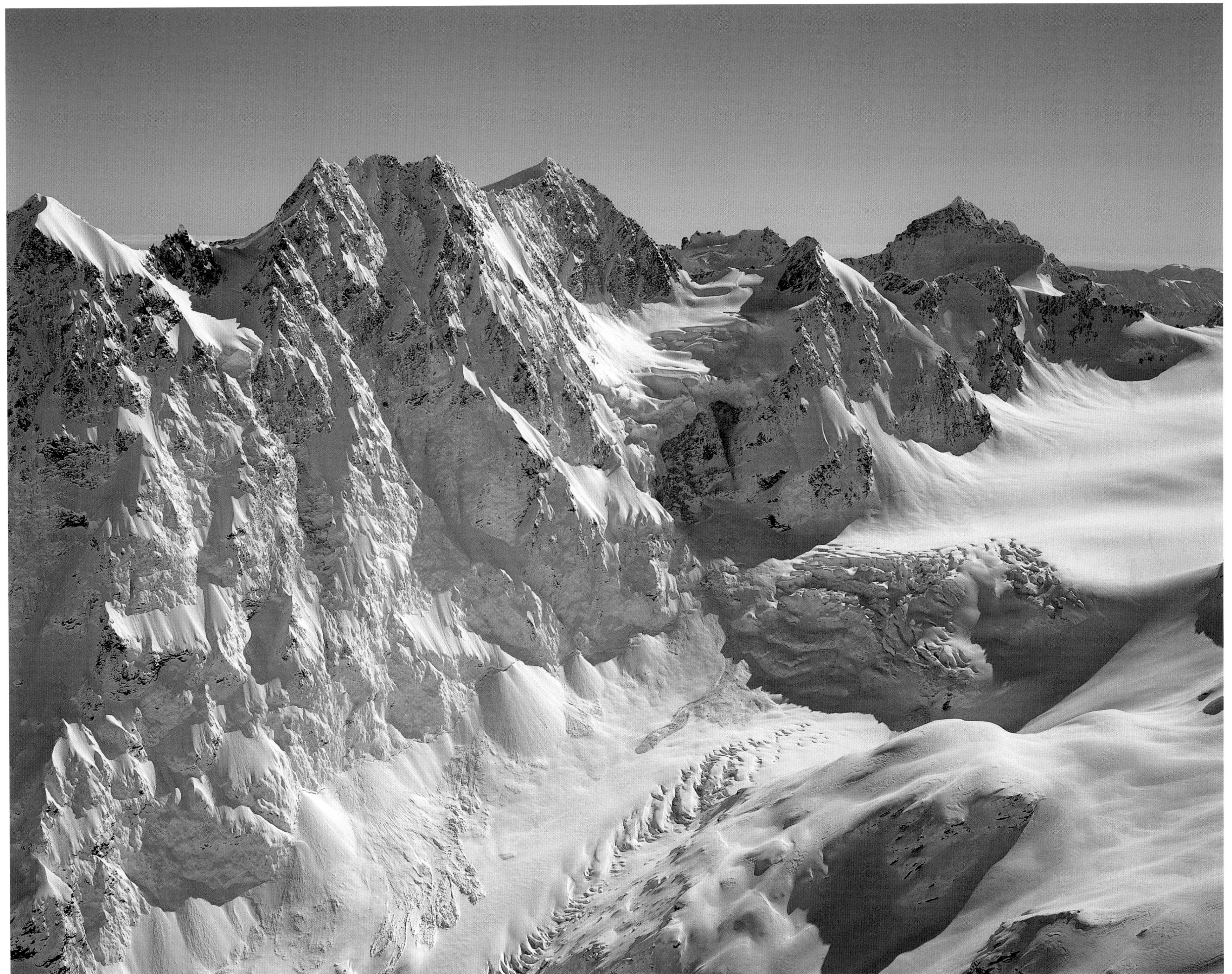

Ramsay Face of Mt Whitcombe

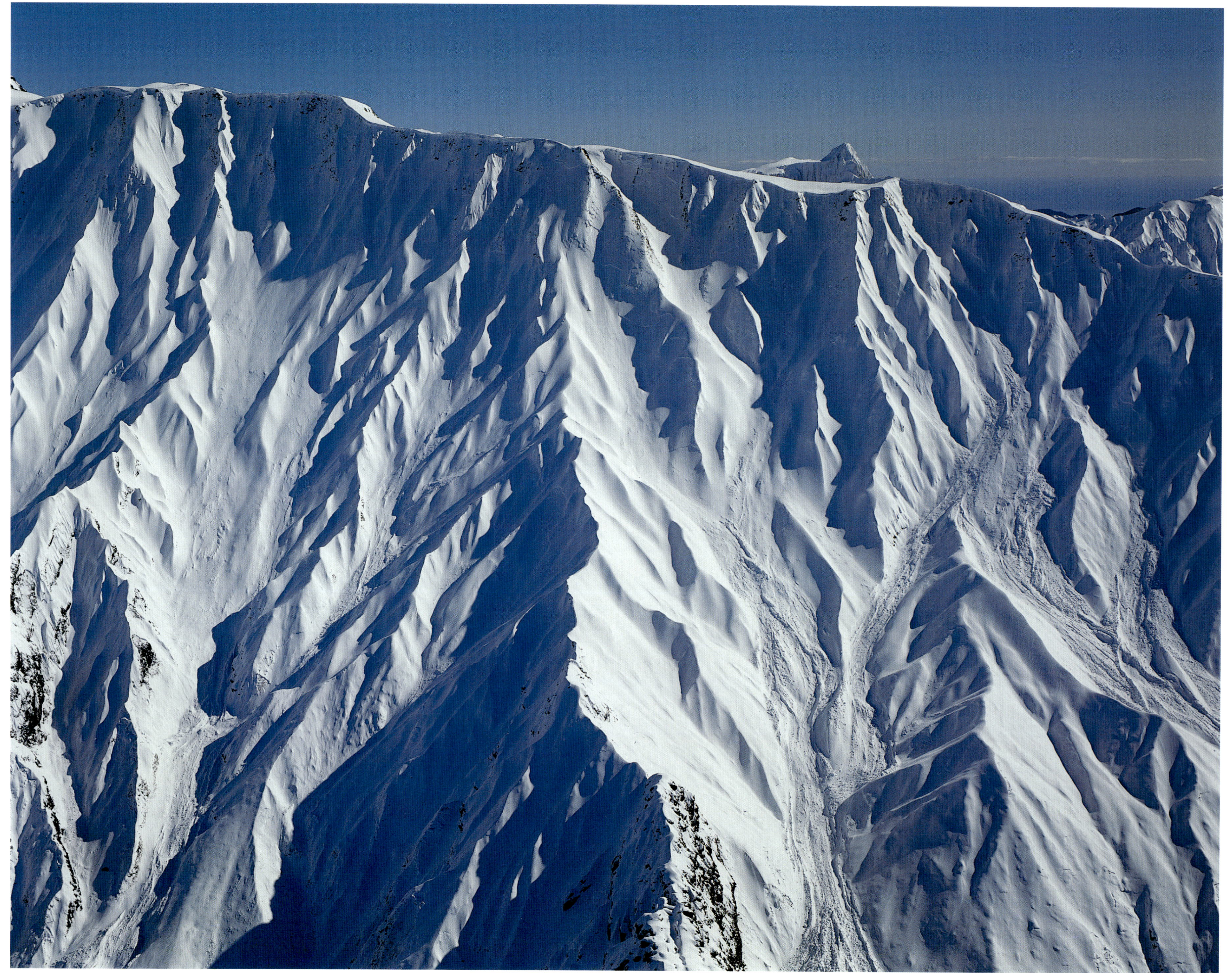

Snow-covered ridge, Whitcombe Valley

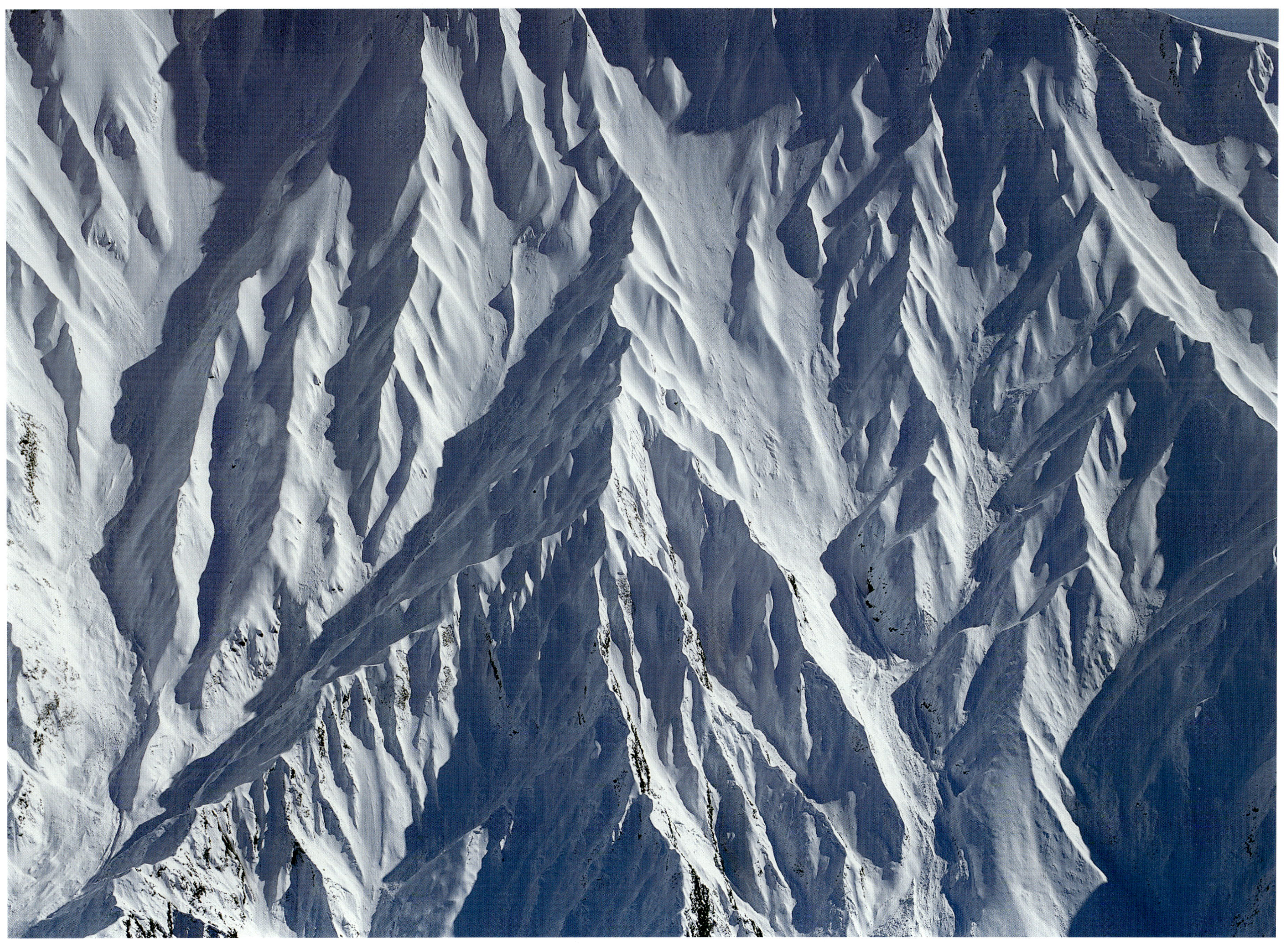

Patterns of gully erosion masked by winter snow, Whitcombe Valley

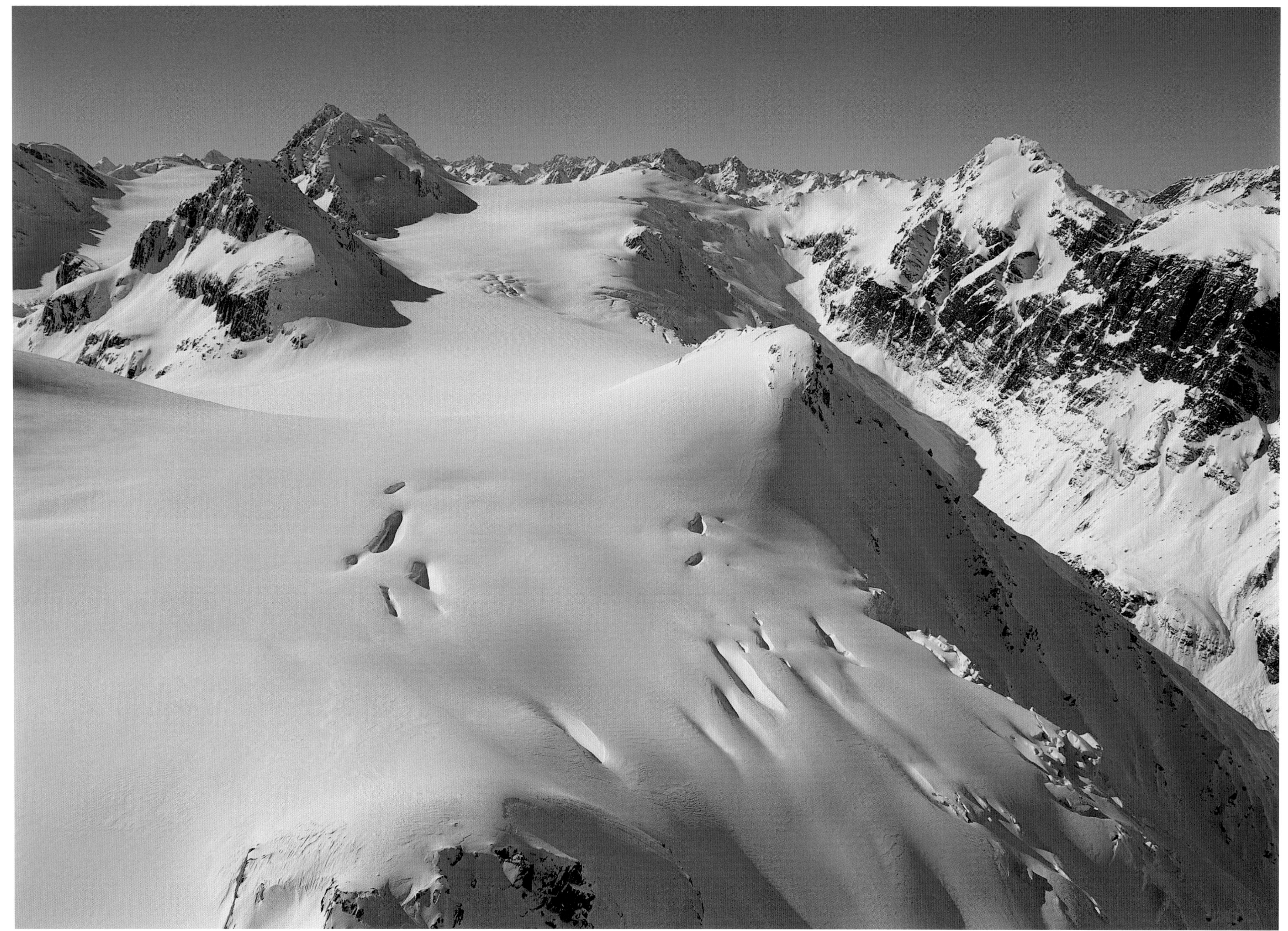

The Garden of Eden from the west

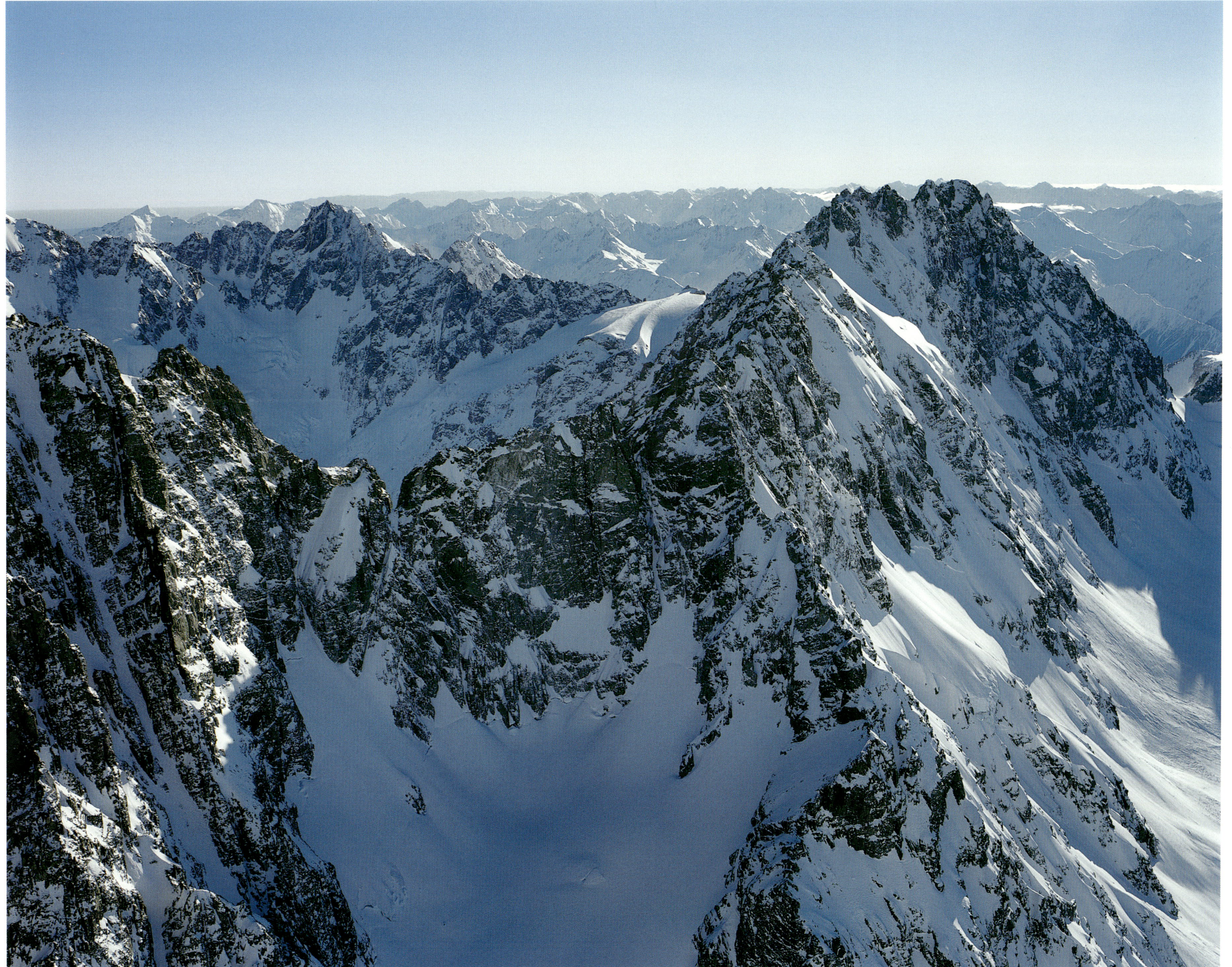

Jagged Peak, Arrowsmith Range

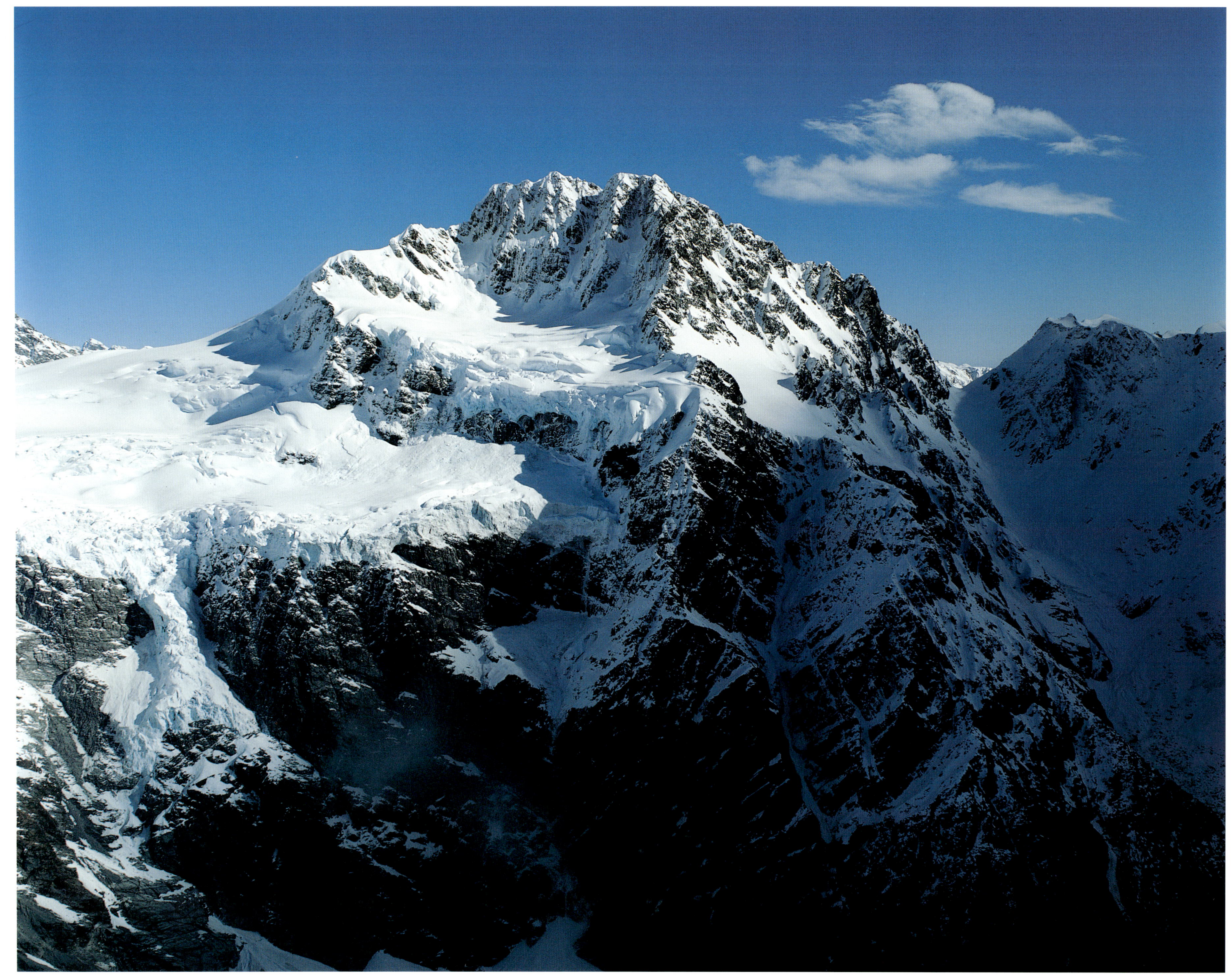

Mt Evans and the Upper and Lower Shelf glaciers

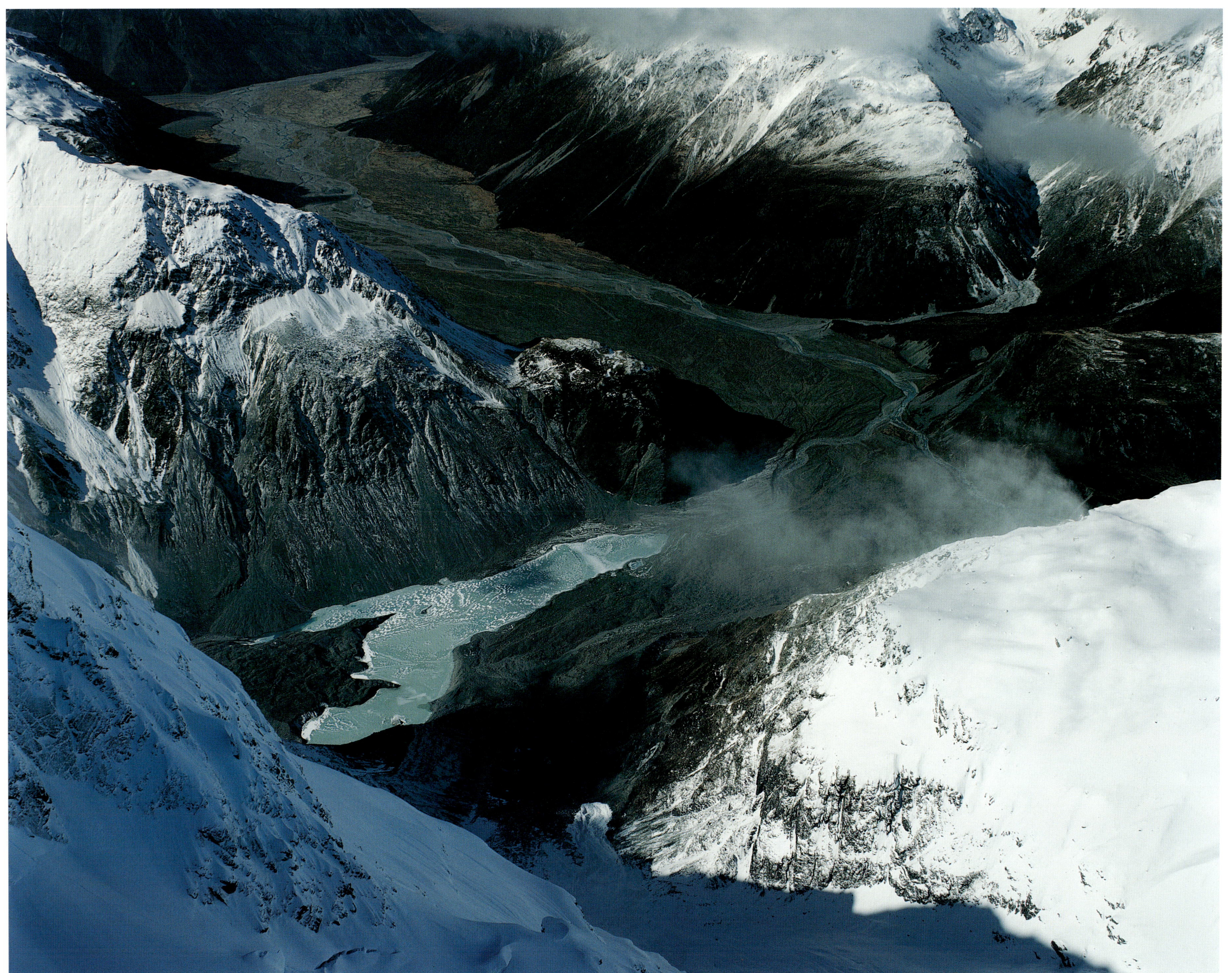

Ramsay Glacier terminal lake

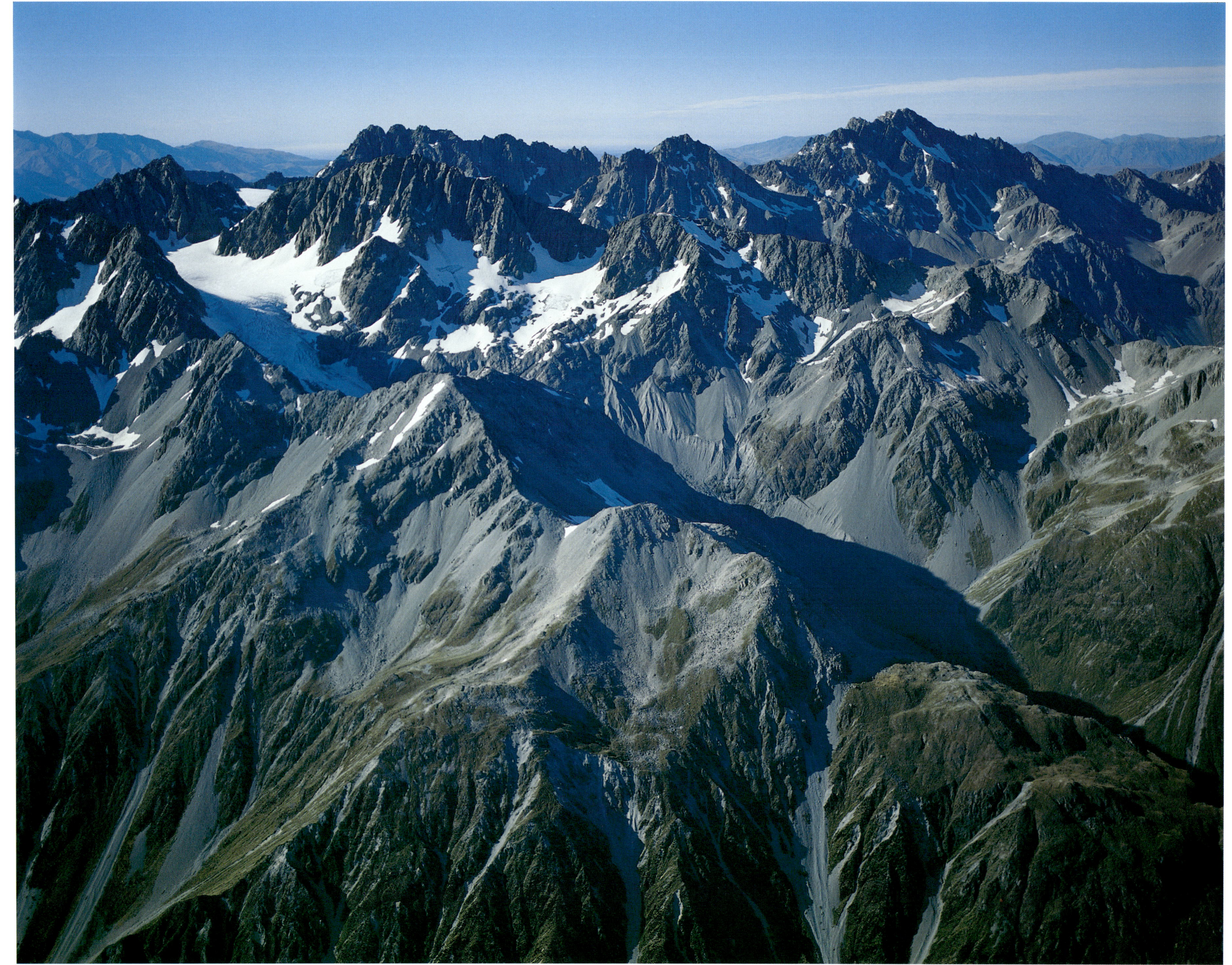

Arrowsmith Range

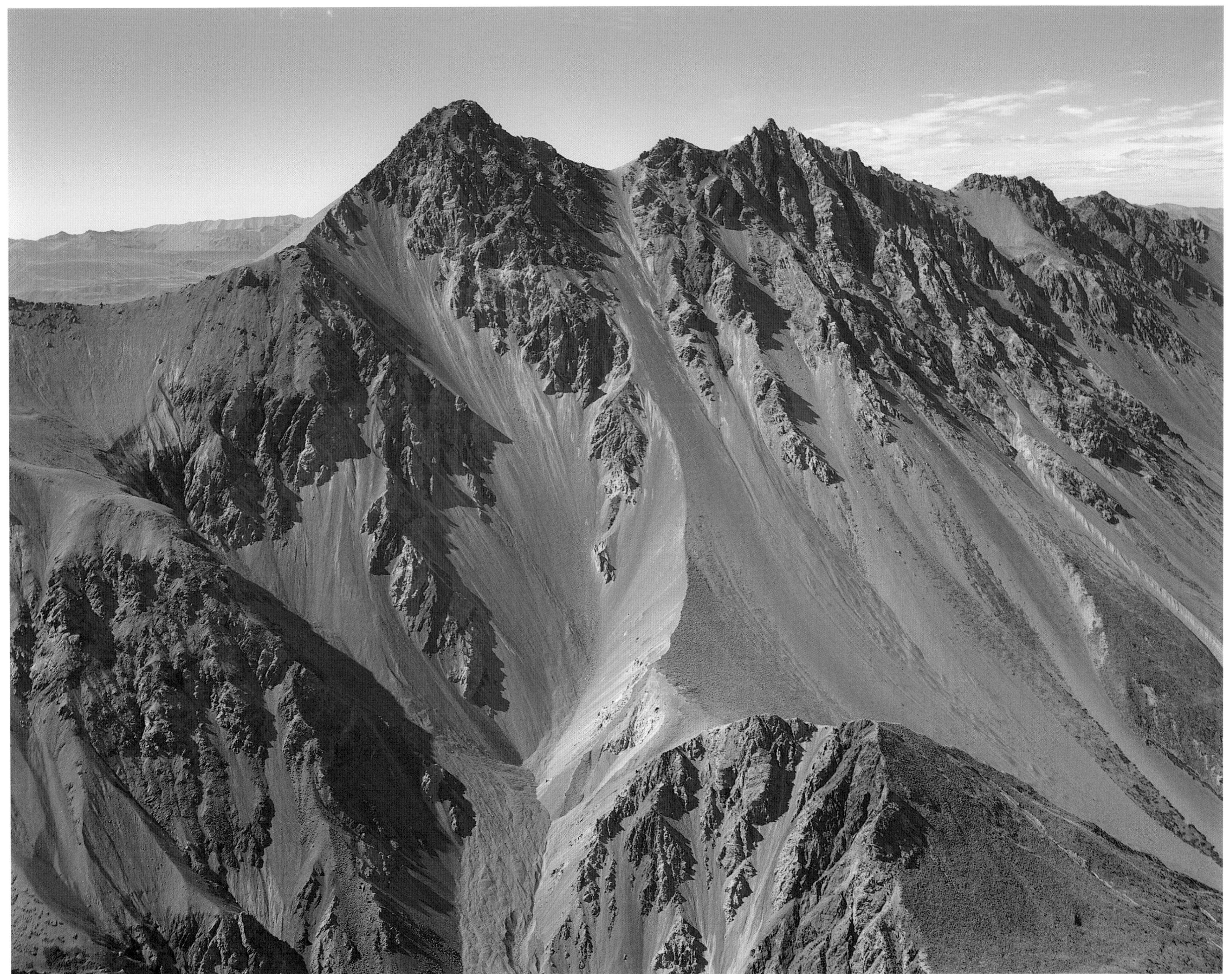

Scree-scarred ridge, inland Canterbury

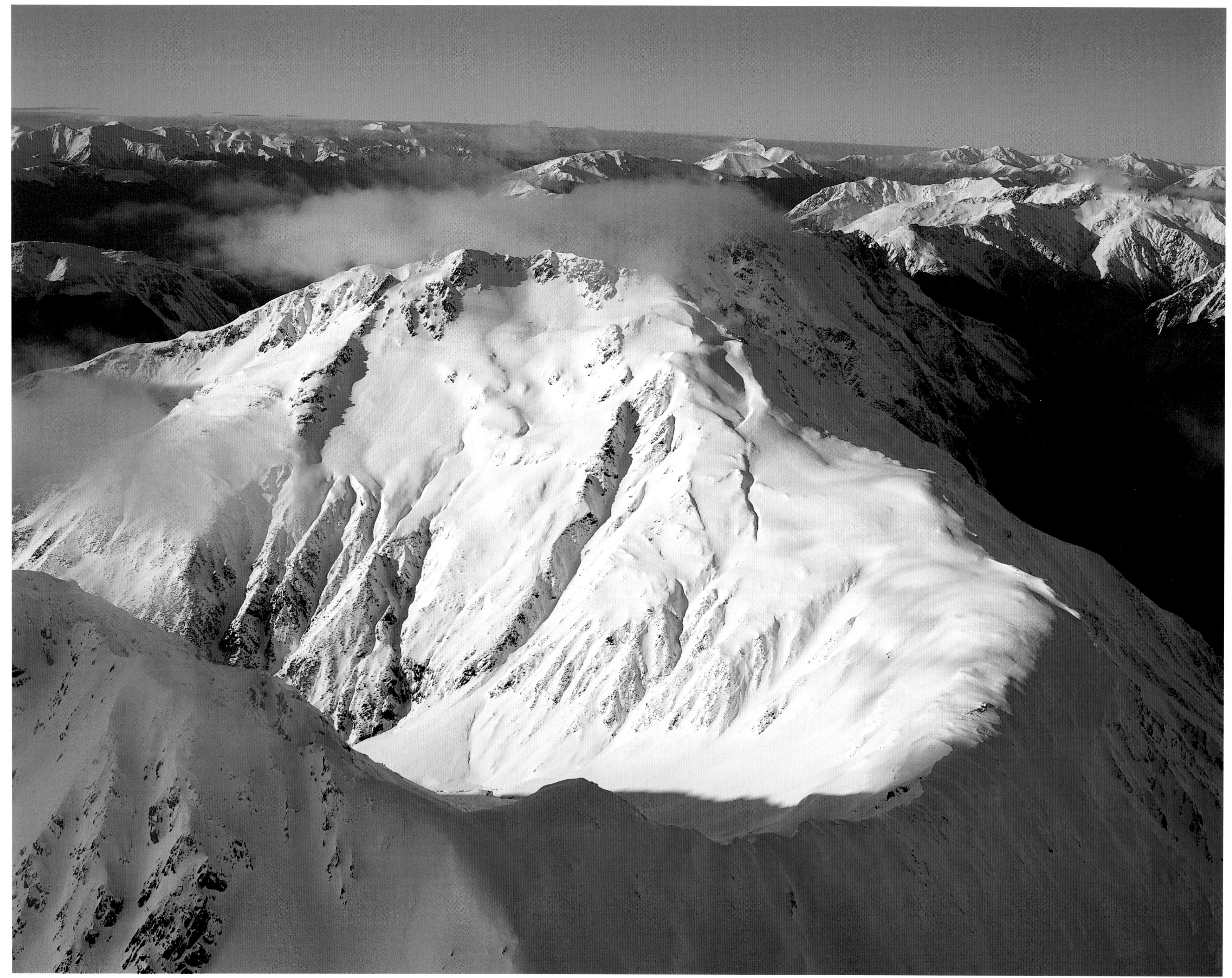

Doubtful Range south of Lewis Pass

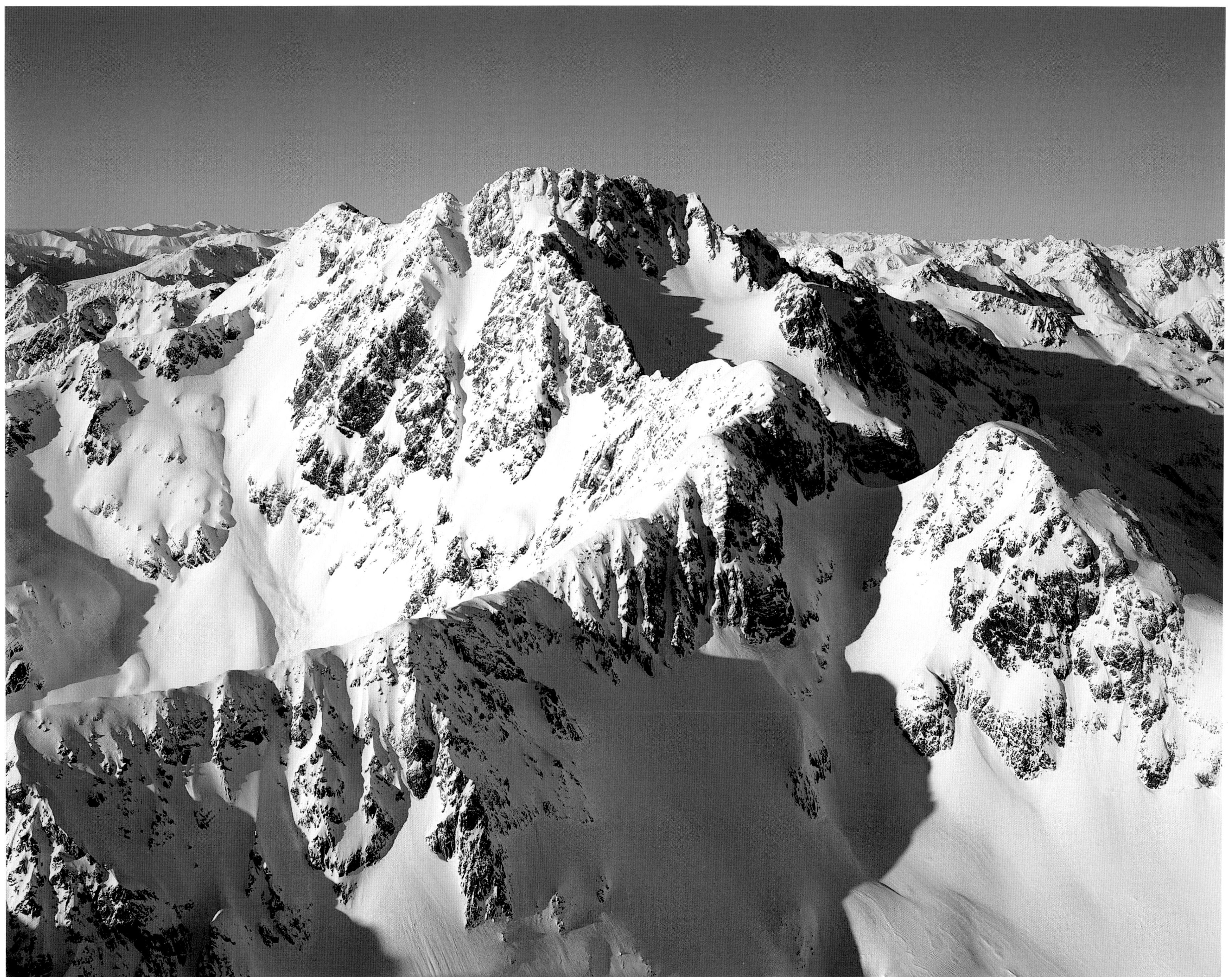

Mt Rolleston from the north-west, Arthur's Pass National Park

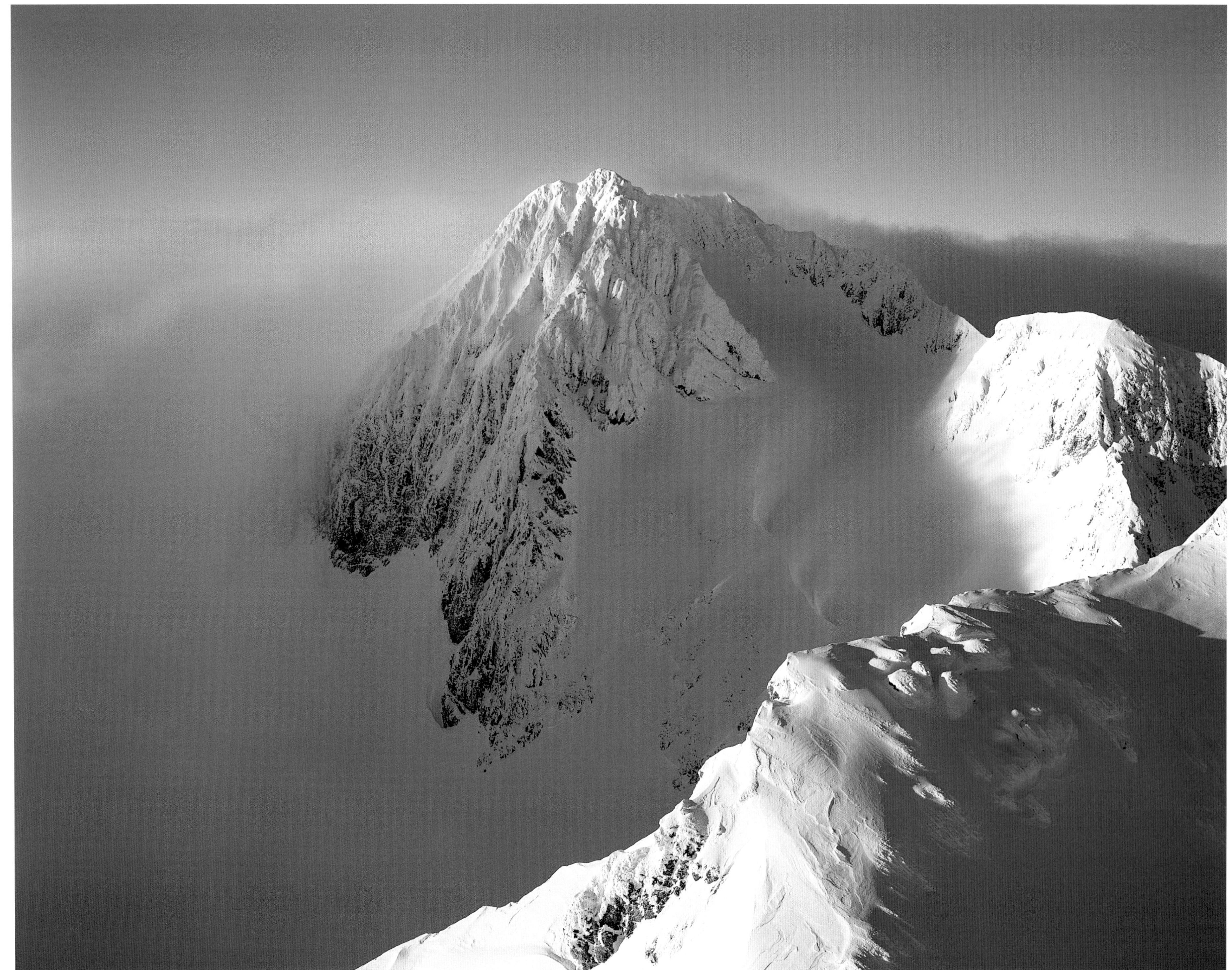

Mt Una, Spenser Mountains

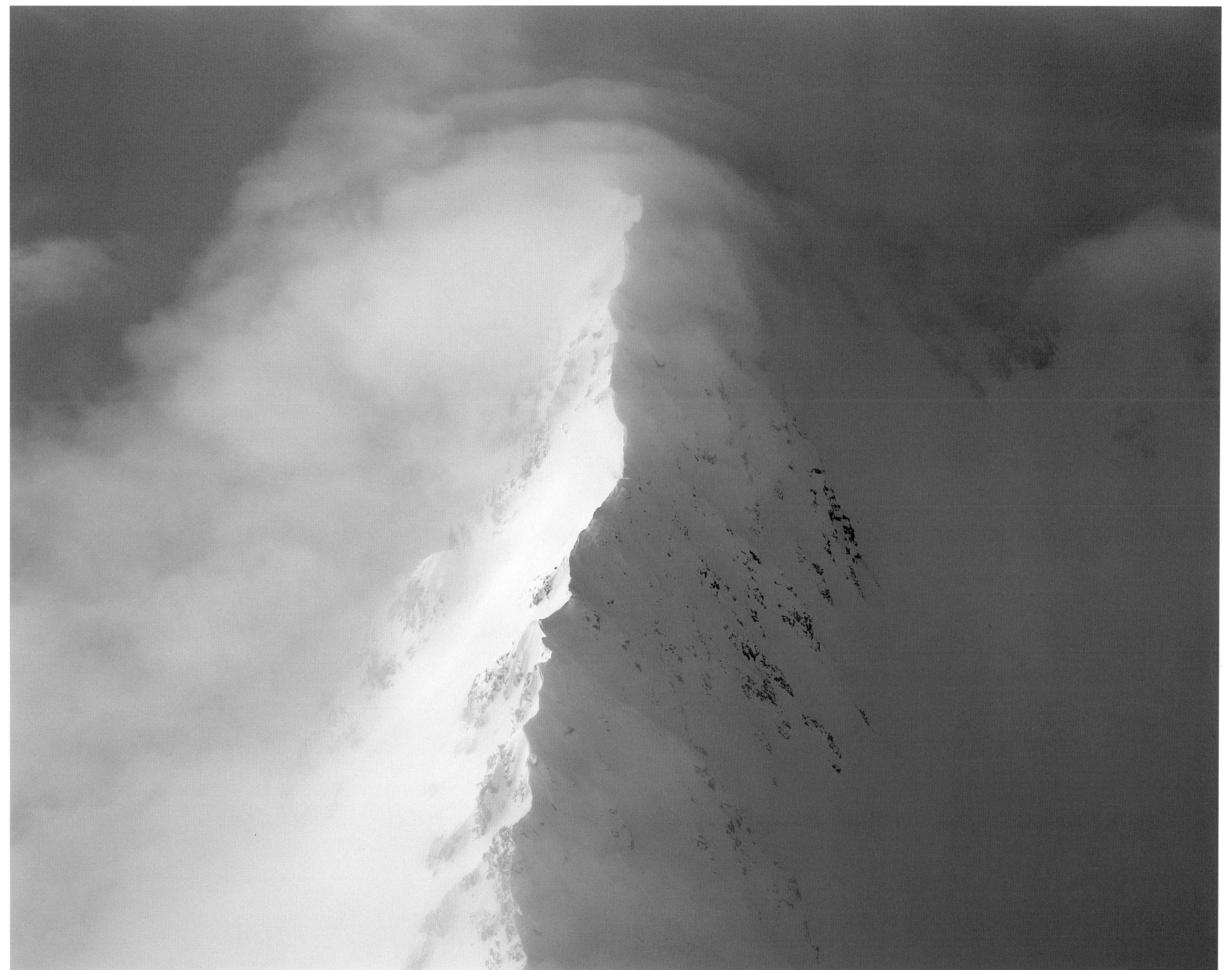

Corniced ridgeline, Mt Una, Spenser Mountains

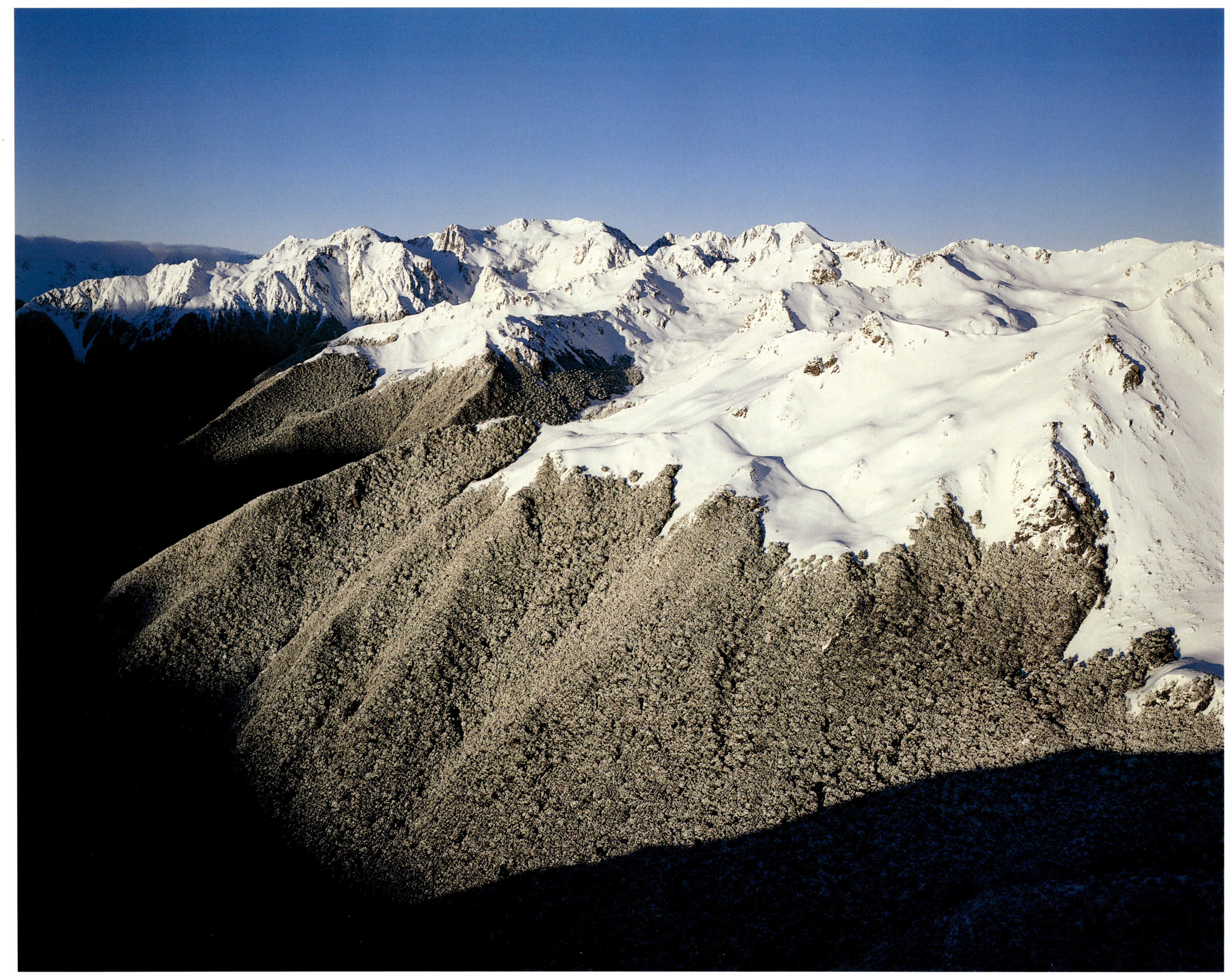

Robert Ridge and Travers Range, Nelson Lakes National Park

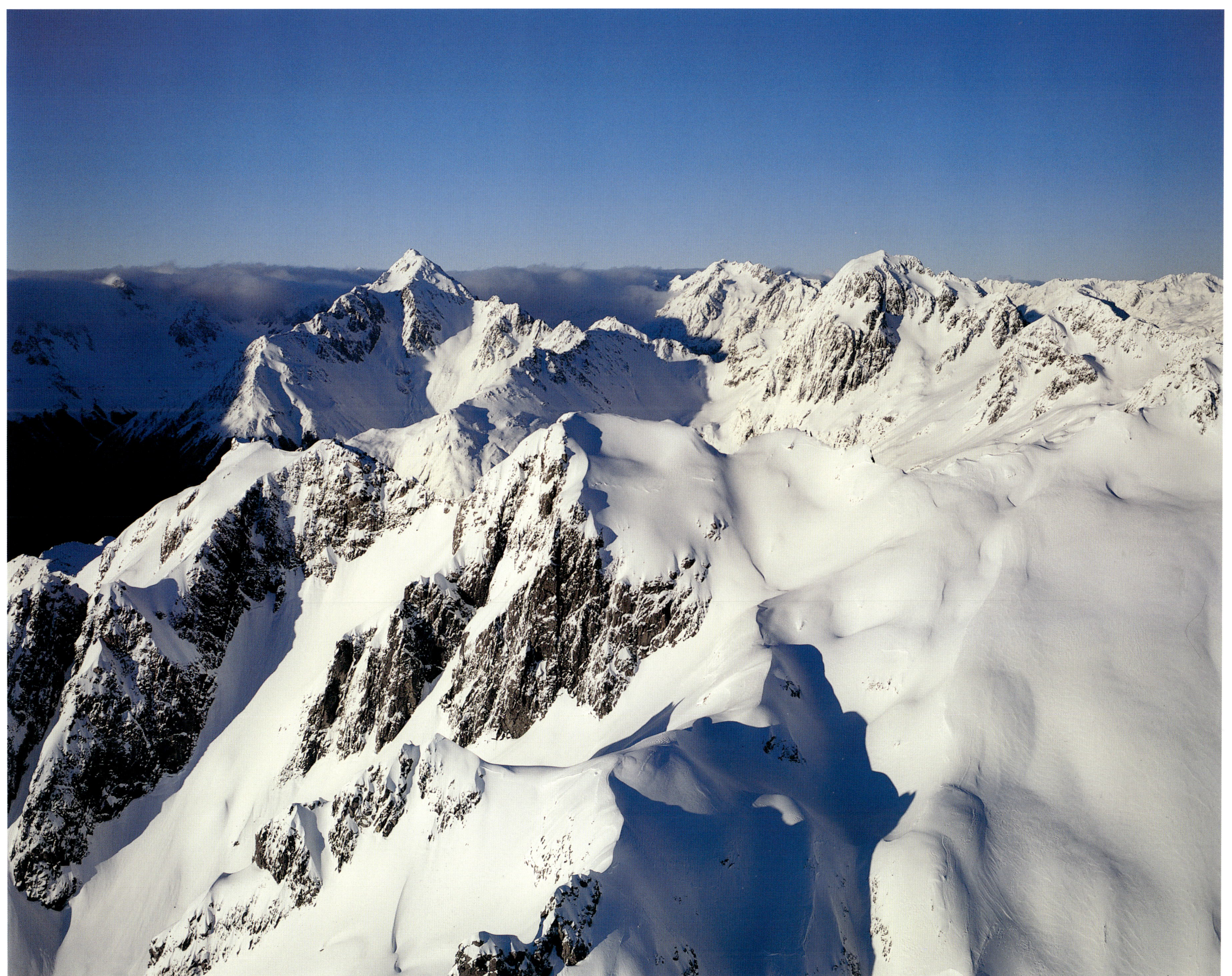

Mt Travers, Mt Franklin and Mt Cupola

Photograph Captions

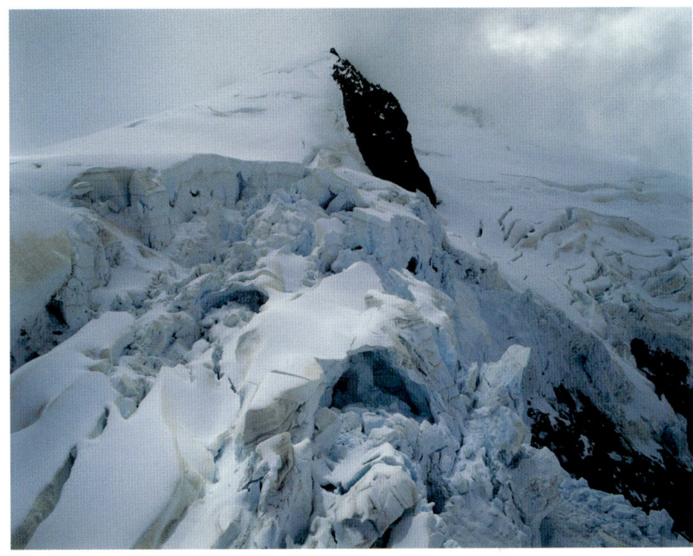

PAGE 14 ICEFALL, MT TUTOKO, DARRAN MOUNTAINS
As well as being the highest peak in Fiordland, Mt Tutoko also carries the area's largest glaciers. The Donne Glacier forms a large sheet on the northern and western sides of the mountain, while the Age (above) falls precipitously down Tutoko's south face. These are mere remnants of the vast ice flows that carved the area's spectacular landscape during the ice ages. Glaciers of the Darran Mountains and nearby Wick Mountains and Lawrenny Peaks are the most southerly in the Southern Alps, mostly small shelf glaciers perched below summits high above valley floors.

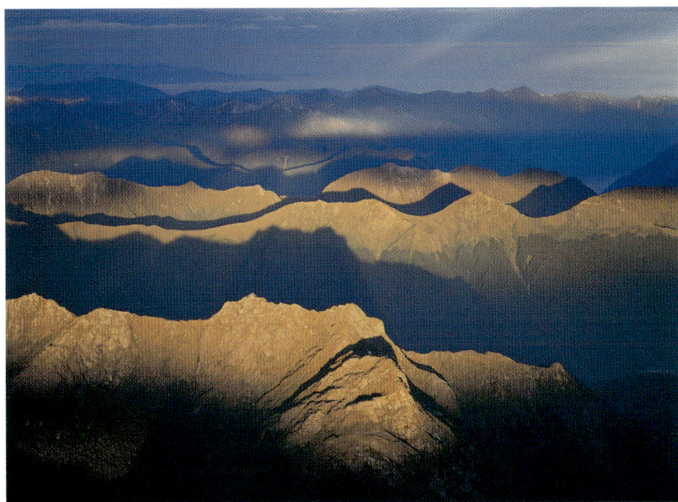

PAGE 16 HEATH MOUNTAINS, FIORDLAND NATIONAL PARK
Southern Fiordland's craggy and rolling glaciated ridgelines and valleys as seen from the Heath Mountains, looking toward the southern coast of the South Island. The head of Lake Hauroko, the deepest of the great southern lakes (462 m), is visible at middle right.

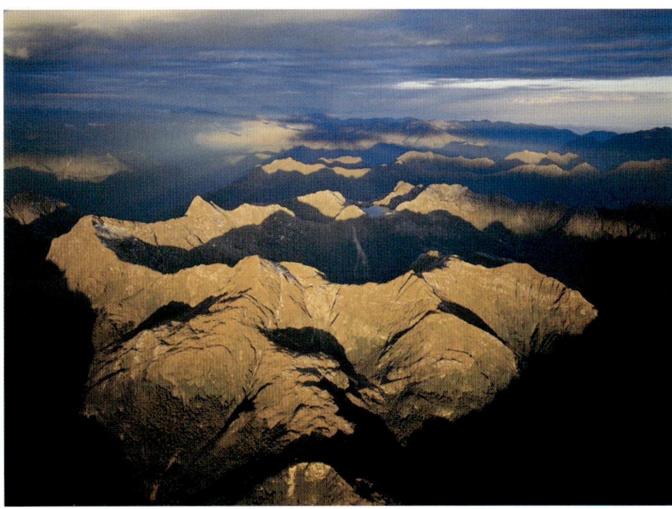

PAGE 17 HEATH MOUNTAINS, FIORDLAND NATIONAL PARK
Last light strikes the Heath Mountains (foreground) and ridgelines beyond in this view south-east across southern Fiordland National Park. Glacial cirques, lakes and hanging valleys are typical geological features of the area's hard rock mountains. The Heath Mountains can be accessed at their northern end from the Dusky Track.

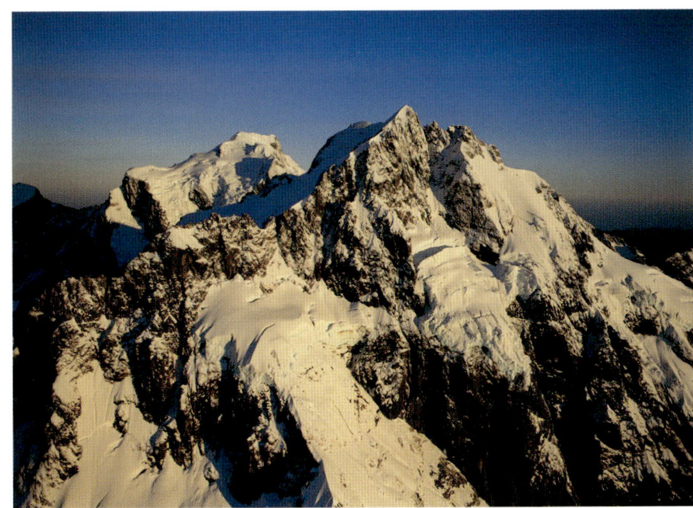

PAGE 18 MTS TUTOKO AND MADELINE, DARRAN MOUNTAINS
The glaciated peaks of Mt Tutoko (left) and Mt Madeline are Fiordland's highest and most spectacular mountains, viewed here from the south-east above the Hollyford Valley. Remote and without straightforward approaches, both peaks remained unclimbed until the 1920s. Madeline (2356 m) was first climbed from the Tutoko Valley approach by the redoubtable Samuel Turner and Alf Cowling in 1920. Turner then claimed the much-prized first ascent of Tutoko (2746 m) in 1924 with guide Peter Graham, climbing from the Donne Glacier on the peak's western side (see page 23).

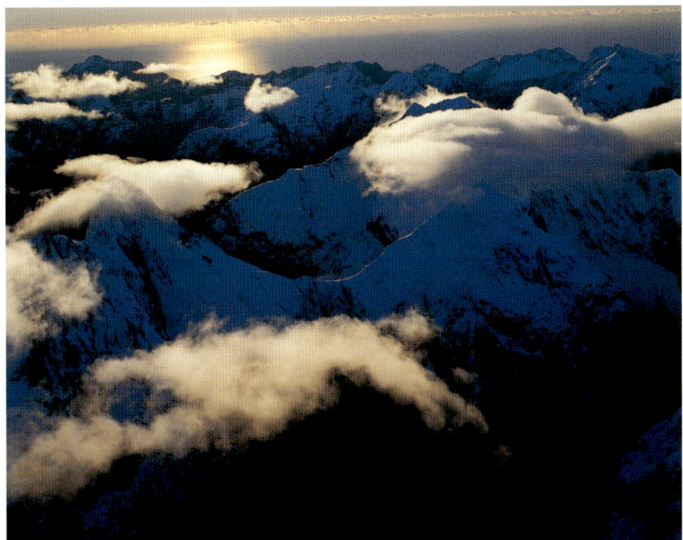

PAGE 19 MOUNTAIN RANGES SOUTH OF MILFORD SOUND
Mountain ridges and peaks south of Milford Sound slip into shadow while wispy clouds catch the last of the sun in this winter evening view looking west toward the Tasman Sea. Much of the 1.3 million hectares of Fiordland National Park consists of inaccessible mountains and valleys like these, making the park one of the most extensive areas of true wilderness left in the world's temperate regions.

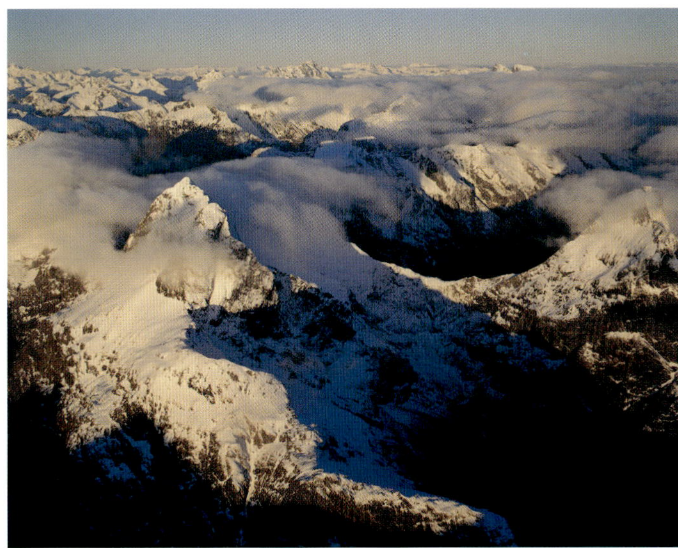

PAGE 20 DARRAN MOUNTAINS
A dramatic winter landscape of peaks and valleys: looking north-east across Fiordland's Darran Mountains from just south of Milford Sound. The hallmarks of the last ice age—sharply defined arête peaks and ridges, hanging valleys, steep faces and cirque walls, deeply incised U-shaped valleys and fiords—are clearly visible in Fiordland. Unlike the schist and greywacke ranges to the north, Fiordland's hard crystalline rocks are far more resistant to erosion, thus preserving the landscape today much as it was left by retreating ice-age glaciers.

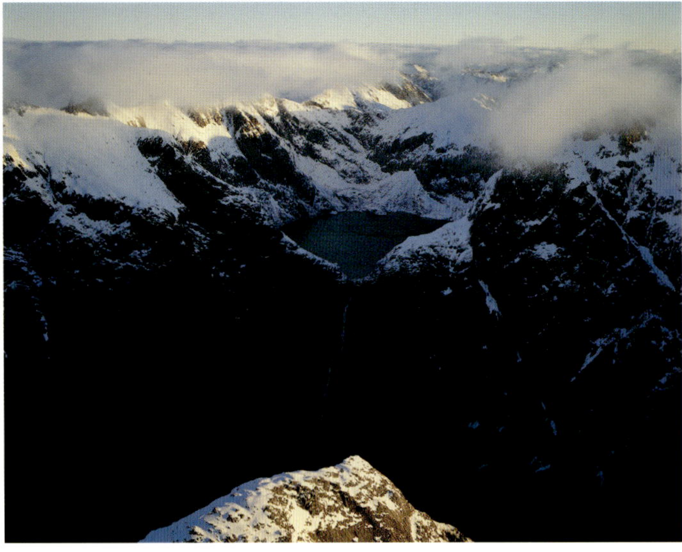

PAGE 21 LAKE QUILL AND SUTHERLAND FALLS
Sutherland Falls begins its 580-metre cascade to the Arthur River from
the hanging valley containing Lake Quill. Named in 1880 by Donald
Sutherland, who was the first European to see them, the falls are the
highest in New Zealand and the fifth highest in the world. Sutherland
was a Milford Sound resident who explored much of the area in the hope
of discovering a route to Queenstown—a quest that was the source of
much rivalry between explorers at the time.

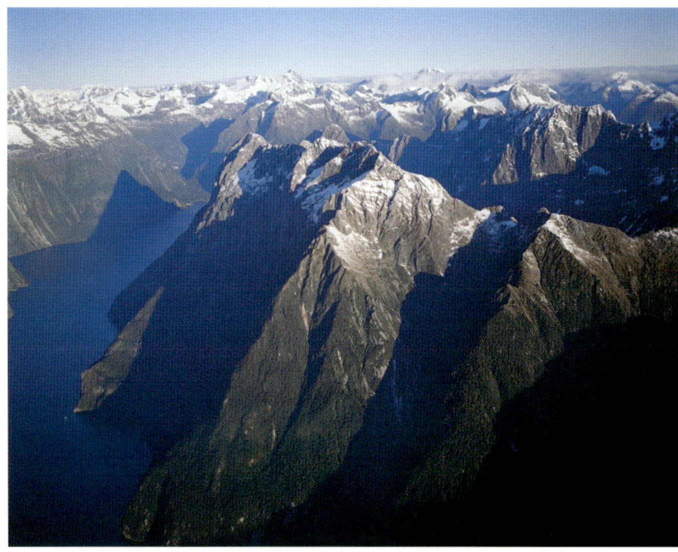

PAGE 22 MITRE PEAK, MILFORD SOUND
The sheer walls of Milford Sound's stunning ice-carved landscape are
dominated by the Mitre Peak massif, photographed here from above the
entrance to Milford Sound. Beyond lie the Darran Mountains, while the
range leading to the Lawrenny Peaks is at right. Mitre Peak (1692 m)
forms a classic silhouette against the sound on the left. Between Mitre
Peak and the Lawrenny Peaks is Sinbad Gully, one of the last places on
mainland New Zealand where kakapo (a gravely endangered flightless
parrot) were found and transferred to island sanctuaries.

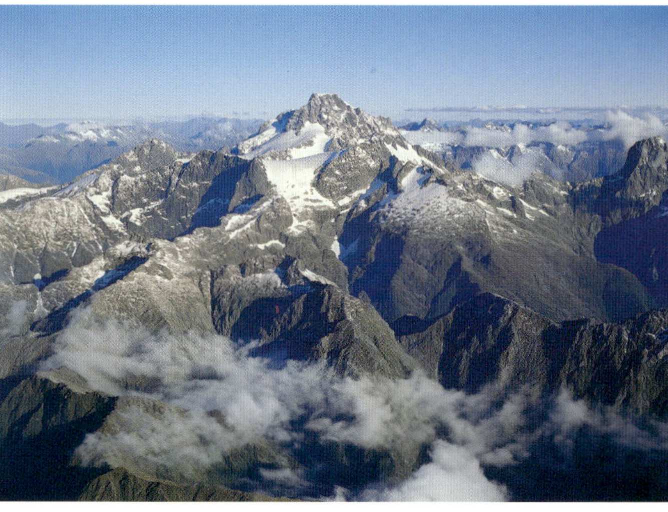

PAGE 23 MT TUTOKO FROM THE WEST
Once believed to be a volcano, Mt Tutoko (2746 m) is the pinnacle
of the Darran Mountains and the highest peak in Fiordland. The first
ascent, by Samuel Turner and Peter Graham, was eventually made via
the north-west ridge, which in this image falls left of the summit to the
Donne Glacier. Tutoko is named after a Maori chief once resident at
Martins Bay at the mouth of the Hollyford River.

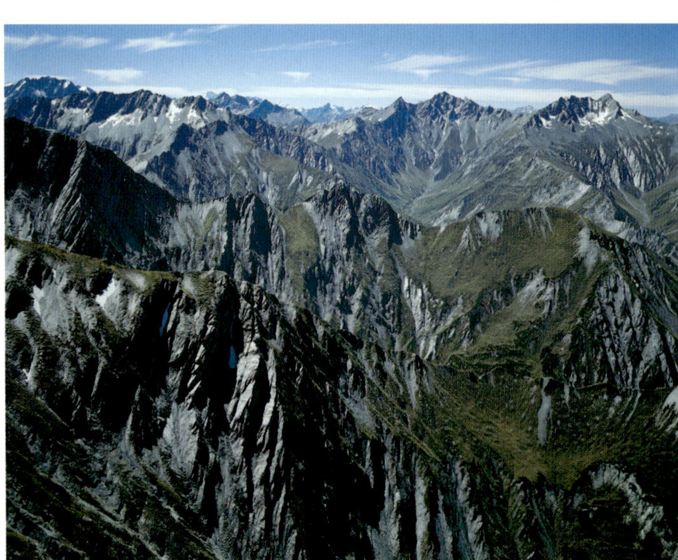

PAGE 25 HARRIS MOUNTAINS
Lying west of Wanaka, the Harris Mountains are a heavily weathered
and bluffed high-country range. The regular slabby faces reflect a
consistency in both the underlying geology and vigorous erosion that is
typical of much of the western Otago schist mountains. The presence
of minerals such as mica often creates a reflective sheen across larger
slabs, as is visible in this photo.

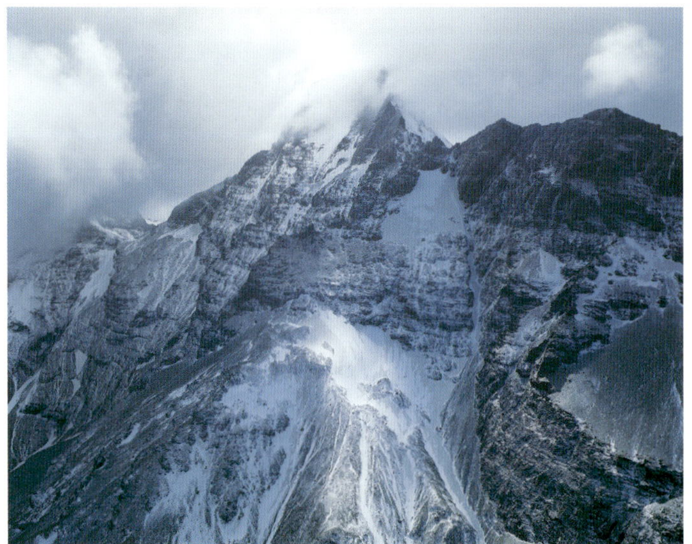

PAGE 26 WEST PEAK, PIKIRAKATAHI/MT EARNSLAW
Pikirakatahi/Mt Earnslaw's West Peak (10 metres lower than the 2030 m
East Peak) swathed in cloud under a dusting of snow, photographed
from the west. Called Pikirakatahi by Ngai Tahu, Mt Earnslaw is the
highest peak in southern Mount Aspiring National Park's Forbes Range.
In stark contrast to its South Face (see page 31), this northern aspect of
Earnslaw has little permanent snow.

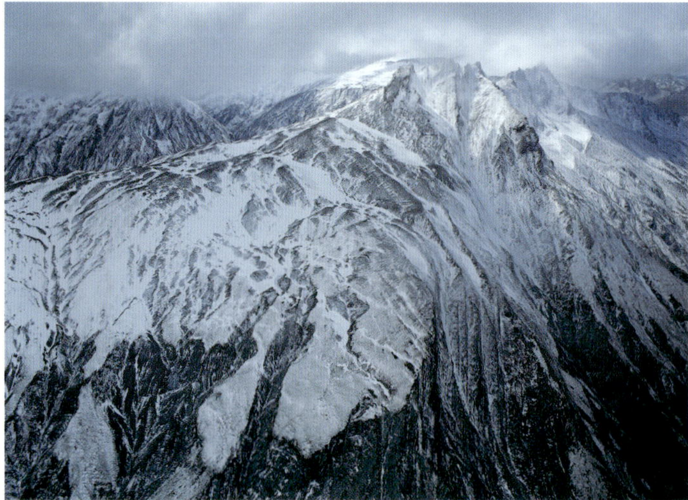

PAGE 27 RICHARDSON MOUNTAINS—RIDGE ABOVE LOCHNAGAR
A broad ridge rises to almost 2200 metres above Lochnagar (out of shot
to the right) and Snowy Creek (in the headwaters of the Dart Valley,
upper left) in the Richardson Mountains. Photographed here during
an early winter snowfall, the ridge forms the boundary between Mount
Aspiring National Park and the Upper Shotover Conservation Area,
which adjoins Mount Aspiring National Park between Lake Wanaka and
Lake Wakatipu.

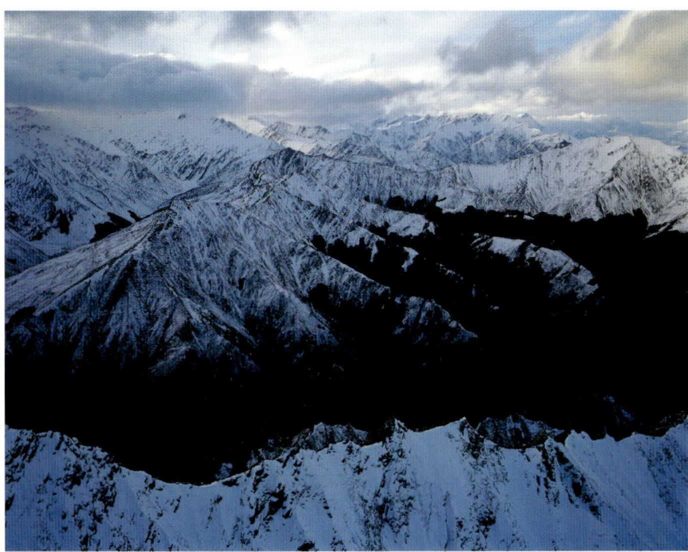

PAGE 29 RICHARDSON MOUNTAINS

The Richardson Mountains occupy high country north-east of Lake Wakatipu. Viewed here under winter snow, the photograph is taken from above Stony Creek looking north. With 2500-metre peaks featuring New Zealand's distinctive subalpine and alpine vegetation, the Richardson Mountains are part of the huge belt of Haast Schists which extends from Mount Aspiring National Park to the coastal hills near Dunedin.

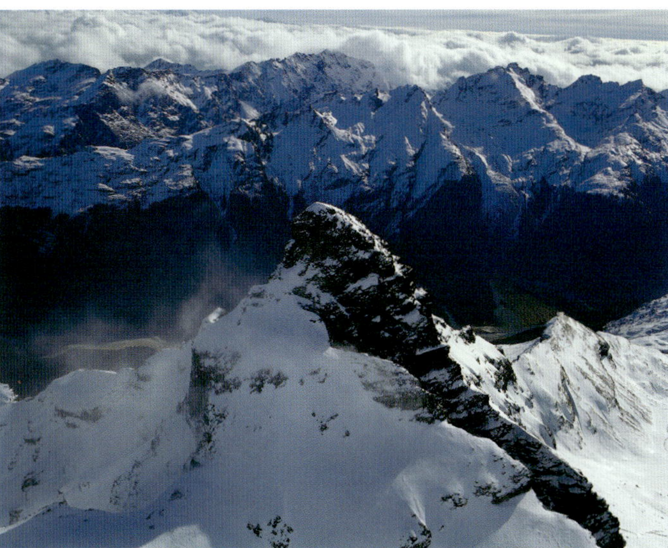

PAGE 30 PLUTO PEAK

Pluto Peak (2480 m) is a spectacular spire immediately north-west of Pikirakatahi/Mt Earnslaw in the Forbes Range, southern Mount Aspiring National Park. It was on top of this peak that 'Gandalf the White' stood in the film of *Lord of the Rings*. An easy route to the summit follows ledges on the far side of the peak to the right-hand ridge below the top. Beyond lies the Dart Valley, the Cosmos Peaks and the Humboldt Mountains.

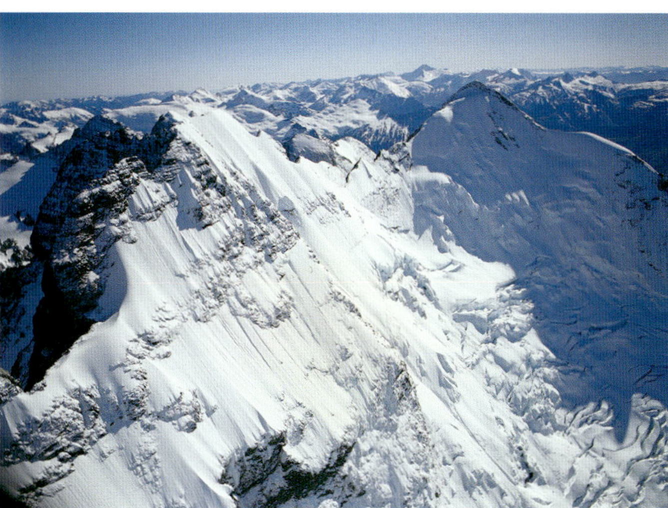

PAGE 31 SOUTH FACE OF PIKIRAKATAHI/MT EARNSLAW

The Earnslaw Glacier is a dramatic sweep of ice filling the southern aspects of Pikirakatahi/Mt Earnslaw's West and East peaks (left and right respectively). The face was first climbed in 1973. Most ascents of Earnslaw are made from the easier northern approach via the Birley Glacier and Wright Col. Of the two peaks, the higher East Peak, first climbed in March 1890, receives the most attention. The more imposing West Peak was not climbed until February 1914 via a gully on its North Face. The traverse between the peaks is a challenging classic route (Grade 3−).

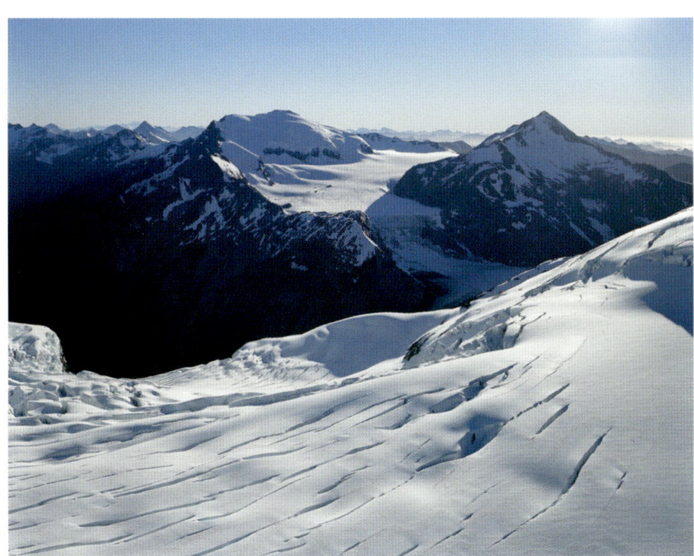

PAGE 32 THERMA AND UPPER VOLTA GLACIERS

Beyond the Therma Glacier north-west of Tititea/Mt Aspiring lie the remote Glacier Dome (left) and Fastness Peak above the Upper Volta Glacier. Both glaciers flow into the head of the Waiototo Valley. Access to the Upper Volta is from the East Matukituki Valley. While there are several straightforward routes up Fastness from the Volta, its East Face (not in shot) has yielded one of the park's most demanding winter routes (Storming the Barbican, Grade 6+), and a long rock route with a Grade 17 crux.

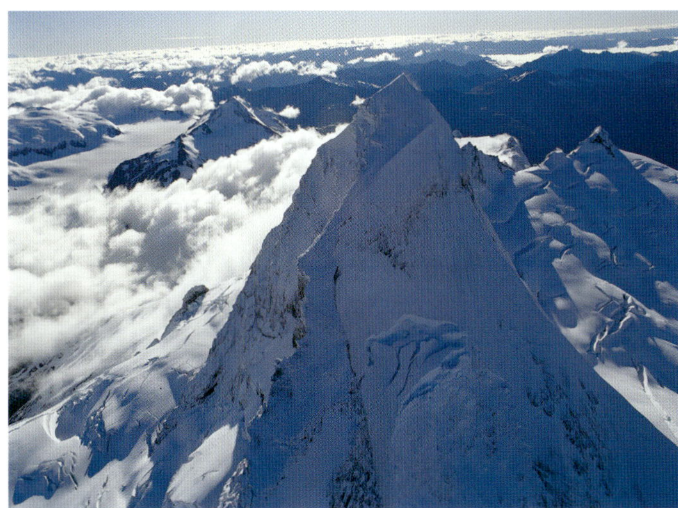

PAGE 33 TITITEA/MT ASPIRING FROM THE WEST

The summit of Tititea/Mt Aspiring (3033 m) from above the North West Ridge, in late spring/early summer conditions. Aspiring's elegant South West Ridge runs up from the right to the route's crux at the base of the gully below the summit. At right is Popes Nose at the end of the Coxcomb Ridge. Fastness Peak (2383 m) lies left of Aspiring's summit above the Upper Volta glacier. Tititea/Mt Aspiring, the only 3000 metre peak in New Zealand outside the Mount Cook region, was first climbed in 1909 by Alec Graham, Jack Clarke and Bernard Head.

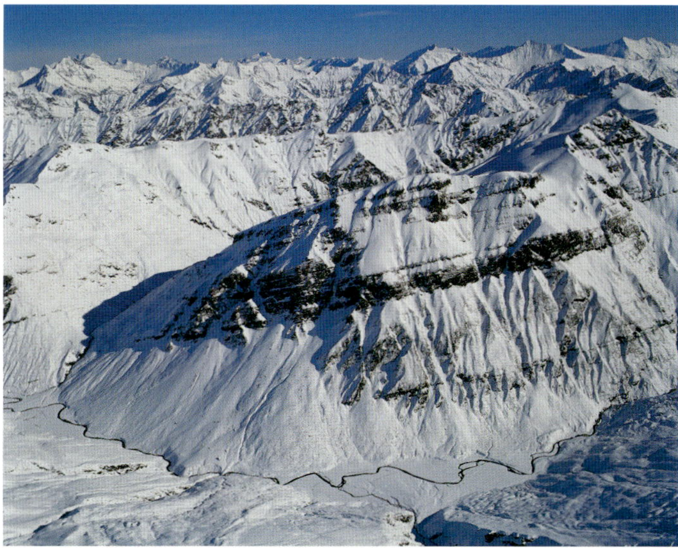

PAGE 34 HARRIS MOUNTAINS

Bands of schist are revealed beneath snow in the Harris Mountains west of Wanaka. The range, an outlier of the Southern Alps, is renowned for heli-skiing. Formed from sediments subjected to intense heat and pressure before being raised, schist has a high quartz content and tendency to split. At its most weathered schist is loose and friable but this varies from place to place, with the many high quality schist crags and good clean and steep mountain routes belying its crumbly reputation.

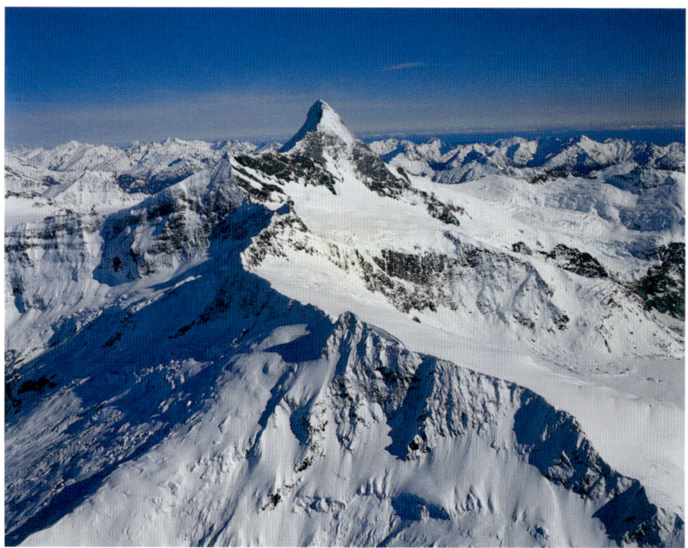

PAGE 35 TITITEA/MT ASPIRING FROM THE EAST
Known to Ngai Tahu as Tititea, the 'upright glistening one', Mt Aspiring (3033 m) commands the landscape in this view from the east. The main dividing ridge of the Southern Alps rises from lower right, separating the Volta Glacier (right) and Kitchener Glacier (left), as it climbs to Aeroplane Peak and Popes Nose (2700 m) at the base of Aspiring's Coxcomb Ridge. The broad glacier visible right of Aspiring's summit is the Therma. Below Popes Nose is the East Face which forms the dramatic headwall of Kitchener Cirque and which has yielded three sustained winter and summer routes graded 5 and 6.

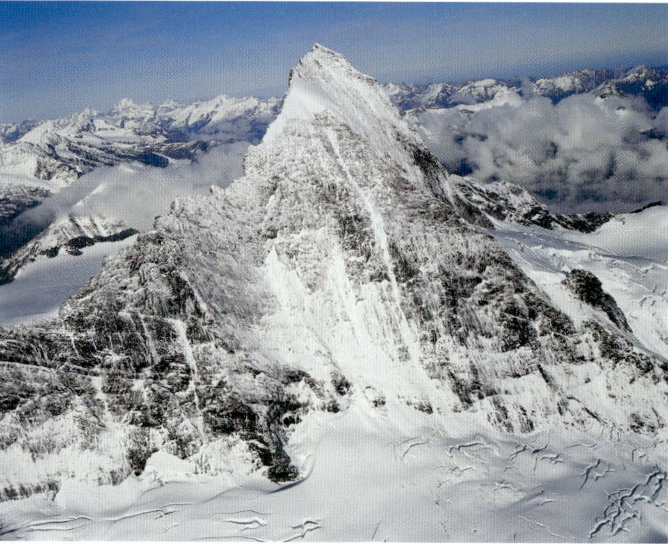

PAGE 36 TITITEA/MT ASPIRING—THE COXCOMB RIDGE AND NORTH EAST FACE
The North East Face of Tititea/Mt Aspiring above the Volta Glacier was climbed in 1978 following a route that began left of the main ice streak in the middle of the face before eventually traversing into the streak and following it to the ridge. It is a hard (Grade 6) and committing climb which is best done when iced up, due to the poor rock. Rising from left to right is the Coxcomb Ridge, an impressive and challenging route crowded with towers, rock steps and ice arêtes that was first climbed in January 1953 and which is still regarded as a classic test piece.

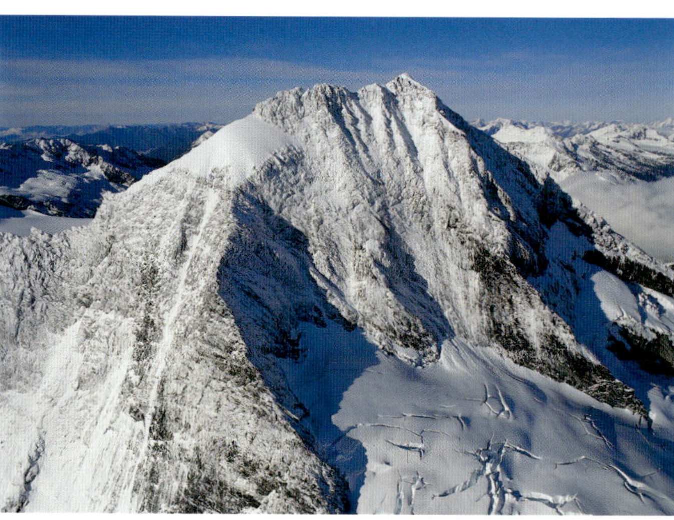

PAGE 37 NORTH FACE, TITITEA/MT ASPIRING
Tititea/Mt Aspiring's North Face above the Therma Glacier, with the top of the North East Face at left (see page 36). The principal climbing routes follow the North East Ridge (Grade 3, rising between the North East and North faces), North Face (Grade 3+, the prominent rib in the centre of the face) and the North Buttress (Grade 3) on the right. Beyond the buttress is the North West Ridge, the mountain's popular standard route. Despite relatively easy access from Colin Todd Hut, north face routes are not often climbed, with some perhaps being put off by routes that involve the top sections of the Coxcomb Ridge.

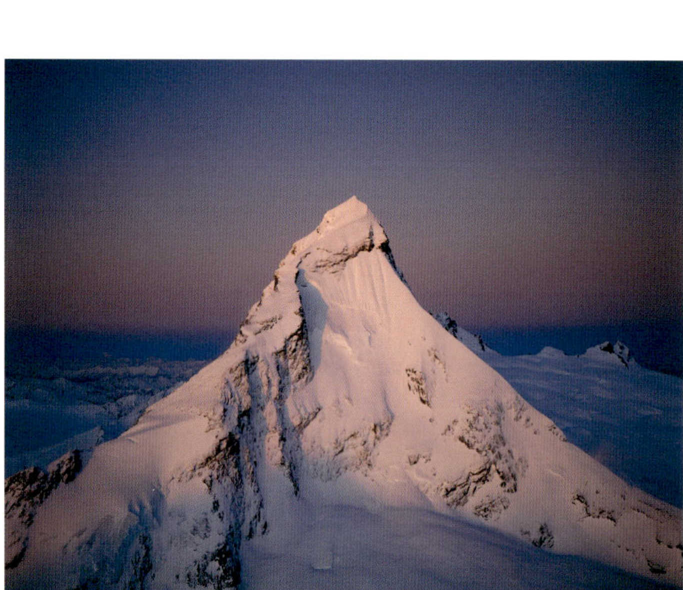

PAGE 38 TITITEA/MT ASPIRING FROM THE WEST
Piercing the evening sky above the Bonar Glacier, Tititea/Mt Aspiring is a beacon to mountaineers. Many have been attracted by the 'appealing purity' of the South West Ridge (Grade 3–, rising from the right), a mountaineering classic first climbed in 1936. But the mountain's most climbed route is the easier North West Ridge (Grade 2+, left) 'a broad highway sweeping to the summit', often sought out by those hoping to bag their first 3000-metre peak. Between the ridges lies the West Face, route of the mountain's first ascent in 1909—a remarkable climb that went unrepeated for 56 years.

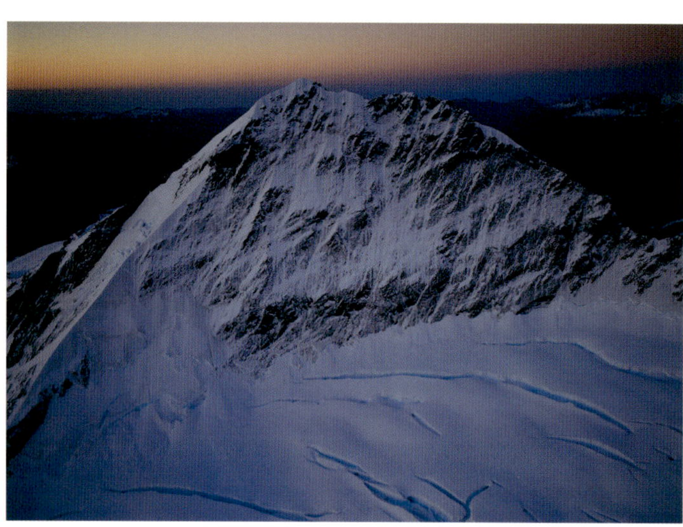

PAGE 39 TITITEA/MT ASPIRING—THE SOUTH FACE
As the peak holds the last daylight, yawning crevasses gather deep shadows in the upper reaches of the Bonar Glacier. Framed by the South West Ridge (left) and the Coxcomb Ridge, Aspiring's South Face sports more than a dozen ice or mixed routes and variations ranging from 250–530 metres in height. First climbed in 1971 in a storm, routes on the face range from Grade 4 to 5+.

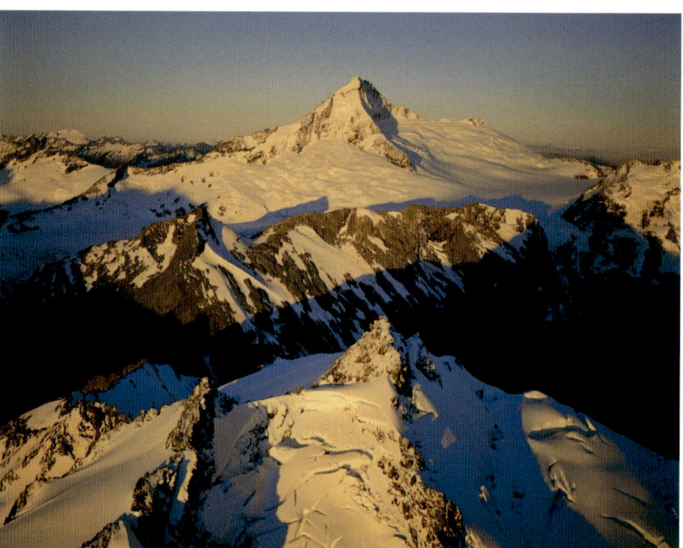

PAGE 40 TITITEA/MT ASPIRING FROM ABOVE THE WAIPARA RANGE
Tititea/Mt Aspiring and the Bonar Glacier from the south-west above the Waipara Range. The glacier breaching the Bonar's impounding ridge at right (with Mt French to the right) is called the Breakaway. On the ridge well to the left of the Breakaway is Bevan Col, the partly shaded snowy pass beneath Mt Bevan. The route from the shadowy Matukituki Valley (right) to the col is the most common way to reach Colin Todd Hut, the starting point for ascents of Aspiring's popular North West Ridge to the left of the summit.

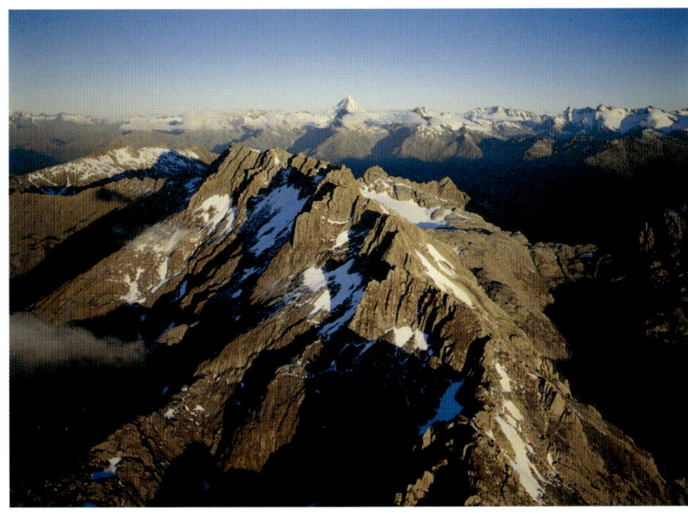

PAGE 41 THE OLIVINE RANGE WITH TITITEA/MT ASPIRING AND THE MAIN DIVIDE PEAKS BEYOND
Tititea/Mt Aspiring and Main Divide peaks from above the Olivine Range, late spring. The Main Divide peaks right of Aspiring are part of the Snowdrift Range, with the Snowball Glaciers visible at right. The Olivine Range lies in some of the remotest parts of South Westland between the Cascade and Arawhata Rivers.

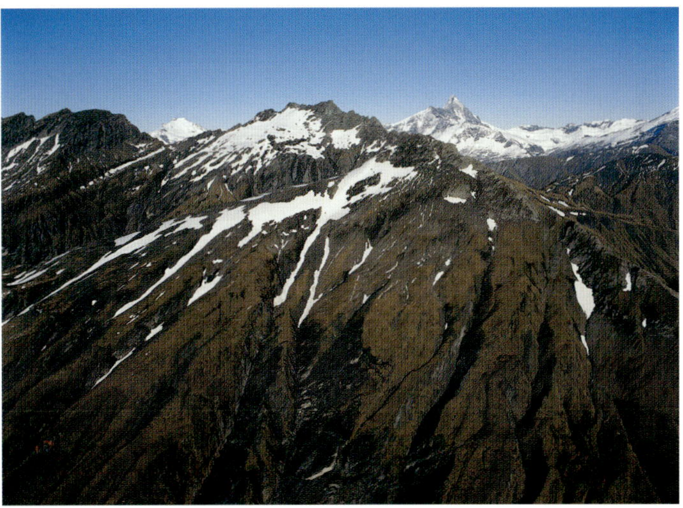

PAGE 42 HEAD OF THE ALBERT BURN
Mt Avalanche (2606 m, left), the North Face of Tititea/Mt Aspiring and the Volta and Therma glaciers form a distant backdrop to overlapping tussock-covered slabs of schist at the head of the Albert Burn on the eastern boundary of Mount Aspiring National Park.

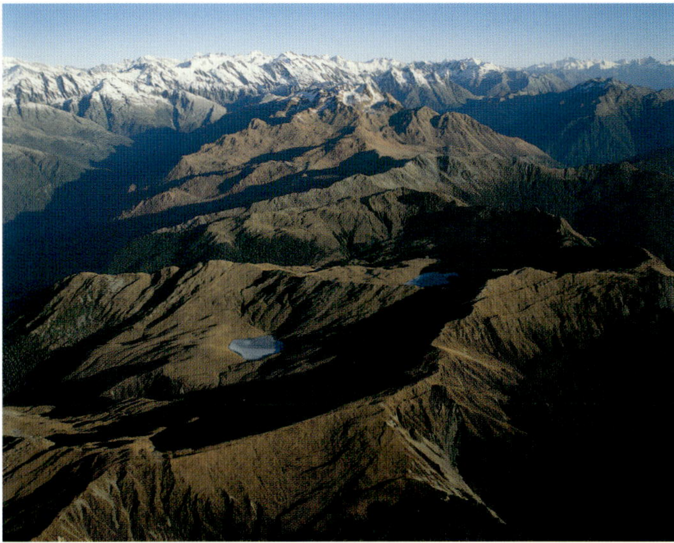

PAGE 43 RED HILLS RANGE, OLIVINE WILDERNESS AREA
The Red Hills Range, in the western region of Mount Aspiring National Park, is notable for its striking reddish ultramafic rocks. High levels of magnesium and other toxic materials in these rocks mean only the hardiest of plants survive, giving rise to a distinctive sparse vegetation. The range is at the northern end of a 150-kilometre belt of ultramafic rocks that extends to Lake Ronald south of Milford Sound. Similar rocks reappear some 450 kilometres north of here in Nelson—evidence of massive lateral displacement along the South Island's Alpine Fault.

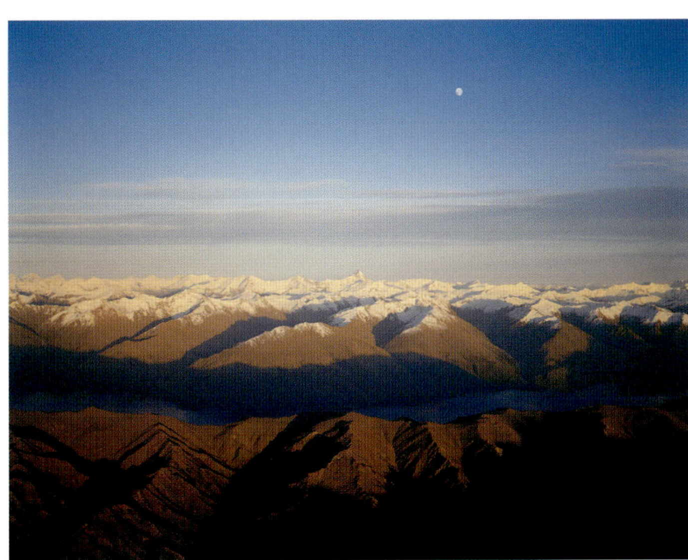

PAGE 45 LAKE WANAKA AND TITITEA/MT ASPIRING
A winter sunrise casts long shadows into the valleys of north-west Otago in this view of the distant snowy ranges of Mount Aspiring National Park, seen across the deep glacial trough now occupied by Lake Wanaka. Lake Wanaka and the Makarora Valley at its head (right) lead to the Haast Pass, the southernmost—and, at 562 metres, the lowest—of only three road routes that cross the Southern Alps.

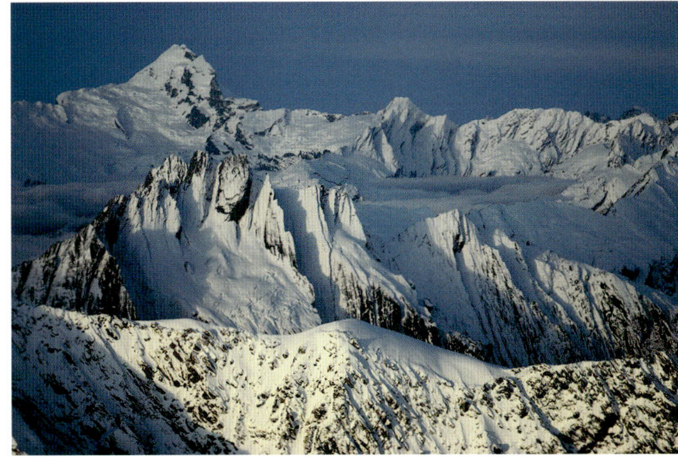

PAGE 46 MT SEFTON, WESTLAND/TAI POUTINI NATIONAL PARK
The last light of winter sun steals briefly under heavy cloud cover, highlighting the contrasting ridges south-west of Mt Sefton (3151 m, top left) and the Douglas névé in the southern region of Westland/Tai Poutini National Park.

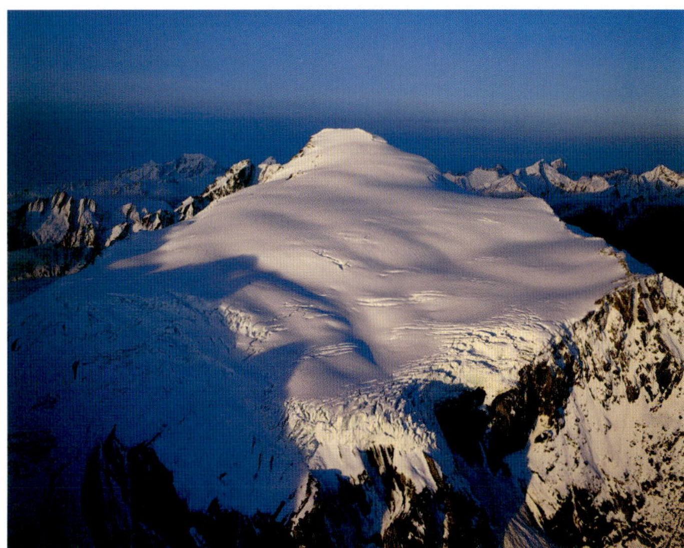

PAGE 48 MT DECHEN, HOOKER RANGE
Mt Dechen (2643 m) is a remote and beautiful glacier-capped peak near the southern end of the Hooker Range in the Hooker/Landsborough Wilderness Area, which adjoins Westland/Tai Poutini National Park to the south. This winter view of the peak, located just north of Mt Hooker, is from the south-west above the upper Otoko Valley looking onto the McCardell Glacier. Aoraki/Mt Cook and Mt Tasman loom in the distance left of the summit.

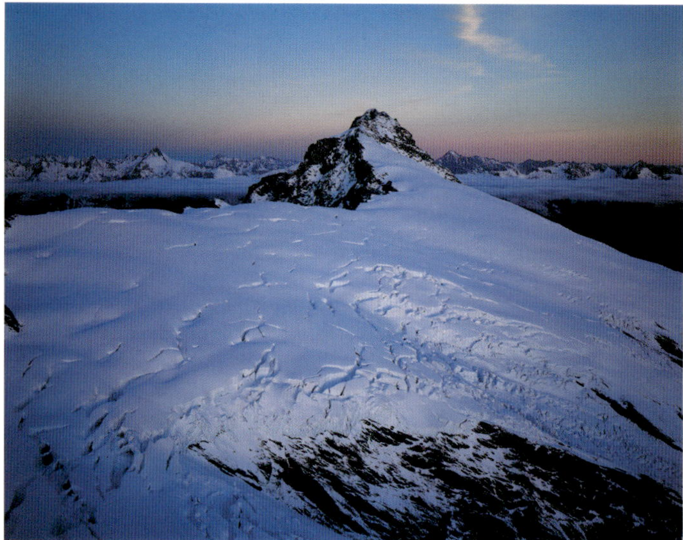

PAGE 49 MT HOOKER AND HOOKER GLACIER
This fine peak (2652 m) lies in remote country at the southern end of
the Hooker Range in the Hooker/Landsborough Wilderness Area south
of the Mount Cook region. First climbed in 1928 by Samuel Turner, Mt
Hooker is an adventurer's mountain, requiring two to three days hard
tramping to reach. The most commonly climbed route (Grade 2) crosses
the Hooker Glacier to a ridge below the low peak (pictured) following
more or less the right-hand ridgeline. A traverse is then made behind
the peak to the main summit.

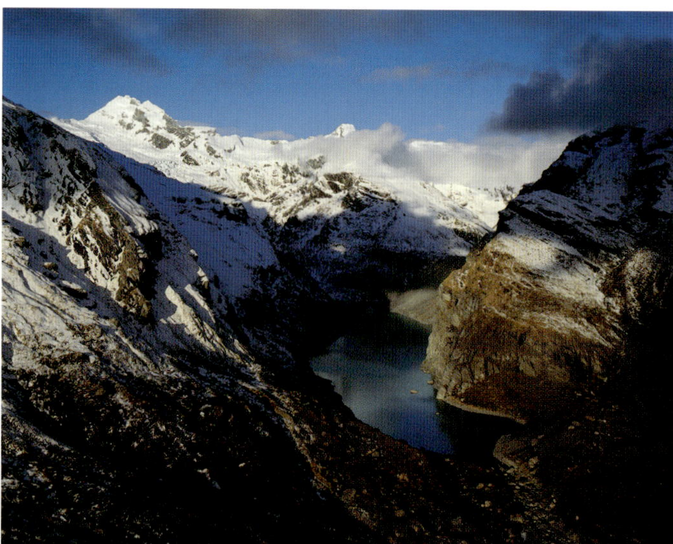

PAGE 50 MT SEFTON AND THE TERMINAL LAKE OF THE DOUGLAS
GLACIER
Mt Sefton (3151 m) above the Douglas névé and the terminal lake of
the Douglas Glacier, in Westland/Tai Poutini National Park. Sefton's
stepped south ridge (Grade 4, first climbed in 1948 from the Mueller
Glacier on the Aoraki/Mt Cook side) rises from the right. The climb of
Sefton from the Copland Valley, Scotts Creek, Tekano Glacier and the
West Ridge (left) is the peak's most accessible route, though one that
still requires good routefinding and fine weather.

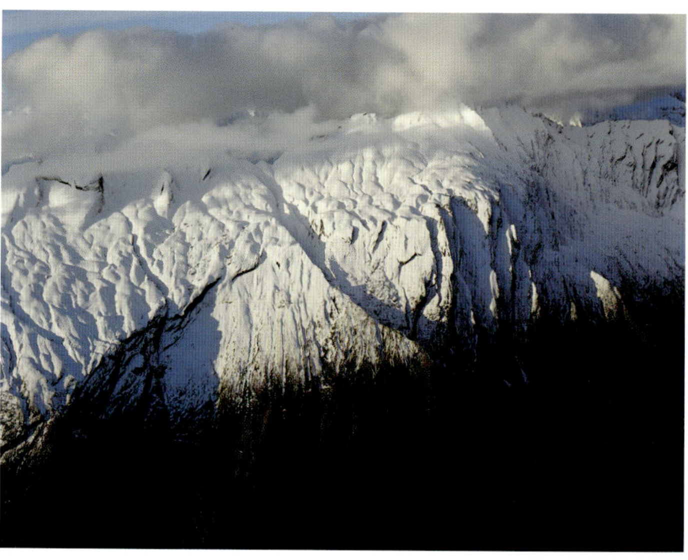

PAGE 51 RIDGE WEST OF THE LANDSBOROUGH VALLEY, SOUTH
WESTLAND
Winter snow clings to gentler slopes close to a ridgeline running west
from the Hooker Range in the Hooker/Landsborough Wilderness area.
The abrupt schist slopes below bear testimony to the immense power
of the ice-age glaciers which issued from all the major valleys of South
Westland to beyond the present coastline.

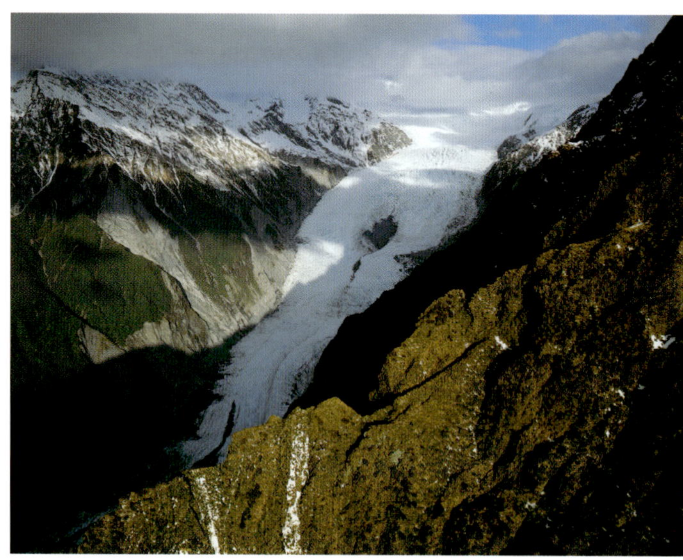

PAGE 52 FRANZ JOSEF GLACIER
Like the neighbouring Fox Glacier, the Franz Josef (Ka Roimata o
Hine Hukatere—the tears of Hine Hukatere) descends rapidly to the
lowlands, terminating in rainforest only 300 metres above sea level.
Periodic advances of both glaciers have been recorded in recent years
as the glaciers respond to heavy winter snows, though as with glaciers
worldwide, the overall trend has been very obvious retreat.

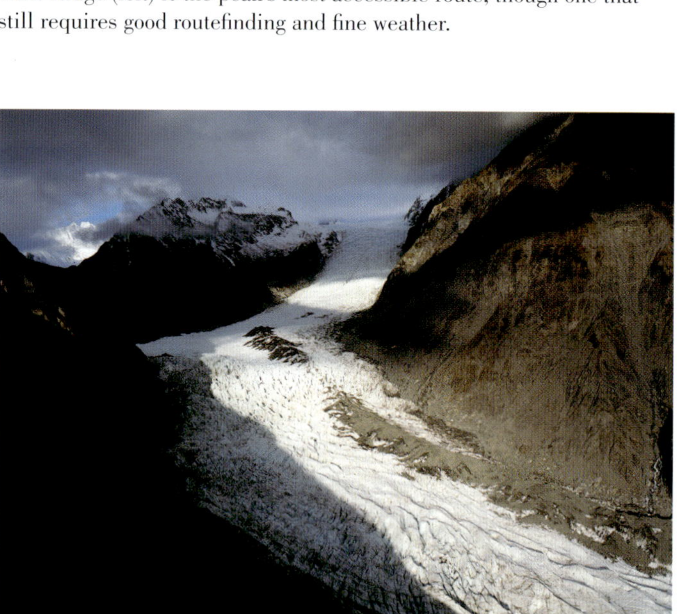

PAGE 53 FOX GLACIER
The heavily crevassed icefall of the Fox Glacier (Te Moeka o Tuawe) is
caused by the glacier's steep descent to the lowlands. Despite the appar-
ent chaos of crevasses and pressure ridges, a relatively straightforward
route up or down the glacier remains feasible, though most climbers and
ski tourers prefer to bypass the icefall by flying to Pioneer Hut on the
Albert Glacier névé (see pages 60 and 79).

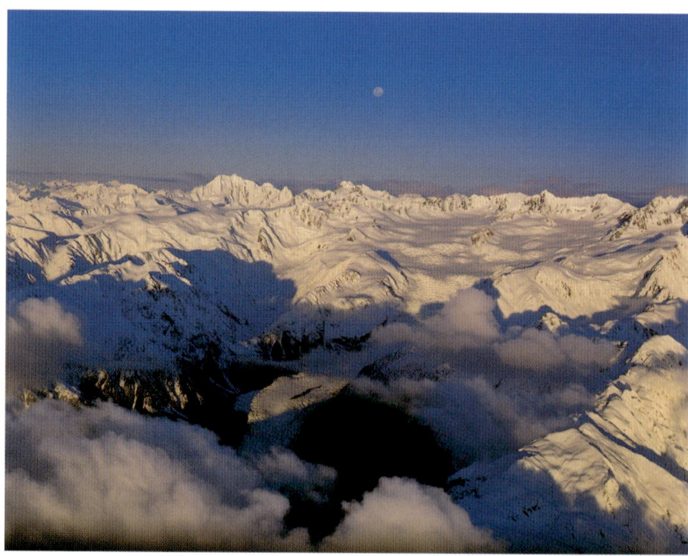

PAGE 54 FOX GLACIER AND NÉVÉ BELOW THE MAIN DIVIDE
Clouds melt away from the Southern Alps in the late afternoon above
Fox Glacier, revealing the glacier's extensive tributary icefields—a ski-
tourer's paradise in winter and spring. At left is the Elie de Beaumont
massif (3109 m) whose snows feed several large western and eastern
glaciers.

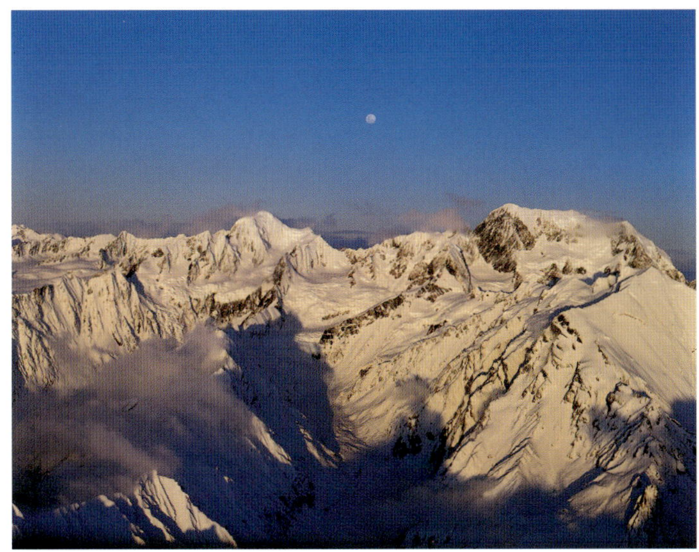
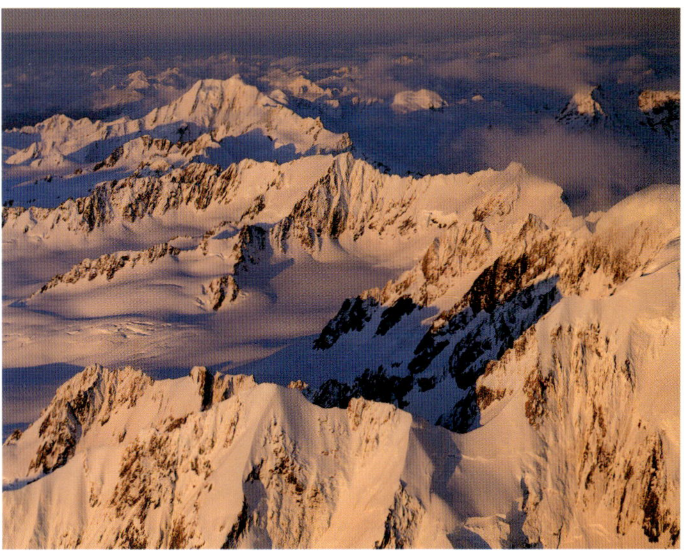
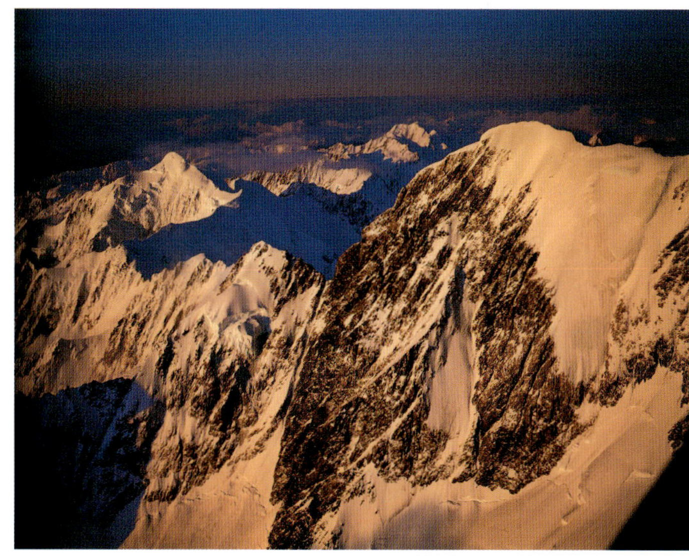

PAGE 55 MT TASMAN AND AORAKI/MT COOK ABOVE THE UPPER
LA PEROUSE VALLEY
The La Perouse Glacier (centre) climbs to the Main Divide between the
western aspects of Mt Tasman (3491 m, centre left) and Aoraki/Mt Cook
(3754 m, right). Rising from lower right is the West Ridge of La Perouse
(3078 m), while left of the glacier in cloud is the Balfour Range.

PAGE 56 UPPER FOX AND FRANZ JOSEF NÉVÉS
Elie de Beaumont (3109 m) stands in the distance in this view north
along the Main Divide from Torres Peak (foreground) in late evening
light. In the middle distance the Fritz Range separates the shadowy
snowfields at the head of the Franz Josef Glacier from the extensive
sunlit névés of the Fox Glacier.

PAGE 57 AORAKI/MT COOK: SHEILA AND HOOKER FACES
Aoraki/Mt Cook's high peak (3754 m) above the Hooker and Sheila
faces. The route of the first ascent by New Zealand amateurs Tom Fyfe,
Jack Clarke and George Graham on Christmas Day in 1894 followed
the prominent gully left of the Sheila Face to Green Saddle, and then up
the North Ridge. This was a remarkable achievement for the time given
the difficulties of this climb (Grade 4) compared with the easier Linda
Glacier approach (see page 83) on the mountain's eastern side, which
had been the focus of all previous attempts.

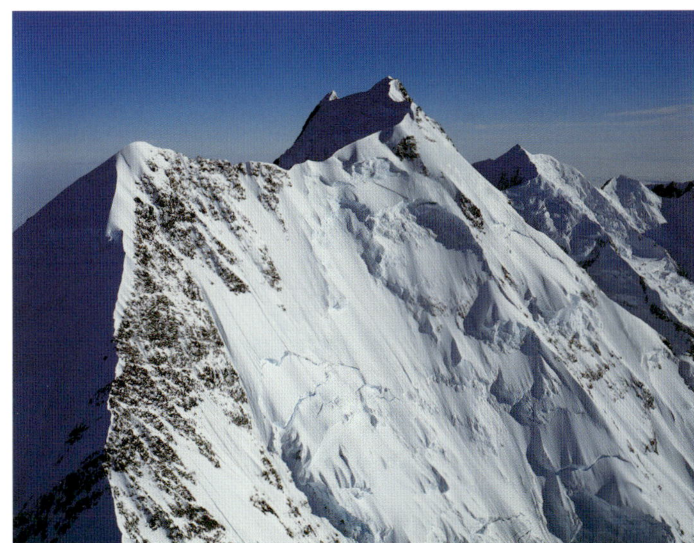
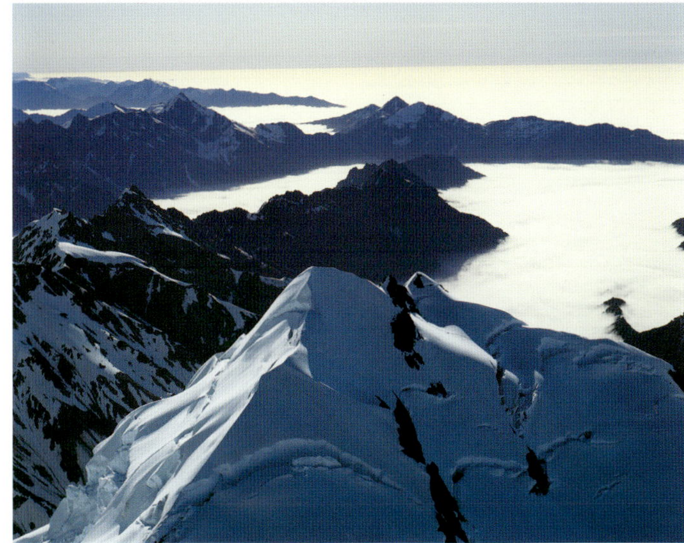
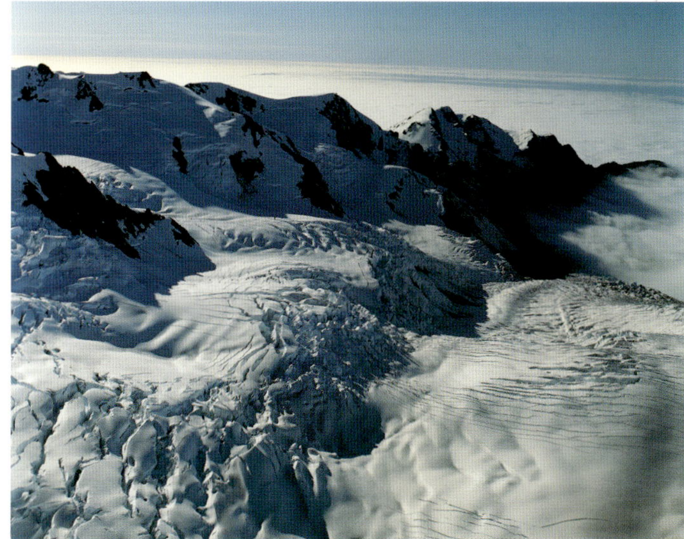

PAGE 58 AORAKI/MT COOK AND MT TASMAN
The Grand Traverse of the 1.6-kilometre summit ridge of Aoraki/
Mt Cook is an exhilarating and demanding Grade 3 climb, particularly
on the exposed and corniced ice ridge between the Middle and High
peaks. The traverse was first completed in 1913 by a party that included
the remarkable Freda du Faur, who in 1910 was the first woman to
ascend Aoraki. Aoraki's South Ridge, a Grade 4– climb, rises to the Low
Peak (foreground) and the top sections of the Caroline Face and East
Ridge lie to the right. North of Aoraki are Mt Tasman and Lendenfeld
Peak.

PAGE 59 TORRES PEAK WEST OF MT TASMAN, WESTLAND/TAI
POUTINI NATIONAL PARK
Torres Peak (3160 m), looking south over West Coast ranges and cloud-
filled valleys. An afternoon build up of cloud rising from the west during
fine weather is a common occurrence that can lead to white-out conditions and navigation difficulties for climbers on West Coast névés. This
cloud often clears away during the evening however, revealing spectacular sunsets over the Tasman Sea.

PAGE 60 ALBERT GLACIER
Patterned by crevasses and flanked by Paschendale Ridge, which tapers
westward to become the Fox Range, Westland/Tai Poutini National
Park's Albert Glacier is the large névé that collects and feeds ice into
the narrow trough containing the Fox Glacier (see page 53). Jumbled
seracs to the right mark the point where the main icefall drops into the
cloud-shrouded valley.

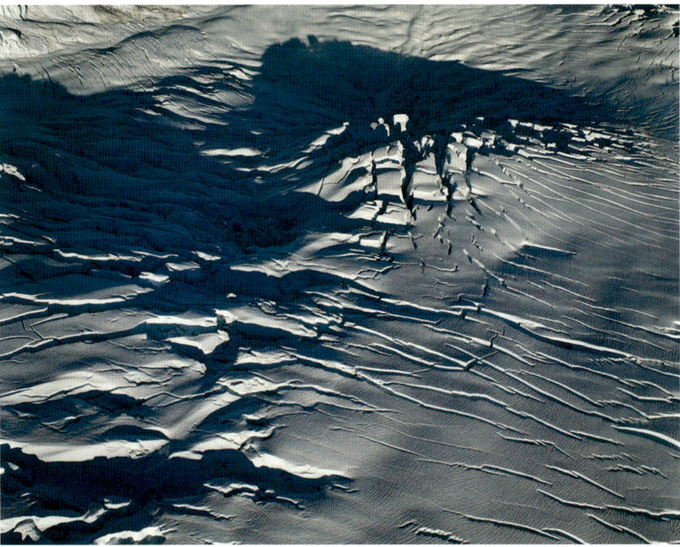

PAGE 61 ALBERT GLACIER DETAIL
As the ice of the Albert Glacier works its way to lower altitudes under
the pull of gravity, variations in the underlying bedrock are reflected in
the surface patterns of crevasses and seracs.

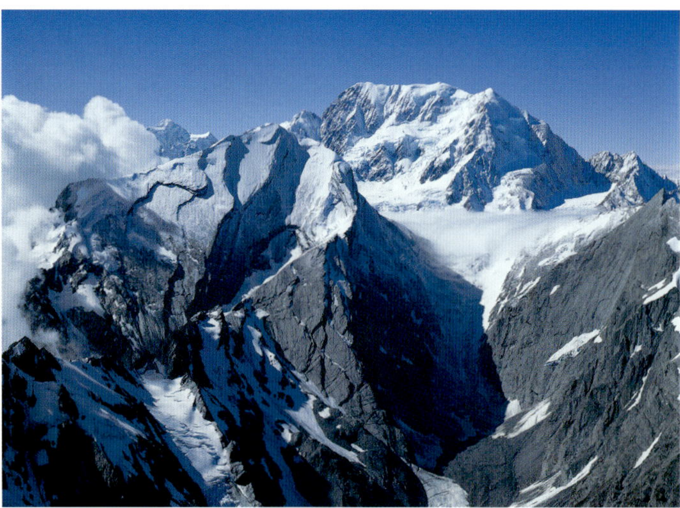

PAGE 62 ROCK SLABS ON THE GULCH FACE OF LA PEROUSE AND
AORAKI/MT COOK
The western and southern faces of La Perouse (foreground, 3078 m) and
Aoraki/Mt Cook from above the Navigator Range. In this photograph the
West Ridge of La Perouse, a Main Divide peak, rises from the left above
the mountain's Gulch Face. East across the Hooker Valley are Aoraki's
Sheila and Hooker faces and the shaded South Face. At extreme right
are the Strauchon faces of Dilemma Peak (2602 m) and the neighbour-
ing Unicorn (2557 m), both of which feature several superb alpine rock
routes.

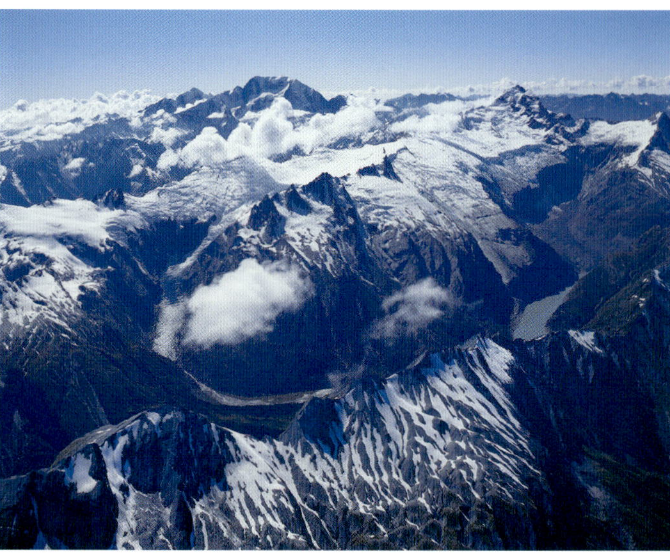

PAGE 63 MT SEFTON WITH AORAKI/MT COOK BEYOND, FROM
ABOVE THE KARANGARUA VALLEY
This photograph looks north-east across the Douglas River and the
Sierra Range to Aoraki/Mt Cook and Mt Tasman on the distant skyline.
The glacier-covered Sierra Range rises to the Douglas névé below
the West and South ridges of Mt Sefton. Directly below Sefton is the
moraine-covered Douglas Glacier and its terminal lake, which are con-
stantly fed by ice thundering over 300-metre bluffs from the névé above.

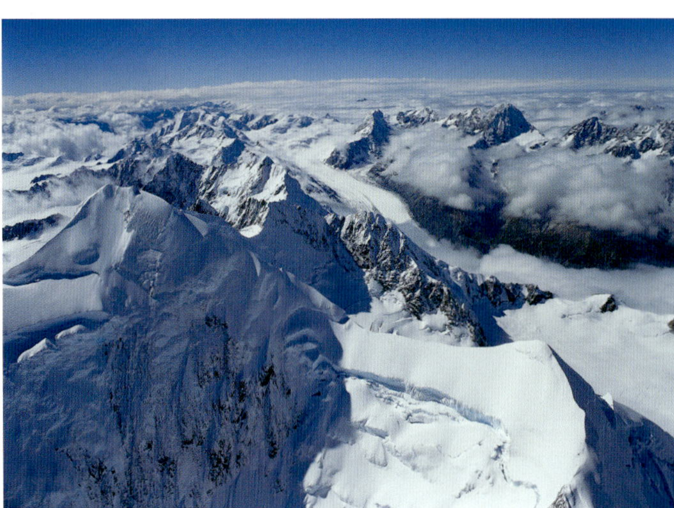

PAGE 64 MT TASMAN, BALFOUR FACE
The shaded Balfour Face of Mt Tasman (3491 m, see also page 85) in
winter conditions, with Silberhorn at lower right. The upper reaches of
the 28-kilometre Tasman Glacier, which cuts through the centre of the
photograph, separates the peaks of the Main Divide (left) from the Malte
Brun Range to the east (right).

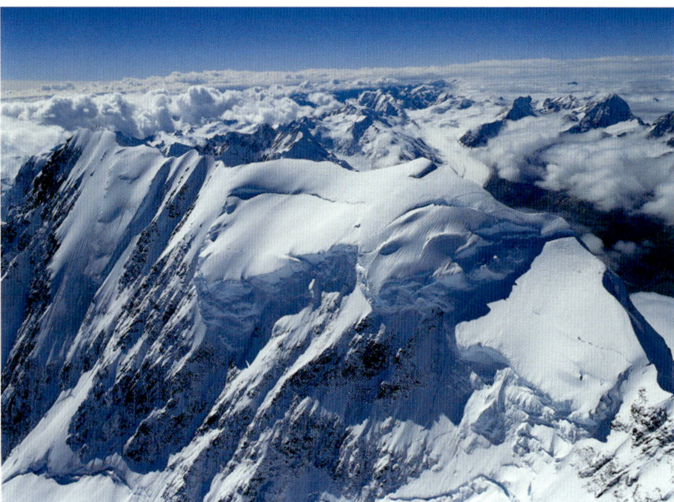

PAGE 65 HOOKER FACE, AORAKI/MT COOK
The Hooker (West) Face of Aoraki/Mt Cook above the Hooker Valley.
Principal routes up the face follow rock ribs from the Empress Ice Shelf
to the summit ridge left of the prominent ice cliff beneath the Middle
Peak, or further left up the ice sheet toward the High Peak (Grade 4+,
far left). The prominent schrund on the Middle Peak (dubbed 'Middle Peak Hotel') has often provided shelter for climbers caught by bad
weather or nightfall, most famously in 1982 when two climbers survived
14 nights in the schrund while a storm raged before they were rescued.

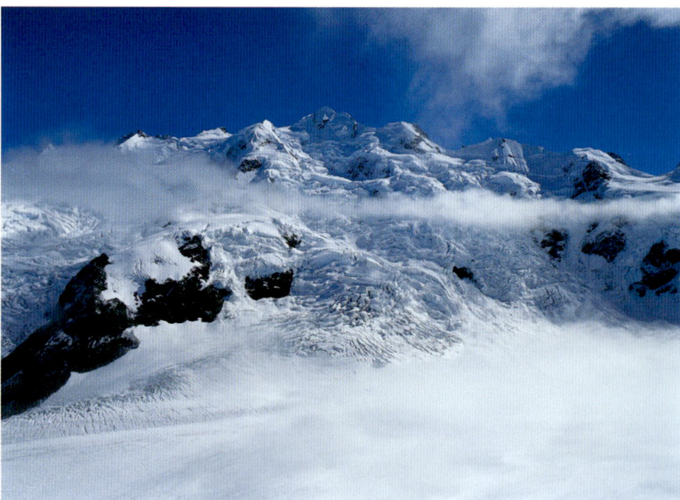

PAGE 66 THE MINARETS FROM THE TASMAN GLACIER
The heavily crevassed Ranfurly Glacier on the eastern flanks of the
Minarets (3040 m), a Main Divide peak viewed from the Tasman Glacier
in Aoraki/Mount Cook National Park. The most popular route to the
Minarets follows De La Beche Ridge which rises from the left to a
plateau beneath the summit.

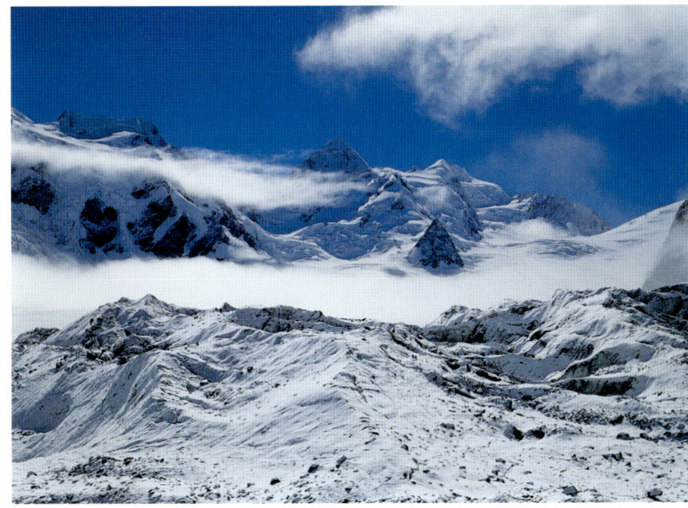

PAGE 67 MT GREEN AND MT WALTER FROM THE TASMAN GLACIER
Mt Green (centre, 2837 m) and Mt Walter (right, 2905 m) from the
moraine-covered ice of the upper Tasman Glacier near the confluence
of the Darwin Glacier. Mt Green was named after the Reverend William
Green who, with Swiss guides Emil Boss and Ulrich Kaufmann, made
the first—and almost successful—attempt on Aoraki/Mt Cook in 1882.

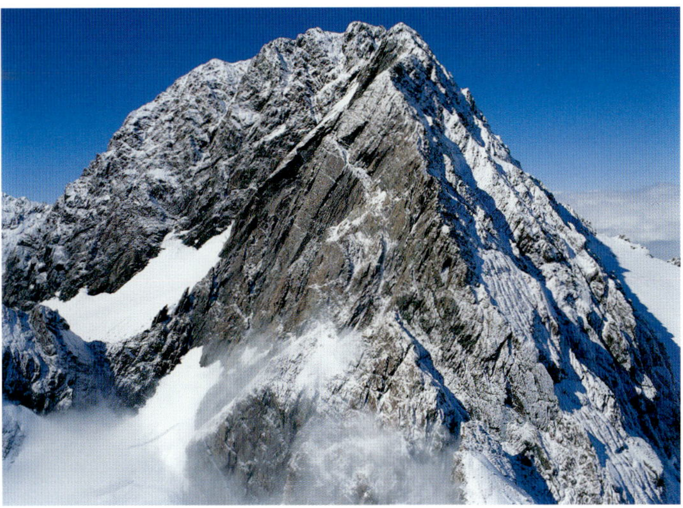

PAGE 68 WEST RIDGE AND NORTH WEST FACE OF MALTE BRUN
Malte Brun (3199 m) is the high point of the Malte Brun Range east
of the Main Divide between the Tasman and Murchison Glaciers. This
image looks directly onto the West Ridge and across to the North West
Face (left). The West Ridge route (Grade 3–) is justifiably popular, with
firm rock and an exposed cheval section high on the climb. At lower left
is the head of the Malte Brun Glacier, while the snow above is the head
of the Bonney Glacier below the North West Face. This face also has
several good quality climbs on firm rock.

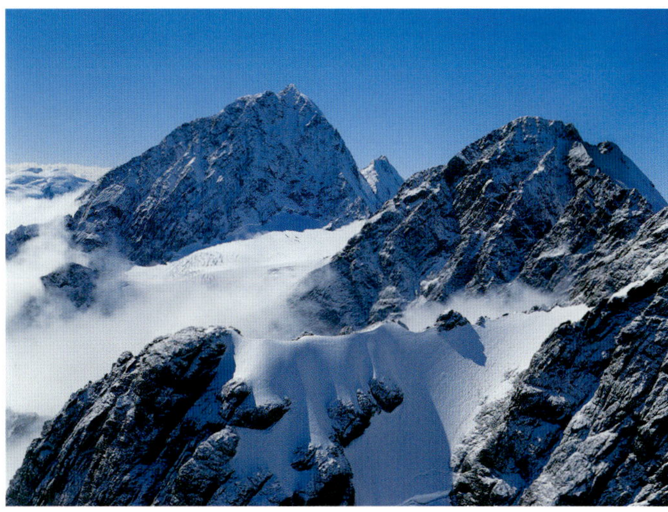

PAGE 69 AIGUILLE ROUGE WITH THE SOUTH FACE OF MALTE
BRUN BEYOND
The South Face of Malte Brun (left) has several ice and mixed routes
up to Grade 4+. The West Ridge is on the left, while the South Ridge
falls on the right to Malte Brun Pass and the Beetham Glacier. Aiguille
Rouge (2193 m), so named for weathered red sandstone and argillite
rock found on the Malte Brun Range, is more commonly climbed from
the Beetham Valley where there are several sunny north- and west-fac-
ing rock routes. The distant peak between Malte Brun and Aiguille
Rouge is Mt Hamilton.

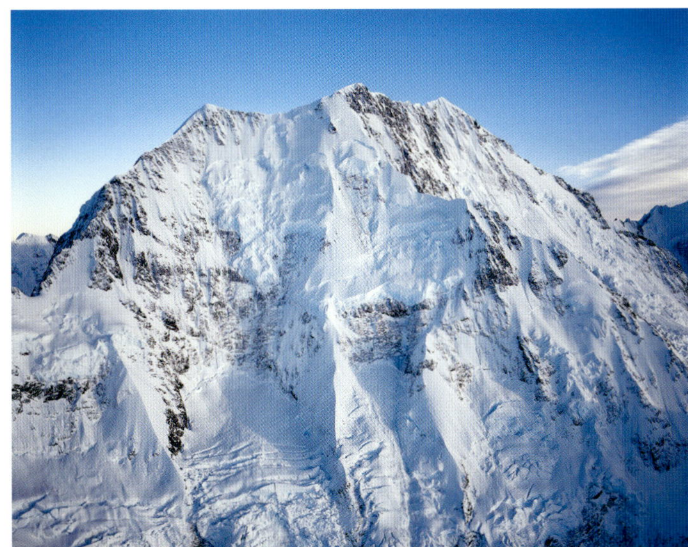

PAGE 70 CAROLINE FACE, AORAKI/MT COOK
The first ascent of the enormous 2000-metre Caroline Face of Aoraki/
Mt Cook was the subject of intense competition—the first and second
recorded ascents of the mountain were made within two days in 1970.
The route taken (Grade 5) followed avalanche-prone lower slopes to the
central spur leading to the Middle Peak. Breaching the ice cliff at half
height provided the technical crux. Flanking the Caroline Face is the
South Ridge to the Low Peak (Grade 4-), and the classic East Ridge
(Grade 4), first climbed in 1938.

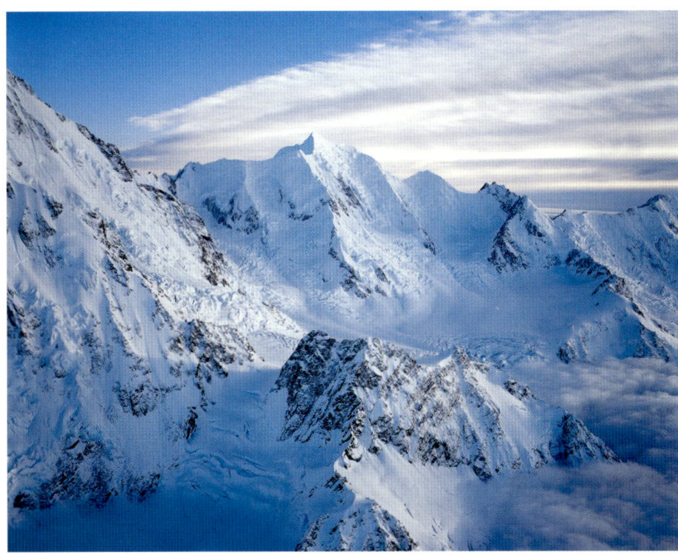

PAGE 71 MT TASMAN AND THE GRAND PLATEAU
The Grand Plateau (centre) from the south, looking across the lower
sections of the East Ridge and East Face of Aoraki/Mt Cook toward Mt
Tasman. Lendenfeld Peak, the castellated summit of Mt Haast and Mt
Dixon (3004 m) lie to the right of Tasman. In the foreground at the base
of Aoraki's East Ridge are the Anzac Peaks.

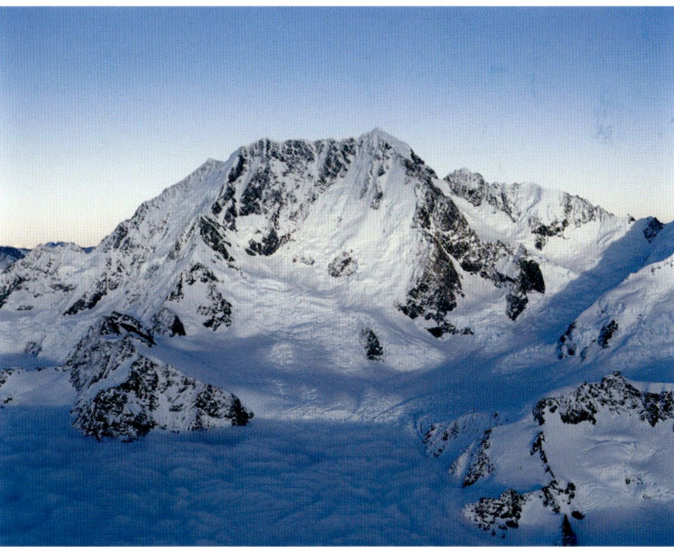

PAGE 72 THE EAST FACE OF AORAKI/MT COOK AND THE GRAND
PLATEAU
The 1800-metre East Face of Aoraki/Mt Cook, photographed before the
1991 summit collapse. The first ascent of the face in November 1961,
up a route leading virtually to the summit, was an important develop-
ment in the coming of age of New Zealand mountaineering (the route
was subsequently obliterated by the 1991 collapse which lowered the
summit by 10 metres to 3754 m). Flanking the face are Zurbriggens
Ridge (Grade 3+, right, first ascent 1895) and the classic East Ridge
(Grade 4, first ascent 1938). Right of Zurbriggens Ridge is the Linda
Glacier, the standard Grade 3 route to the summit from Plateau Hut.

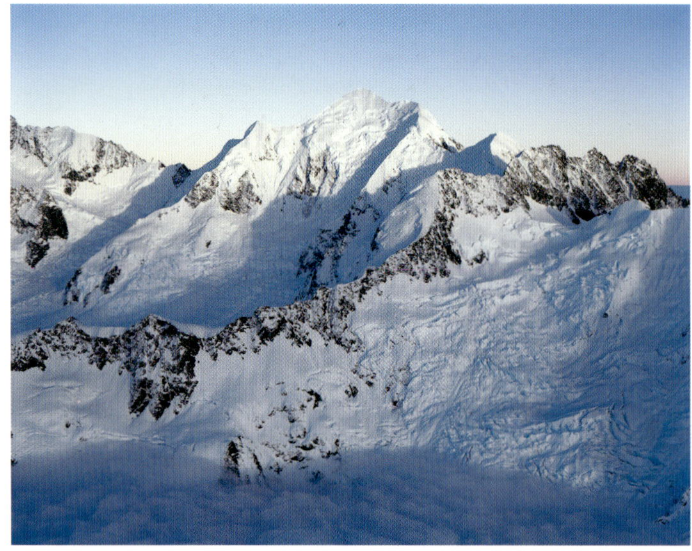

PAGE 73 MT TASMAN FROM THE NORTH-EAST
Mt Tasman is a beautiful ice-climbing peak, with two elegant ridges leading from the Grand Plateau to its summit. On the left is the Silberhorn Ridge, the route used for the first ascent in 1895. The Syme Ridge route to the North Shoulder was first climbed in 1931. Both routes are Grade 3+. Lendenfeld Peak (3194 m) and the three rocky peaks of Mt Haast (3114 m) lie to the right (north) of Tasman; both are most commonly climbed from the upper Fox Glacier on the western side.

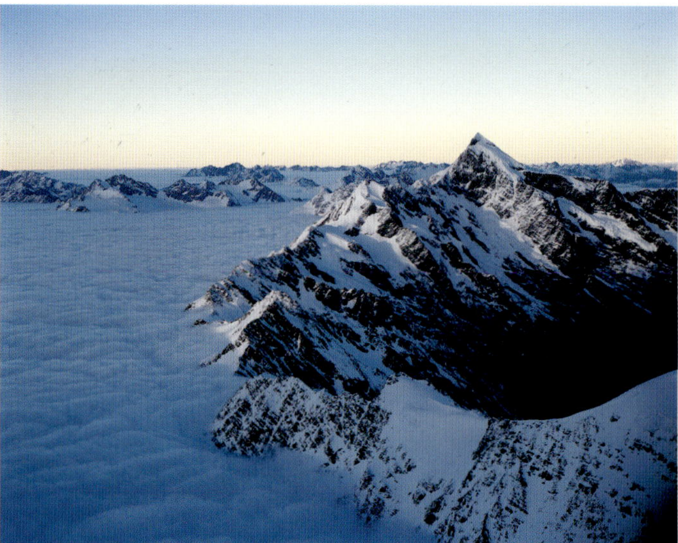

PAGE 74 MT SEFTON FROM ABOVE THE HOOKER VALLEY
Mimicking the massive ice sheets of glaciers of past millennia, a sea of early morning cloud drowns valleys east of the Main Divide, making islands of ranges and mountains. This photograph is taken above the Hooker Valley in Aoraki/Mount Cook National Park looking south to the North Face of Mt Sefton. Below the peak is the cloud-free Copland Valley which drains to the West Coast. The first ascent of Sefton, in 1895, was up the East Ridge which falls left of the summit. The classic North Buttress (Grade 3+) rises between the East and West ridges right of the North Face.

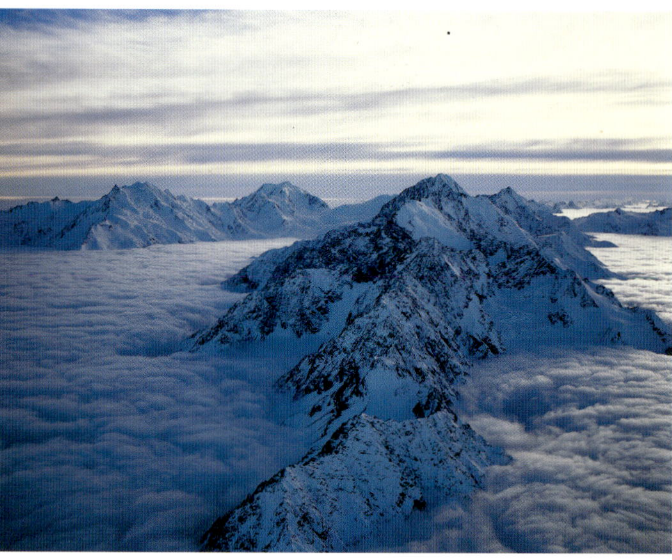

PAGE 75 MALTE BRUN RANGE WITH THE MINARETS AND ELIE DE BEAUMONT BEYOND
Early morning on the Malte Brun Range above an inversion layer of dense valley cloud. The rock pyramid of Malte Brun (3199 m) dominates the range, with Mt Hamilton (3025 m) beyond, while to the west across the Tasman Valley are the massifs of the Minarets (left) and Elie de Beaumont.

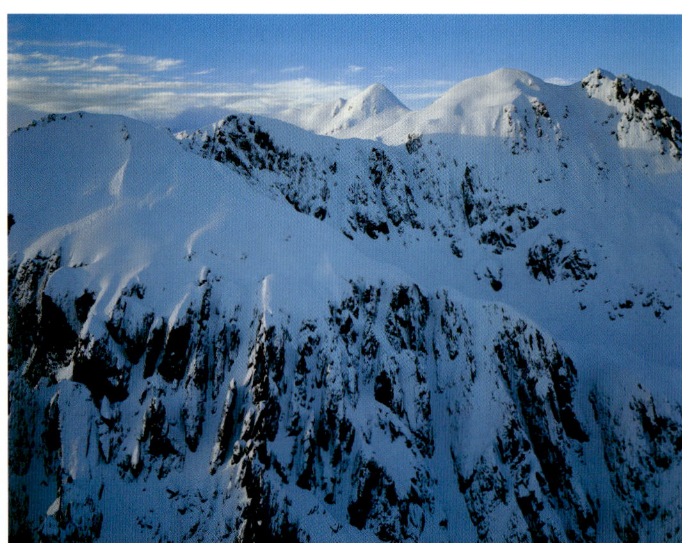

PAGE 77 RIDGE NORTH OF FRANZ JOSEF GLACIER
A heavy snowfall mantles sunlit and shadowy ridges on the West Coast side of the Main Divide north of Franz Josef Glacier. As often occurs elsewhere on this western side of the Southern Alps, precipitous valley walls carved by ice-age glaciers give way above 1500 metres to terrain of gentler contours.

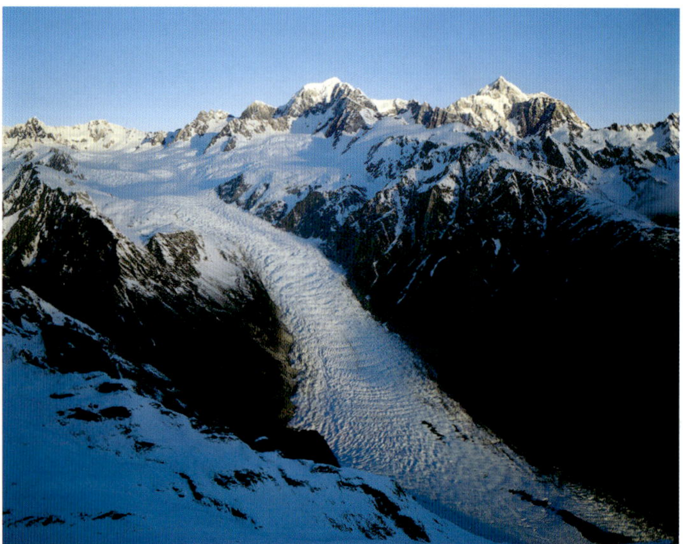

PAGE 78 FOX GLACIER WITH MT TASMAN AND AORAKI/MT COOK BEYOND
Known also as Te Moeka o Tuawe (the resting place of Tu Awe, a Ngai Tahu ancestor), the Fox Glacier is a dramatic icefall that channels ice accumulated on the vast snowfields west of Mt Tasman (centre) down to the West Coast lowlands. Like the Franz Josef Glacier to the north, a combination of high precipitation, large névé, and steep descent enables the Fox to fall 1500 metres over just 7 kilometres, terminating in temperate rainforest at an altitude of only 300 metres above sea level.

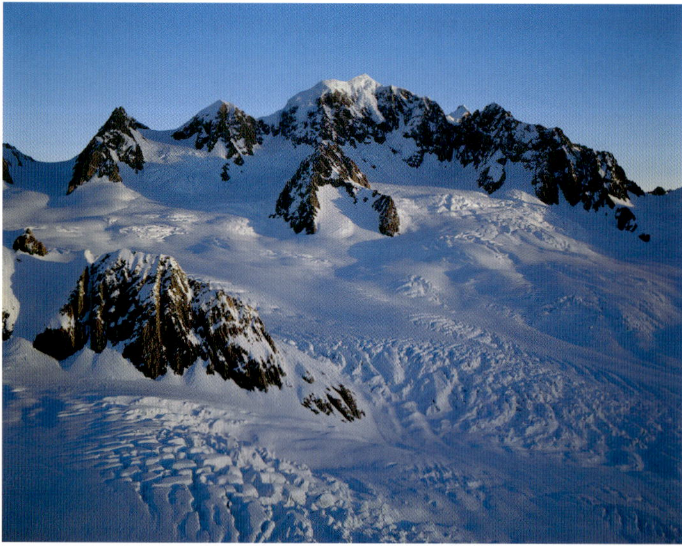

PAGE 79 MT TASMAN AND SURROUNDING PEAKS ABOVE THE ALBERT GLACIER
The amphitheatre of peaks, crevasses and snowfields at the head of the Fox Glacier. This photograph looks south across the western end of Pioneer Ridge to Mt Haast (left), Lendenfeld Peak, Mt Tasman, the tip of Aoraki/Mt Cook and Torres Peak. Pioneer Hut, base for climbs and ski-touring in this area, is located higher up Pioneer Ridge. The most popular approach to Mt Tasman from Pioneer Hut is via Marcel Col (right of Haast), over Lendenfeld and up to Tasman's North Shoulder, a route graded 3+. Some continue the traverse by descending Tasman's West Ridge to Torres Peak and Katies Col (at extreme right).

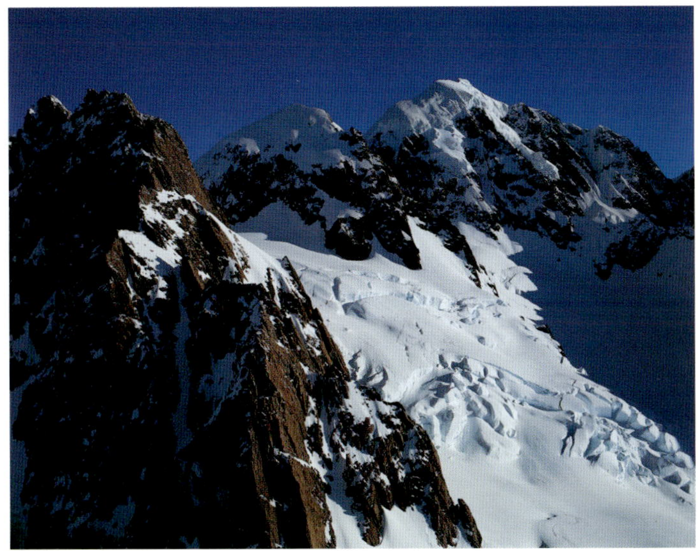

PAGE 80 MT HAAST, LENDENFELD PEAK AND MT TASMAN
The craggy peaks of Mt Haast (left), Lendenfeld Peak and the Heem-skirk Face of Mt Tasman loom above the Heemskirk Glacier, on the Westland/Tai Poutini National Park side of the Main Divide. All three peaks are regular objectives for climbers based at Pioneer Hut about 2 kilometres away. The lengthy, though relatively straightforward route to Tasman over Lendenfeld (see page 79) is one of the Southern Alps' classic alpine climbs. Rock routes on Haast and Lendenfeld are of varying quality.

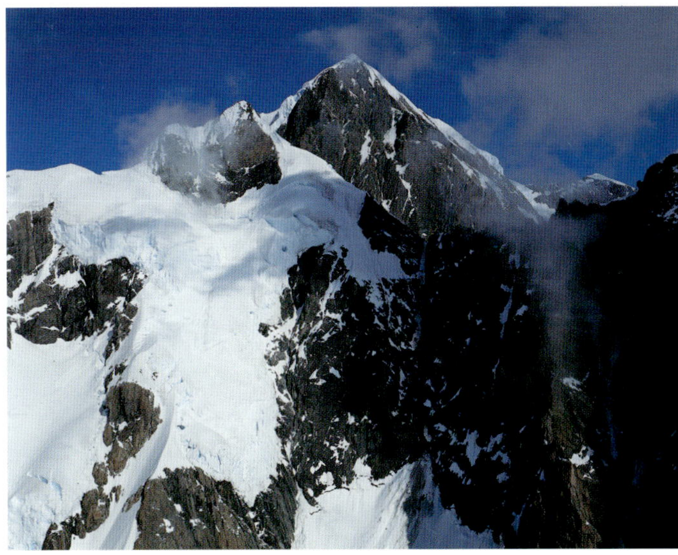

PAGE 81 SHEILA FACE OF AORAKI/MT COOK ABOVE THE DAMPIER-HICKS RIDGE
The Sheila (north-west) Face of Aoraki/Mt Cook rises above the Mt Dampier-Hicks Ridge. This western side of Mt Dampier (left, 3440 m), New Zealand's third-highest peak, is rarely visited—the peak is more commonly climbed from the Grand Plateau via the Linda Glacier.

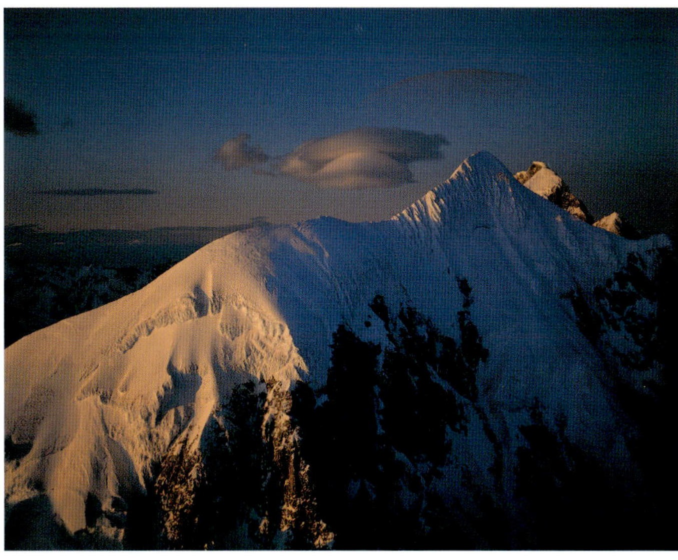

PAGE 82 NORTH SHOULDER, MT TASMAN
The first sunlight of a winter morning highlights the summits of the three highest peaks of the Southern Alps. In the foreground the still shaded Abel Janszoon Face of Mt Tasman falls away abruptly from the sunlit North Shoulder, beyond which soar the peaks of Mt Tasman (3491 m), Aoraki/Mt Cook (3754 m) and Mt Dampier (3440 m, right).

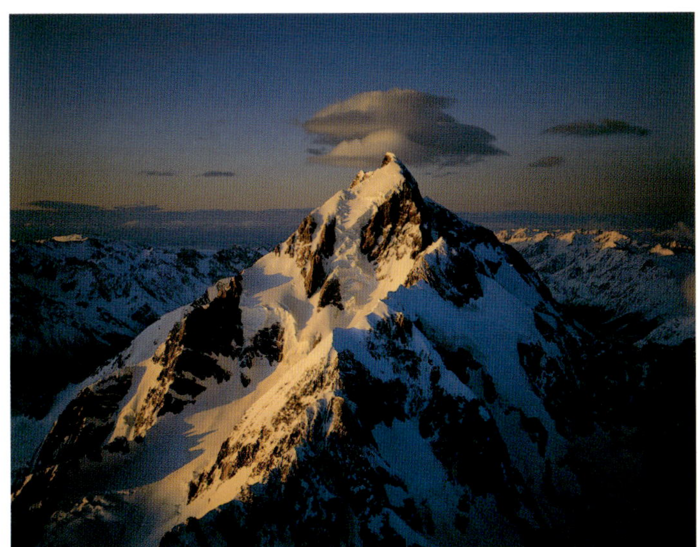

PAGE 83 AORAKI/MT COOK FROM THE NORTH
Capped by lenticular cloud, a sign of approaching bad weather, Aoraki/Mt Cook is pictured here from the north soon after dawn. This northern side of the mountain offers the easiest route to Aoraki's high peak via the Linda Glacier (Grade 3, rising from lower left) and the Linda Shelf (above the large ice cliff beneath the Summit Rocks where the route meets Zurbriggens Ridge). It is, however, a route threatened in many places by ice avalanches and often heavily crevassed. The North Ridge, route of Aoraki's first ascent in 1894, falls directly towards the camera from the summit to the col between Aoraki and Mt Dampier.

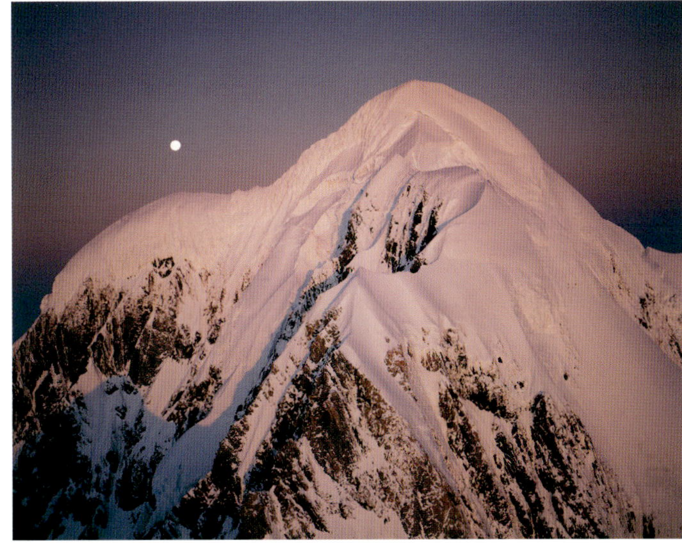

PAGE 84 MT TASMAN
A full moon rises over the North Shoulder of Mt Tasman (3491 m) in this image from the west at dusk. The top of the Abel Janszoon Face lies between the shoulder and the West Ridge, while the classic Silber-horn Ridge rises from the right above the Balfour Face. New Zealand's second highest peak was first climbed in 1895 from the Grand Plateau (a Grade 4 route on the eastern side, see page 71) but three-quarters of a century were to pass before successful ascents of these western faces were made.

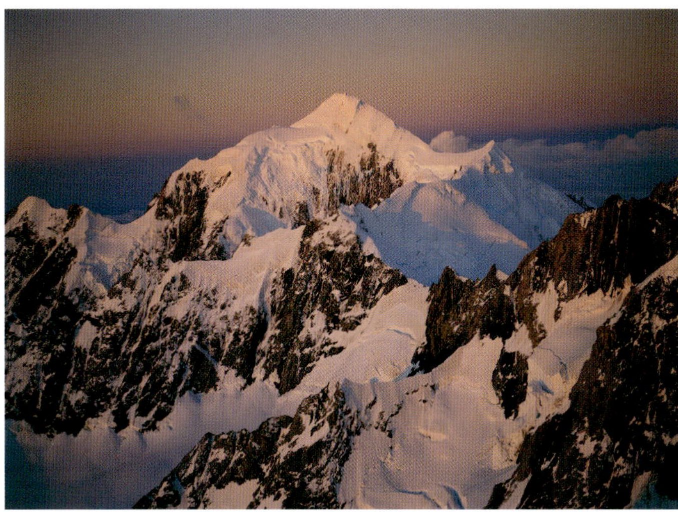

PAGE 85 THE MAIN DIVIDE, LOOKING NORTH TOWARDS THE BALFOUR FACE OF MT TASMAN
The Balfour Face of Mt Tasman (top centre) has yielded some of the hardest and most committing alpine routes in New Zealand. Attention turned to the face in the early 1970s, with Bill Denz and Bryan Pooley completing the first ascent in 1971. The first winter ascent, made by Denz and Phil Herron in 1975, was one of the most outstanding of the period. Tasman's West Ridge from Torres Peak (3160 m, far left) and the Torres-Tasman col leads from the left.

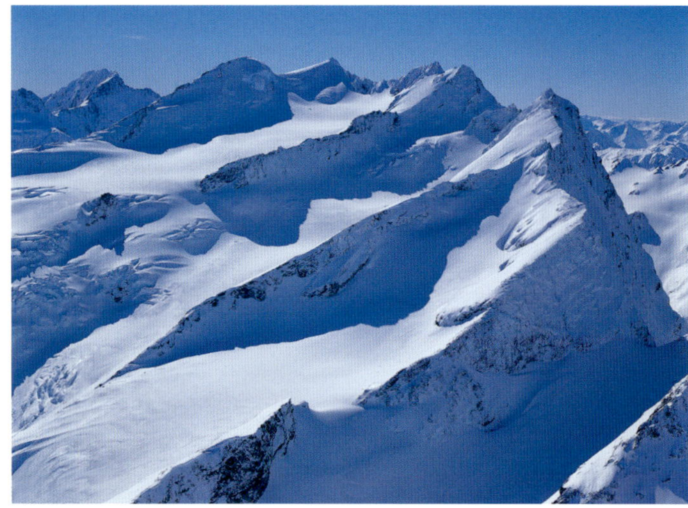

PAGE 86 WESTERN FLANKS OF MT WHITCOMBE
Mt Whitcombe's 3-kilometre summit ridge looking north from Menace
Gap (in shade at extreme right) to the high peak (2650 m) right of Snow
Dome (2624 m). Mt Evans (2620 m) is in the distance at top left. Scene
of more than a few epic adventures, Whitcombe is a challenging pros-
pect given its remoteness and its lengthy climbing routes. The peak is
most often climbed from the headwaters of the Wanganui River via the
Evans Glacier and Bracken Snowfield, which straddle the Main Divide
between Mt Whitcombe and Mt Evans.

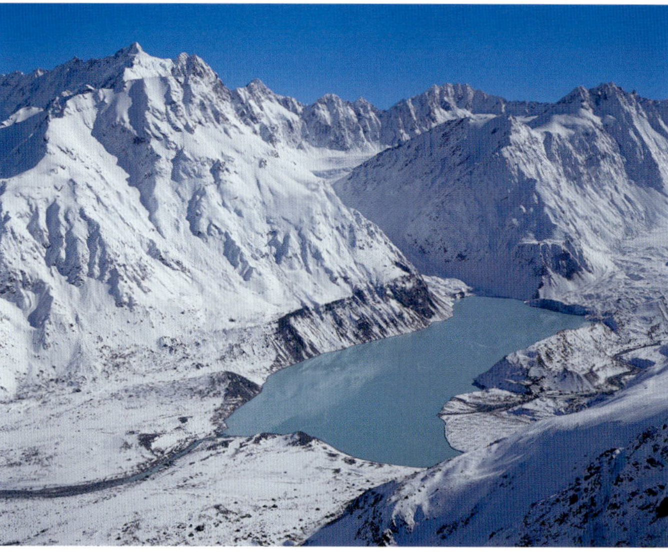

PAGE 88 TERMINAL LAKE, GREY AND MAUD GLACIERS, WITH THE
MAIN DIVIDE BEYOND, GODLEY VALLEY
The view west over the terminal lake of the Grey and Maud glaciers,
looking toward the Main Divide from above the upper Godley Valley.
The names of the peaks in this region recall past explorers, settlers and
the First World War. From left are Mt Moffat (2638 m), Mt Livingstone
(2561 m), Casino Peak (2450 m), Alamein Peak (2361 m), Takrouna
Peak (2357 m) and the flat-topped Mt Loughnan (2590 m).

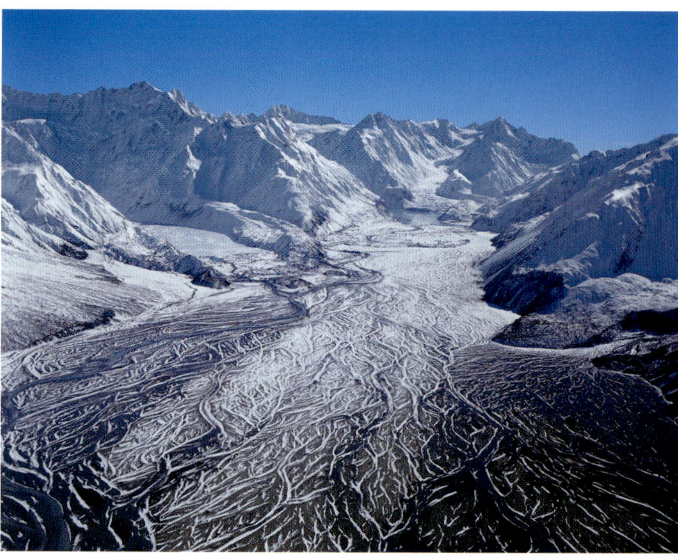

PAGE 89 HEAD OF THE GODLEY VALLEY
Main Divide peaks of the Godley region, in the north-east of Aoraki/
Mount Cook National Park, tower above river braids snaking south
toward Lake Tekapo along the path taken by the Godley Glacier at the
height of the last ice age. Large lakes in the terminal regions of the
tributary Classen and Grey/Maude glaciers impound meltwaters behind
moraine dams formed as the glaciers retreated rapidly during the twentieth century.

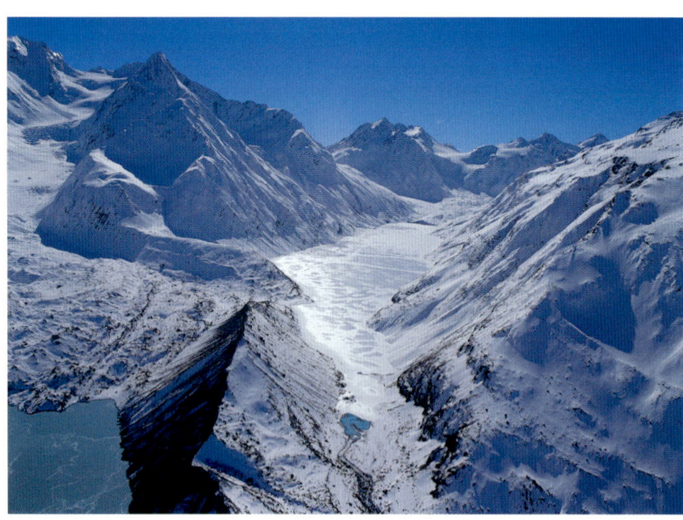

PAGE 90 GODLEY GLACIER TERMINAL LAKE
Looking north toward the frozen terminal lake (centre) of the Godley
Glacier in midwinter. Located in the north-east corner of Aoraki/Mount
Cook National Park, this part of the park is remoter and less frequently
visited than the peaks and glaciers of the upper Tasman Valley, with no
aircraft access allowed on the glaciers. Nonetheless, the area has excellent mountaineering objectives and winter ski touring terrain. At the
head of the valley is Mt Shyness (2337 m, see page 91), with Mt Wolsely
(2558 m) at left above the Maud Glacier and terminal lake.

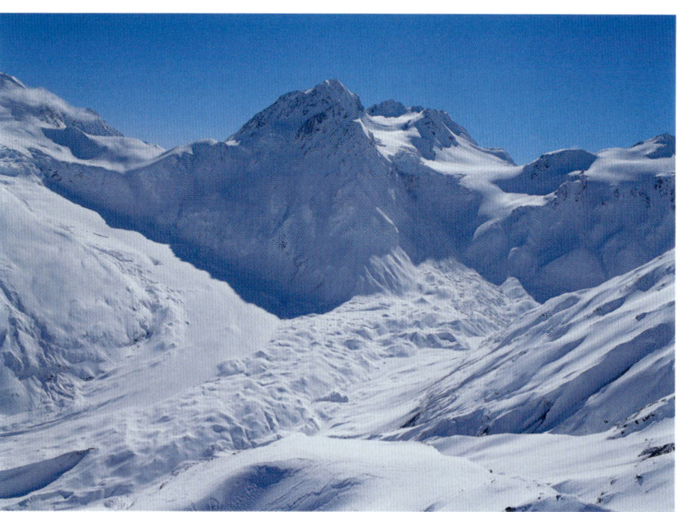

PAGE 91 SEALY PASS AND MT SHYNESS, UPPER GODLEY VALLEY
Mt Shyness (2337 m), a beautiful Main Divide peak at the head of the
Godley Glacier. Left of Shyness is Sealy Pass, which lies between the
Godley Valley and the Perth Valley on the West Coast side. The pass is
named after Timaru surveyor Edward Sealy, whose long excursions to
the Mount Cook region between 1867 and 1870 with heavy wet-plate
cameras resulted in the first photographs ever taken of New Zealand's
highest mountains.

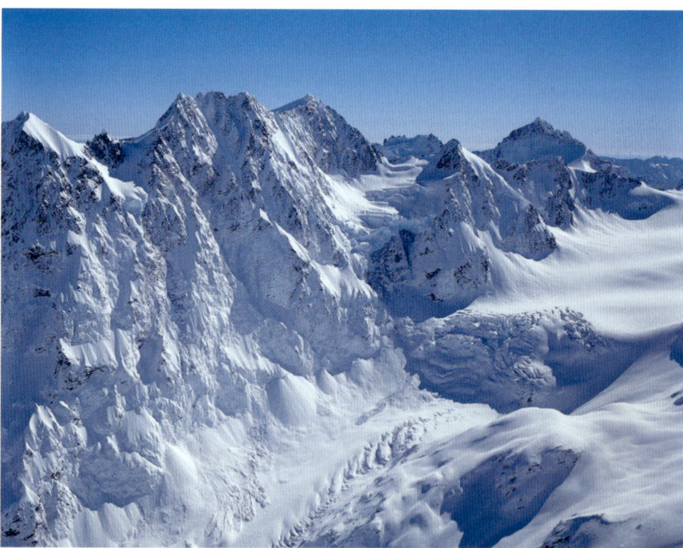

PAGE 93 RAMSAY FACE OF MT WHITCOMBE
Standing 1100 metres above the Ramsay Glacier, the Ramsay Face of
Mt Whitcombe has just two routes on it, both so far climbed only in
summer. The route to the low peak (at left) was first climbed in 1962.
The middle peak followed in 1972. Few have repeated these climbs
given the face's reputation for dangerously rotten rock, and the face
remains unclimbed in winter when conditions are arguably better. The
high peak (2650 m) was first climbed in December 1931 by its North
Ridge (right of the summit). Mt Evans (2620 m) is to the right.

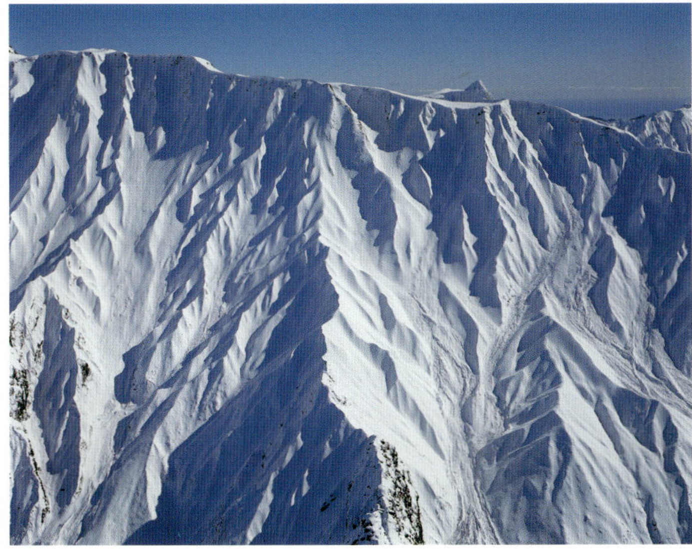

PAGE 94 SNOW-COVERED RIDGE, WHITCOMBE VALLEY
A mid-winter snowfall plasters a ridge west of the Whitcombe Valley in
central Westland, with Remarkable Peak and the Tasman Sea visible
beyond. With precipitation on this western side of the Southern Alps
often well in excess of 5000 millimetres a year, snowfalls like this can
occur at any time of year, and mostly maintain snow cover above the
treeline throughout the winter.

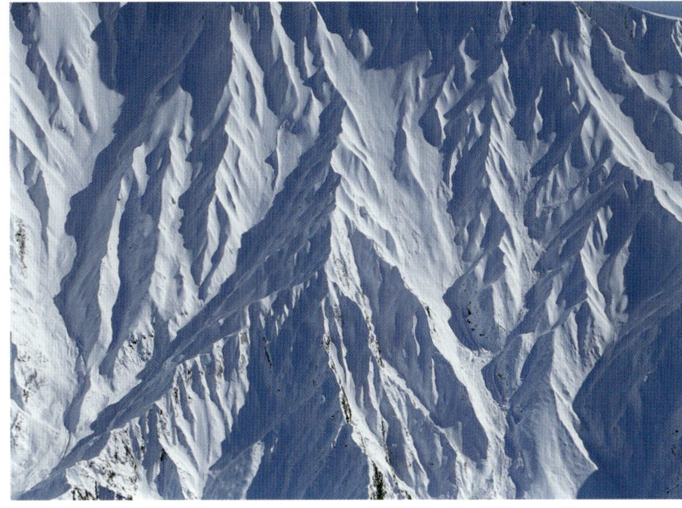

PAGE 95 DETAIL, SNOW-COVERED RIDGE, WHITCOMBE
VALLEY
In summer, areas of the Southern Alps that are free of ice and snow
show the effect of the vigorous erosion that results from rapid uplift,
high rainfall and widespread freeze/thaw shatter. This is much less evident in winter, when snow and lower-angled light convert even the most
gully-scarred faces into abstract works of geomorphological art.

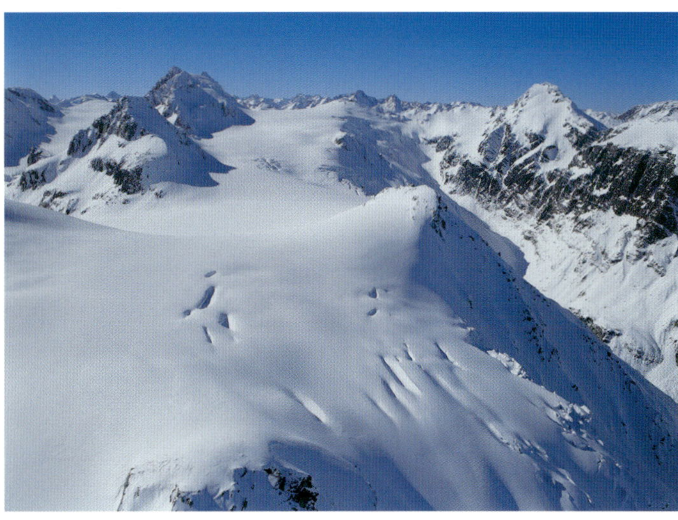

PAGE 96 THE GARDEN OF EDEN FROM THE WEST
The Gardens of Eden and Allah are two high ice plateaus abutting the
western side of the Main Divide between the headwaters of the Perth
and Wanganui Rivers. Highly valued for their remoteness, a crossing
of the Main Divide via the Gardens is a demanding and adventurous
wilderness mountaineering undertaking. Pictured above is the lengthy
sweep of the Garden of Eden looking east toward the Main Divide, with
Newton Peak the high point left of the plateau (2543 m). Perth Col is at
the head of the Perth Glacier (right).

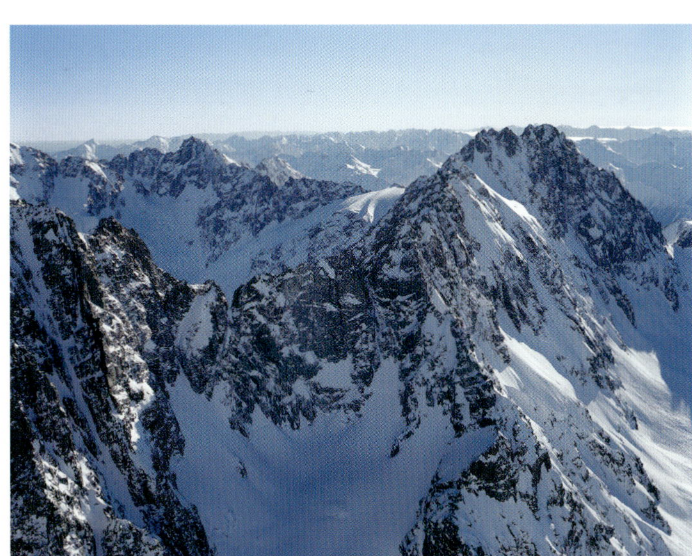

PAGE 97 JAGGED PEAK, ARROWSMITH RANGE
The aptly named Jagged Peak (2696 m) stands above the Cameron Glacier in the Arrowsmith Range, a high eastern outlier of the Main Divide
between the headwaters of the Rakaia and Rangitata rivers. Although
renowned for its rotten rock, several hard winter ice routes on Jagged
Peak's south-east face (pictured) have been climbed. The couloir route
on Couloir Peak (at the extreme left of the photograph) is another challenging climb. The highpoint of the ridge visible behind Jagged Peak is
Red Peak (2637 m).

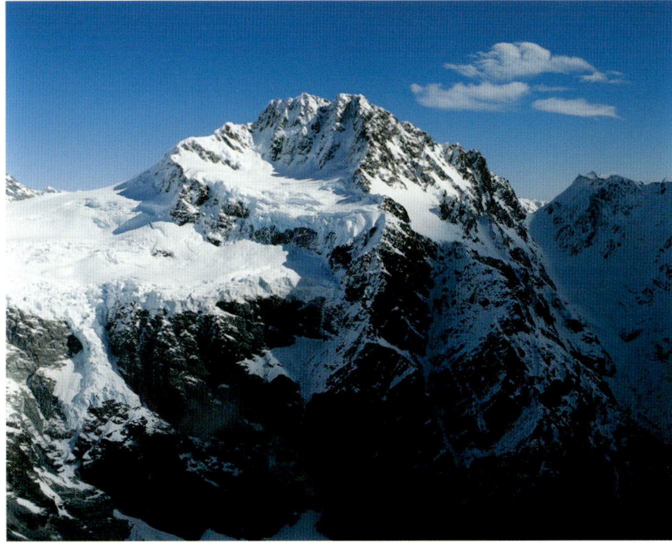

PAGE 98 MT EVANS AND THE UPPER AND LOWER SHELF GLACIERS
The unclimbed East Face of Mt Evans (2620 m) above the Wilkinson
Valley. An isolated peak immediately north of Mt Whitcombe (see pages
86 and 93), Mt Evans remained unclimbed until 1933, when a party
succeeded on a route from the Wilkinson to the upper North Ridge
(rising from the right above McKenzie Col). The East Ridge (on the left)
then fell in 1940, the North East Ridge in 1955 and the complete North
Ridge from McKenzie Col in 1958.

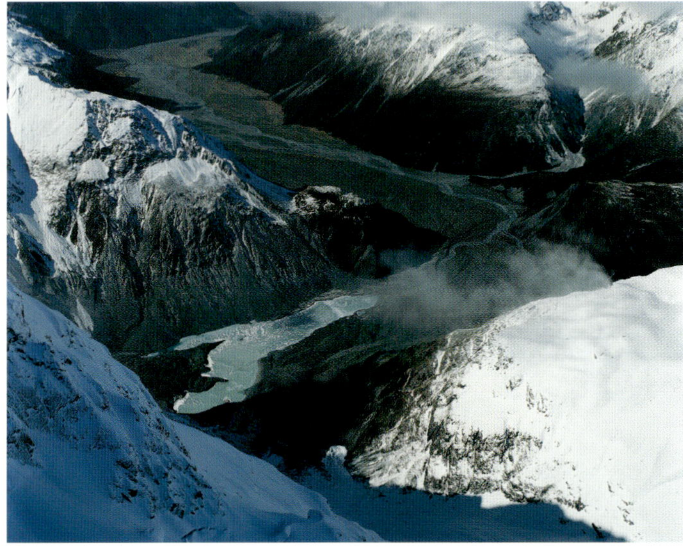

PAGE 99 RAMSAY GLACIER TERMINAL LAKE
Looking down onto the terminal lake of the Ramsay Glacier and the
Rakaia Valley from above the Main Divide south of Mt Whitcombe.
This is the northernmost of a series of terminal glacial lakes which have
expanded rapidly over recent decades on the eastern side of the central
Southern Alps, filling deep troughs left by retreating valley glaciers (see
also pages 88–90).

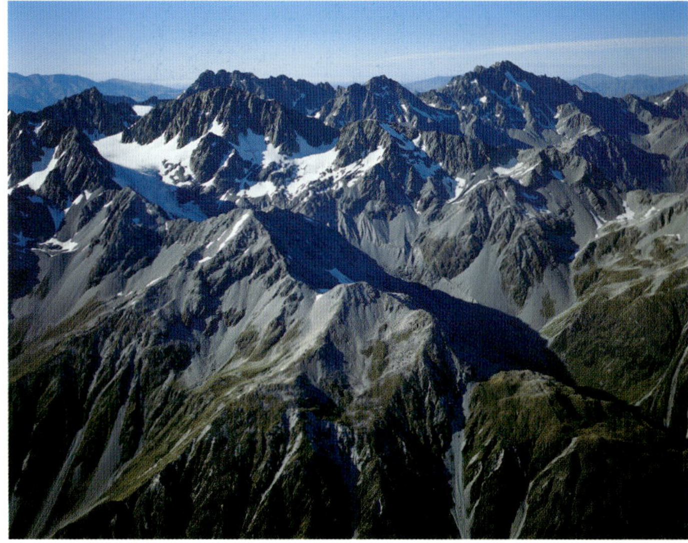

PAGE 100 ARROWSMITH RANGE
The Arrowsmith Range from the west above the headwaters of the Rakaia River. Jagged Peak is the on the left-hand skyline and Mt Arrowsmith (2800 m) is at right. This landscape is typical of much of the drier eastern side of the Southern Alps north of Fiordland, with broken rocky ridges, small remnant glaciers, extensive screes and snow tussocks. Many of New Zealand's endemic alpine plants and animals thrive in these tussock communities.

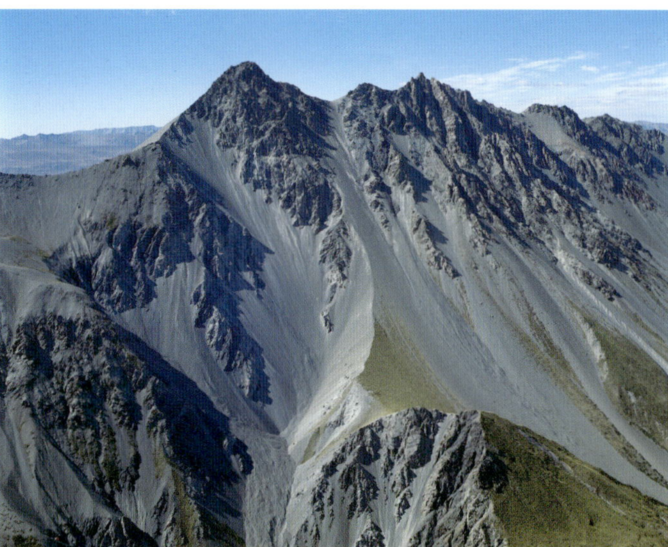

PAGE 101 SCREE-SCARRED RIDGE, INLAND CANTERBURY
Much of the topography of inland Canterbury provides textbook examples of the vigorous erosion countering the rapid uplift of the Southern Alps. As is clearly evident in this photograph, crumbling rock ridges feed ubiquitous screes, which over millennia have supplied the materials for much of the lowland landscape on both sides of the Alps.

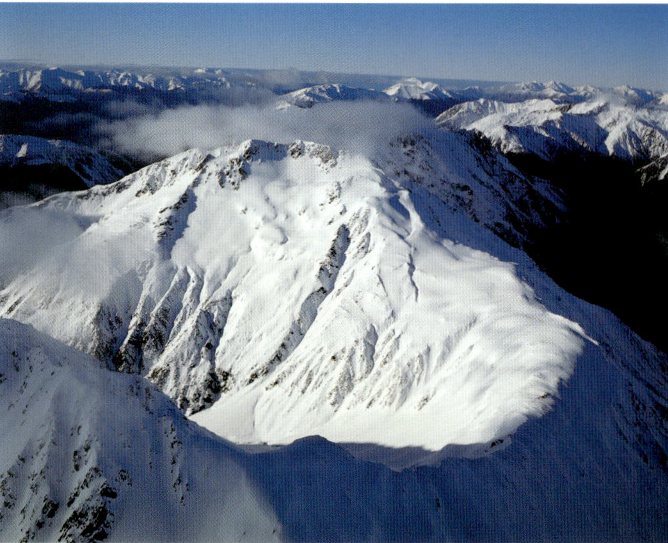

PAGE 102 DOUBTFUL RANGE SOUTH OF LEWIS PASS
With peaks rising to 1800 metres, the Doubtful Range is one of several ranges radiating east and west from the Main Divide in the Lewis Pass region. The easily accessible tops provide extensive opportunities for tramping and mountaineering both in summer and winter.

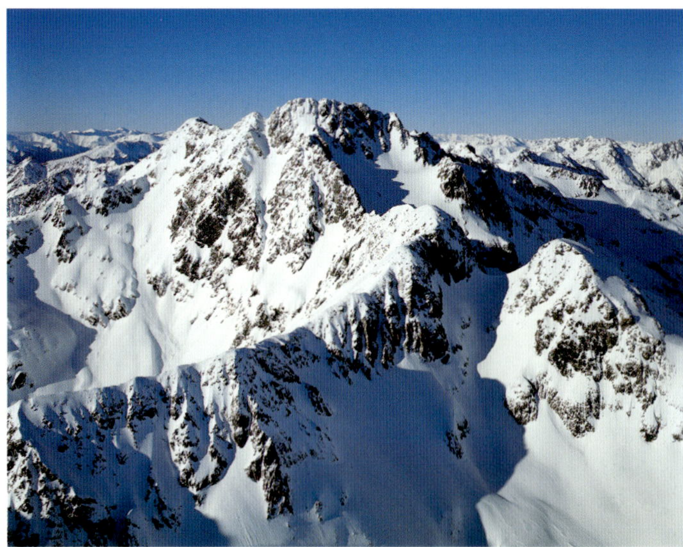

PAGE 103 MT ROLLESTON FROM THE NORTH-WEST, ARTHUR'S PASS
Mt Rolleston (2275 m), in Arthur's Pass National Park, viewed from the north-west looking across the Philistine–Rolleston ridge to the sunny Otira Face. With reasonably firm rock, the Otira Face has several popular summer routes, including a route up the buttress leading directly to the highest of Rolleston's three summits—a mid-grade route on firm greywacke sandstone. The Otira Slide, a straightforward ascent and descent route, is the broad gully at the left of the face.

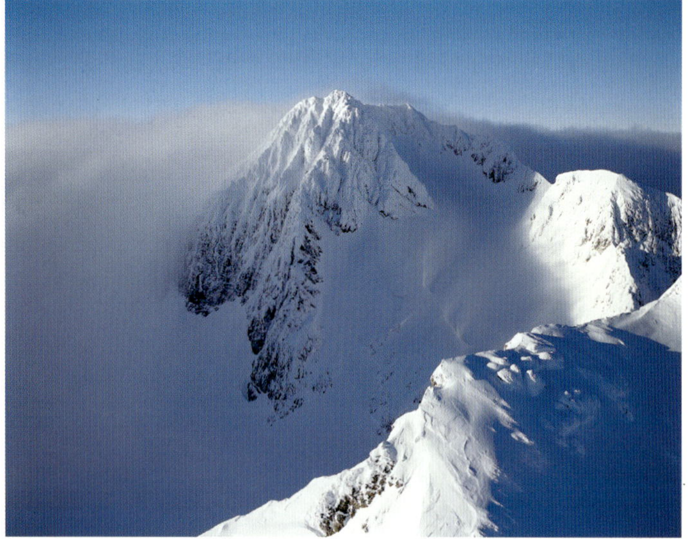

PAGE 104 MT UNA, SPENSER MOUNTAINS
Mt Una (2300 m) is one of several spectacular Southern Alps peaks in the Spenser Mountains between Lewis Pass and Nelson Lakes. This view is of Mt Una's heavily snow-plastered west buttress (accessed from the Matakitaki Valley), with the South Ridge rising from the right. Other notable peaks in this range are Gloriana Peak (2218 m) and Faerie Queen (2236 m) both within a day's walk from Lewis Pass and set among fine tramping country.

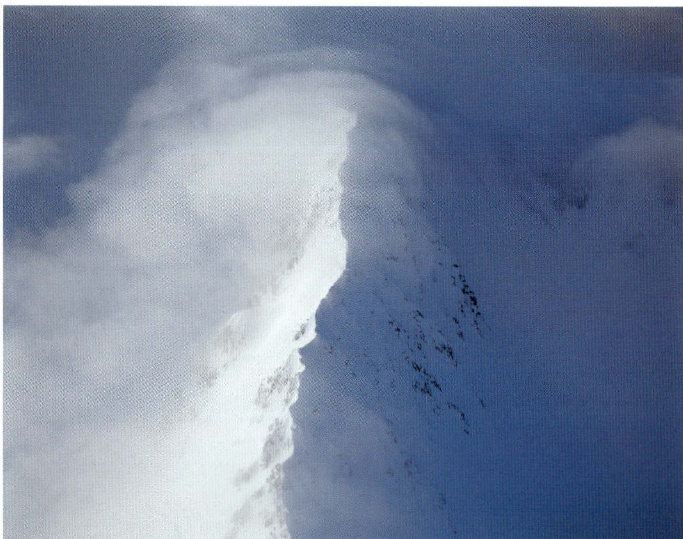

PAGE 105 CORNICED RIDGELINE, MT UNA, SPENSER MOUNTAINS
A mid-winter storm blasts snow plumes across a ridge on Mt Una, creating a potentially dangerous corniced ridge crest. Snow storms of this nature can occur at any time of year, although for the most part these ridges are snow free in summer.

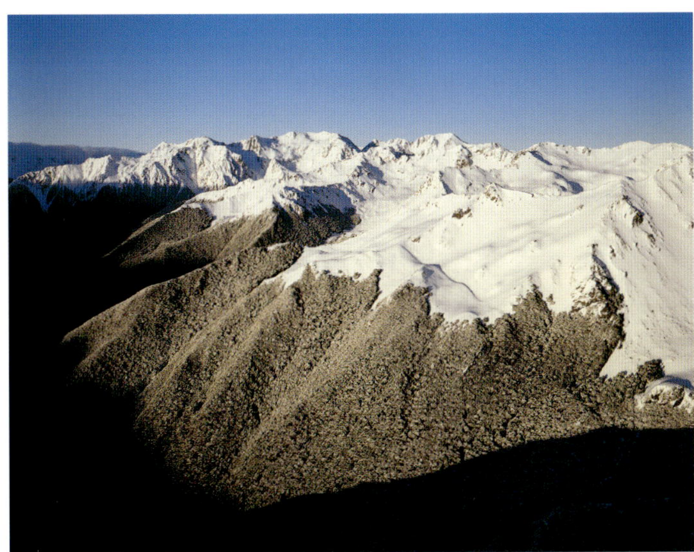 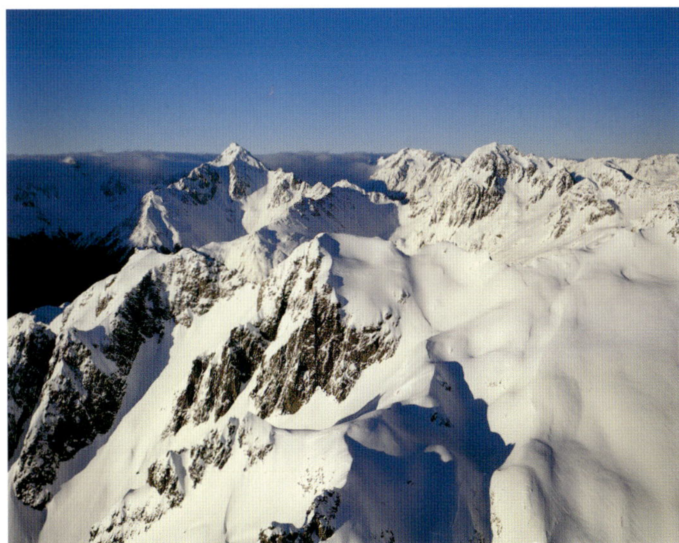

PAGE 106 ROBERT RIDGE AND TRAVERS RANGE, NELSON LAKES NATIONAL PARK
The gentler mountain topography of the Travers Range at the northern end of the Southern Alps. This photograph is taken above the head of Lake Rotoiti looking onto the glaciated basins flanking the east side of Robert Ridge under heavy snow. The edge of the beech forest is at approximately 1400 metres, and peaks in the region reach no higher than 2350 metres. The flatter rolling terrain of Robert Ridge provides excellent ski touring as far as Mt Angelus, the flat-topped peak on the skyline right of centre.

PAGE 107 MT TRAVERS, MT FRANKLIN AND MT CUPOLA
Midwinter on the Travers Range in Nelson Lakes National Park, looking south. To the left, the northern face of Mt Travers (2338 m) is still shaded from the morning sun, with Mt Cupola (2260 m, right of centre) already in full sunlight. Lower buttresses of Cupola's North East Face have several 8–9 pitch rock routes. In the distance between the two is Mt Franklin (2340 m), the park's highest peak, which is usually climbed from the West Sabine Valley.

A Natural History of the Southern Alps

Andy Dennis

It is impossible for me to describe in adequate words the majestic scenery by which we were surrounded…As far as the eye could reach everywhere snow and ice and rock appeared around us, and in such gigantic proportions that I sometimes thought I was dreaming, and instead of being in New Zealand I found myself in the Arctic or Antarctic mountain regions.

—Exploring geologist Julius von Haast on the Tasman Glacier, March 1862

The Southern Alps are a chain of high glaciated mountains that separate the eastern and western sides of the South Island of New Zealand into regions of strikingly different climate, vegetation and landscape. Named from the sea to the west in 1773 by Captain James Cook for their 'prodigious height', they are far and away the highest mountains in Australasia. As such they form the only formidable barrier to the tempestuous westerly airstreams that circle the Southern Oceans apart from the Patagonian Andes, and as a consequence are subjected to regular voluminous deluges of rain. Created over the past 5 million years by a combination of rapid uplift and very vigorous erosion, these geologically youthful mountains along with their neighbouring lowlands provide outstanding examples of major earth-shaping (or geomorphological) processes and climatic fluctuations. As for their biota, the fact that New Zealand has been isolated from other land areas for something like 80 million years means that the vast majority of plants and animals that have evolved in association with these youthful mountains are not found anywhere else in the world.

To the extent that they are defined by a unifying geology and geomorphology the Southern Alps extend for about 500 kilometres (as the kea flies) from Nelson Lakes National Park in the north to Mount Aspiring National Park in the south. Throughout this entire distance virtually the whole of the alpine spine of the South Island has been constructed from a consistently uniform assemblage of basic materials—ancient sedimentary sandstones (or 'greywacke') and mudstones in the east grading into increasingly metamorphic schists towards the west. But for many New Zealanders what constitutes the Southern Alps is not so precisely or scientifically defined but extends southwards into the rugged and glaciated mountains of Fiordland at least as far as Milford Sound, if not all the way to the south-west corner of the South Island. And while it is certainly true that both the rocks and the landforms of Fiordland are strikingly different from those further north, in other no less important respects—climatic patterns and the extent to which they are affected by the mountains; the overwhelming dominance of indigenous vegetation; the obvious wilderness character of so much of the terrain; and the linking together in 1991 of Fiordland, Mount Aspiring, Aoraki/Mount Cook and Westland/Tai Poutini national parks in the vast South-west New Zealand World Heritage Area—the mountains and valleys of Fiordland form a seamless extension of this unbroken chain of pre-eminent South Island mountains.

The most prominent features of the Southern Alps include more than 25 summits over 3000 metres among which the 3754 metre Aoraki/Mt Cook is very much the 'Monarch of the Southern Alps' being more than 250 metres higher than its nearest rival. Of the more than 250 separate glaciers which extend as far north as Arthur's Pass, the 28-kilometre Tasman Glacier on the eastern side of Aoraki/Mt Cook is comfortably the longest, while the 10-kilometre Franz Josef and 13-kilometre Fox glaciers in the west are not only among the fastest-moving glaciers in the world but are also exceptional in the way their terminal regions trespass down into the realm of temperate rainforest. Numerous beautiful ice-carved lakes on both sides of the alps include all of New Zealand's deepest and—with the single exception of the volcanic Lake Taupo in the North Island—largest lakes in the country. And the magnificent fiords of the far south-west are not only classic examples of precipitous fiord topography, but along with the surrounding Fiordland valleys and mountains preserve the shape of a heavily glaciated landscape very much as it was when the most recent ice age glaciers abandoned it 10,000 years or so ago.

In the endless cycles of sedimentation, uplift and erosion which oversee the rise and fall of all mountains, the Southern Alps as we have them today are the result of four major earth shaping processes. The first is New Zealand's somewhat precarious location along the boundary between two of the earth's larger tectonic crustal plates, whose recent (geologically speaking) collision has resulted in one of the world's most rapidly rising mountain ranges. The second is the very considerable barrier these youthful mountains have provided to the moisture-laden westerly airstreams that circle the empty Southern Ocean, and the consequent very large amounts of precipitation that have been dumped upon them. The third is the monumental imprint of ice-age glaciers on the topography of the Southern Alps and Fiordland mountains as well as on most major components of the lowland landscapes which today surround these mountains. And the fourth (which should probably be the first) are the particular characteristics of the basement rocks from which these mountains have been fashioned, and the manner and extent to which these rocks have responded to the attacks of water and ice and gravity and regular earthquakes to produce both the shape and the detail of today's mountain landscapes.

In the South Island of New Zealand the eastern margin of the complex Indian/Australian plate meets the advancing—and subducting—western edge of the Pacific Plate, pushing up 100 to 300 million-year-old sedimentary rocks transported by the Pacific Plate along the line of the Alpine Fault. Defining the more precipitous western edge of the Southern Alps, this fault extends from the Nelson Lakes area in the north to near the entrance to Milford Sound in the south, and is one of the most obvious fractures in the Earth's crust to be clearly visible in satellite photographs. Vertical displacement across the fault of river terraces created by retreating Ice Age glaciers indicates that present rates of uplift in the central parts of the Southern Alps averages more than 10 millimetres per year, and over the past 3 million years may well have amounted to 18,000 metres in total—or approximately twice the height of Mt Everest. However, since the present height of Mt Cook is 'only' 3754 metres, such a rate of uplift indicates that for every 5 metres these mountains have been pushed up, 4 metres has been recycled back to lower altitudes by weathering and erosion. It is also clear that there has been extensive lateral (or sideways) displacement along the Alpine Fault, most strikingly demonstrated by the 480-kilometre separation of the formerly adjacent ultramafic rocks of today's Red Hills in the western part of Mount Aspiring National Park and the Red Hills of the Richmond Range south of Nelson.

If the statistics for tectonic activity associated with the Southern Alps are spectacular then the same can be said for the very large quantities of rain and snow that are annually emptied onto these mountains. At the tourist villages of Franz Josef and Fox Glacier immediately west of Mt Cook and most of the other 3000-metre peaks rainfall averages upwards of 5000 millimetres a year, while closer to the Main Divide it is thought to be between 10,000 and 15,000 millimetres (although here it is virtually impossible to measure precipitation as much of it arrives as blizzard-blown snow). East of the Main Divide a classic 'rain-shadow' effect means that annual precipitation rates fall away very rapidly. Hence while at Mount Cook Village just east of the highest peaks rainfall is about 4000 millimetres a year, places in the nearby Mackenzie Basin receive less than 1000 millimetres. As far as seasonal distribution goes there is no regular rainy season in the Southern Alps, although persistent rain is often a feature of spring in the west while prolonged dry spells in the east tend to occur during the second half of summer. In terms of geomorphology and landforms this high rainfall has (and has had) a major hand in every phase of the land-shaping processes that have created the Southern Alps apart from tectonic uplift—from the creation of both the ice age and present-day glaciers to the relentless process of freeze-thaw shatter which begins the process of recycling the mountains back to the sea—and in so doing has buried so much of the Southern Alps basement rocks under screes, moraines and expansive outwash plains.

For much of the past 2 million years contrasts between the eastern and western sides of the Southern Alps would not have been anything like as obvious as they are today, with much of the whole area being buried under huge ice age glaciers up to 1000 metres thick. In the west, temperatures between 4 and 6 degrees celsius cooler than they are today resulted in great coalescing tongues of glacial ice extending well beyond the present coastline from Hokitika to Fiordland, while their counterparts in the east advanced up to 100 kilometres down the major valleys from their source on the Main Divide. While providing a chronology for these events has proved extremely difficult (largely because each new glacial episode tends to obliterate much of the evidence of earlier advance and retreat), what is beyond doubt is that most of the grander landforms of today's Southern Alps are a direct legacy of the massive carving and carrying work of ice age glaciers. The most graphic manifestations of the ability of these now largely vanished glaciers to carve deep into even the most resistant bedrock are the sheer-walled fiords and valleys of Fiordland and the great depths of the ice-carved Southern Lakes. As for their no less impressive carrying power, the whole of the Canterbury Plains have been constructed from outwash gravels transported from the mountains by ice age glaciers, while to the west of the Alps much of the hill country seawards of the main highway through South Westland is old lateral moraines up to 450 metres high dumped there by huge glaciers that extended 10 to 15 kilometres beyond the present coastline during major advances.

Co-operating in the creation of the Canterbury Plains and lumpy South Westland coastal moraine hills, as well as other depositional features like the ubiquitous screes and expansive gravel-choked riverbeds, are the qualities of the dominant rocks of the Southern Alps. These ancient sandstones and schists have for the most part emerged from their 100 to 300 million years of pressure and heat and the stresses of uplift and other tectonic deformation riddled with a myriad of fractures and faults which readily yield to weathering and freeze-thaw shatter in this environment of high rainfall and temperatures which regularly shift between warm days and freezing nights. The resulting 'rotten rock' is characteristic of ridges and other exposed bedrock surfaces throughout the Southern Alps, and from time to time delivers more dramatic reminders of its inherent instability in the form of major rock avalanches—like the one that broke loose from the summit of Aoraki/Mt Cook in December 1991, hurling 55 million cubic metres of rock onto the surface of the Tasman Glacier 2600 metres below and lowering the height of the country's highest mountain by 10 metres. In contrast the exceptionally obdurate gneiss and diorite of the Fiordland mountains have proved much more resistant to the ravages of freeze-thaw shatter, with the result that the shape of these mountains today is much the same as it was at the end of the last of the ice ages and has not been modified by screes and other post-glaciation erosional 'softening' to anything like the extent of the schist and greywacke mountains further north.

While a textbook on the rise and fall of mountain ranges could be illustrated by examples from the Southern Alps, none of the processes described above are unique to New Zealand. The opposite however is true of the flora and fauna that have evolved in association with these land-shaping process. In the case of plants, 93 per cent of the more than 600 indigenous species that are found today in alpine and sub-alpine zones are endemic to New Zealand (that is they do not occur anywhere else), and many of these are very strongly centred on the Southern Alps. A comparable level of endemism occurs in the native fauna of the Southern Alps, among which are unique examples of adaptation to the rigours of alpine living by a number of creatures whose kith and kin elsewhere in the world are found only in much less hostile environments.

As a general rule treelines throughout the Southern Alps occur at between 1300 and 1500 metres although there are striking differences between the forests to the east and west of the Main Divide. In the east the very much simpler and more open forests are for the most part dominated by a single species of nothofagus or southern beech (mountain beech) and are regularly confined to valleys close to the Main Divide, while elsewhere open landscapes of tawny tussock grasses and scattered shrublands provide the foreground to the lofty peaks. In part this is a legacy of 150 years of pastoral farming throughout the eastern high country in which the deliberate use of fire has almost invariably played a significant role. But even before the arrival of sheep-farmers, beech forest would have been less continuous on the eastern side of the alps as a consequence of both natural fires and fires lit by moa-hunting Maori, and the very slow rate at which beech seed—which is neither wind-blown nor bird-carried—was able to disperse in the aftermath of fire, glaciation or other significant disruption. In the west, much denser and very much more complex forests containing a wide range of podocarp (native New Zealand conifer), beech and broad-leaved species mantle the whole of this side of the Southern Alps, and south of Arthur's Pass often extend all the way to the coast. A notable ecological anomaly of these western forests is the complete absence of beech between Hokitika and the Mahitahi Valley behind Bruce Bay—a distance of about 200 kilometres. This 'beech gap' is believed to be the consequence of the total elimination of beech from this part of the western side of the alps during the ice ages, and the subsequent inability of beech to recolonise this area over the past 10,000 years due to the limitations on seed dispersal mentioned above.

On this western side of the Southern Alps the upper echelons of the forest usually merge into a mosaic of tightly-packed subalpine shrubs, which regularly extend for 500 metres or more of altitude beyond the limit of the larger trees. Dominated by a variety of colourful tree-daisies and 'grass-trees' similar dense sub-alpine shrublands also occur throughout the east, although frequently too on this side of the alps open alpine grasslands and herbfields commence at the treeline with only a relatively minor scattering of shrubs. On both sides of the Main Divide this zone above the treeline often contains terrain of significantly gentler contour than that both above and below and is also the place where many of New Zealand's more distinctive alpine flowers are likely to be encountered. Prominent among these are the giant mountain buttercup or 'Mount Cook lily' (the biggest buttercup in the world); a plethora of large white and yellow mountain daisies; meadows adorned with glistening white late-summer gentians; and numerous plants specially adapted to scree, rock rubble or other unstable environments including the large raoulia and haastia cushion plants aptly described as 'vegetable sheep'.

Among the animals that have adapted to the rigours of the alpine environment the comic and colourful kea—the only mountain parrot in the world and a bird of unusual intelligence—is often the most conspicuous, and would formerly have been very much more so had not sheep farmers decimated the kea population from an estimated 150,000 birds to the present 5000. Other notable birds of the Southern Alps include the elusive New Zealand falcon and even more elusive tiny rock wren, the latter the only New Zealand bird that spends its entire life above the treeline and one of only two survivors of at least six endemic species of wrens that were present in New Zealand at the time of human settlement. (Since neither keas nor rock wrens are found in the North Island mountains both are very much birds of the Southern Alps.) Elusiveness is also a characteristic of most of the other unique creatures of this alpine environment which include several species of powelliphanta (or large carnivorous land-snails); at least two species of deinacrida (or giant wetas); the only alpine gecko in the world (the black-eyed gecko of the dry Marlborough mountains at the northern end of the Southern Alps); and the world's only alpine cicadas. Among the more plentiful inhabitants large numbers of alpine moths and colourful grasshoppers are always very active on sunny summer days, while among the birds the New Zealand pipit is easily the most common open country companion throughout the eastern side of the alps as well as the north-west.

Most of the introduced animals that have made a home in the Southern Alps since human settlement are also often secretive, but the consequences of their invasion most certainly are not. From the time the first European ships reached these shores Norway rats and ship rats spread in vast numbers throughout all mainland parts of the country where their toll on birds and other small native animals—which had evolved in a land free from mammalian predators—has been inestimable. In this they were soon joined by other hugely effective immigrant killers, most notably stoats, ferrets and weasels (all of which were introduced in a misguided attempt at rabbit control) and feral cats. Other deliberately introduced animals have taken a similar toll on the native flora. Deer (principally Scottish red deer), Austrian chamois and Himalayan thar, which were introduced to New Zealand in the latter part of the nineteenth or early twentieth century as game animals, caused massive damage to both forest and alpine ecosystems before effective control was achieved through helicopter hunting from the late 1960s. Extensive damage to forests continues however through the voracious browsing of large numbers of Australian brush-tailed possums which, among much else, have virtually eliminated native mistletoes from the eastern beech forests and decimated rata throughout whole valleys in the west. These too were deliberately introduced to New Zealand—in this case to establish a fur industry—and throughout much of the precipitous and inaccessible terrain of the Southern Alps can only be effectively controlled by aerial poison drops.

While it is difficult to be precise about how many of the more than 40 species of native New Zealand birds that are known to have become extinct since Maori first arrived in New Zealand would have been present in the forests and grasslands of the Southern Alps, it is probable that these would have included several species of moa (including the large, slender and little bush moas, upland moa and crested moa), the gigantic haptagornis (or Haast's eagle) which was the largest eagle the world has known, and the far from diminutive (up to 12 kilograms) adzebill. Among birds that have become extinct since European settlement the piopio (or New Zealand thrush), bush wren, laughing owl and probably extinct South Island kokako were all formerly abundant throughout the forests of the Southern Alps, as were others that are now tottering on the brink of extinction and today are either of very limited distribution (like the takahe and mohua or yellowhead) or are confined to off-shore predator-free sanctuary islands (like the kakapo and little spotted kiwi). As for native New Zealand birds that still remain widely distributed throughout the Southern Alps, even relatively common species like keas, tuis, bellbirds, fantails and tomtits are present only in greatly diminished numbers compared to the still plentiful populations encountered by early explorers and mountaineers in the final decades of the nineteenth century, while robins, kakariki (parakeets), kaka, whio (blue ducks) and rock wrens have today become rare enough to be a cause for celebration each time they are encountered.

Awareness of the impact of human settlement on native plants and animals even in remote places like the Southern Alps resulted in the foundations being laid for New Zealand's extensive system of national parks and reserves. Beginning with the protection of the peaks and valleys close to Aoraki/Mt Cook in the 1880s a network of national parks and other reserves gradually spread along the rest of the Southern Alps until today they form an unbroken tract of protected public lands extending from Nelson Lakes National Park in the north to the southern coast of Fiordland. As a result the magnificent natural wildness of the Southern Alps will henceforth remain not only comprehensively protected but also enhanced as threatened species recovery programmes and new methods of predator control developed by the Department of Conservation begin to rebuild populations of native birds and other rare and threatened creatures.